'The twin challenges of sustainability and ensi
contribute to poverty reduction and social justice
ment are re-framed in this book. The alternative nai
for showing that new thinking can lead to change.'

**David J. Grimshaw, Head of International Prog~ a~~~~~ (~~~~ ~~~~~~~~~ ,
at Practical Action, and Senior Research Fellow (New and Emerging
Technologies) at the Department for International Development**

'This book should be welcomed by all who take an holistic view of sustainable development and poverty reduction. For those of us rooted in the Appropriate Technology
movement, the STEPS team provide analytical rigour for the notion that technological
"silver bullets" are misconceived and that technology users have a range of options.
Drawing from across disciplines, *Dynamic Sustainabilities* provides a contemporary
approach to understanding the complicated and ever-changing world we live in; one
which explicitly recognizes that there are different ways of understanding the world, and
that development is indeed a political process.'

Andrew Scott, Policy and Programmes Director, Practical Action

'Melissa Leach, Ian Scoones and Andy Stirling of the STEPS Centre put the finger on
a fundamental challenge. How can we ensure that science and technology in a highly
complex, dynamic and interconnected world help improve livelihoods and social justice
in the quest for social-ecological sustainability? In their pathways to sustainability
approach they constructively suggest novel and practical ways forward for issues like
empowerment, styles of knowledge-making, governance, political engagement simultaneously confronting uncertainty, ambiguity and ignorance in comprehensive case
studies. Their way of "normative framing" provides inspiring and significant food for
thought and action. Highly recommended reading!'

**Carl Folke, Stockholm Resilience Centre and the Beijer Institute of
Ecological Economics**

'The old economic models are unlikely to serve us well on a planet of six billion, rising
to nine billion people by 2050. A systems approach catalysing a transition to a low
carbon, resource efficient, Green Economy is the only approach possible if all societies
are to thrive let alone survive through the 21st century. *Dynamic Sustainabilities:
Technology, Environment, Social Justice* outlines the challenges and barriers but also the
pathways and opportunities to realize that change not least through illuminating real-
world case studies. In doing so it offers a counterpoint to those trapped in old patterns
of development and an inspiration to those keen to embrace a paradigm shift.'

**Achim Steiner, UN Under-Secretary General and Executive Director UN
Environment Programme (UNEP)**

'This book addresses critical issues associated with transitioning to a more sustainable
world. It is both conceptual and practical – exactly what is needed to address issues such
as climate change, food and water security and human health.'

Professor Robert Watson, Chief Scientist, DEFRA

'This book provides orientation in a complex and uncertain world full of contradictions and ambiguous developments. It takes inclusive governance based on public participation, diversity of values and institutional plurality as an opportunity rather than a risk. Offering a new perspective on social capacity as the main resource for sustainability, the authors have produced an academically fascinating analysis and an innovative set of practical recommendations that link the dynamic interactions between social, technological and ecological processes and facilitate the transition to an alternative, progressive future.'

Ortwin Renn, Director of the Interdisciplinary Research Unit on Risk Governance and Sustainable Technology Development, University of Stuttgart, Germany

'The recent confluence of crises – in financial, climate and social systems – has boosted political will to make fundamental institutional changes. Our leaders know that fixing the banks is not enough. Whether the political and business space is labelled "green economy", "high-sustainability recovery" or simply "sustainable development", a lot now rests on the pathways that will be taken by enlightened leaders. But their courage is also not enough, and – in a fast-changing world – neither is clinging to previous practices that had once helped them to muddle through. There is a need for sound theory and good empirical evidence if we are to make progress with confidence: Leach, Scoones and Stirling offer considerable conceptual advances of real value in this accessible volume.

Steve Bass, Senior Fellow, International Institute for Environment and Development (IIED)

Dynamic Sustainabilities

Pathways to Sustainability Series

This book series addresses core challenges around linking science and technology and environmental sustainability with poverty reduction and social justice. It is based on the work of the Social, Technological and Environmental Pathways to Sustainability (STEPS) Centre, a major investment of the UK Economic and Social Research Council (ESRC). The STEPS Centre brings together researchers at the Institute of Development Studies (IDS) and SPRU (Science and Technology Policy Research) at the University of Sussex with a set of partner institutions in Africa, Asia and Latin America.

Series Editors:
Melissa Leach, Ian Scoones and Andy Stirling
STEPS Centre at the University of Sussex

Editorial Advisory Board:
Steve Bass, Wiebe E. Bijker, Victor Galaz, Wenzel Geissler, Katherine Homewood, Sheila Jasanoff, Colin McInnes, Suman Sahai, Andrew Scott

Titles include:
Dynamic Sustainabilities
Technology, Environment, Social Justice
Melissa Leach, Ian Scoones and Andy Stirling

Avian Influenza
Science, Policy and Politics
Edited by Ian Scoones

Rice Biofortification
Lessons for Global Science and Development
Sally Brooks

Epidemics
Science, Governance and Social Justice
Edited by Sarah Dry and Melissa Leach

Dynamic Sustainabilities

Technology, Environment, Social Justice

Melissa Leach, Ian Scoones
and Andy Stirling

publishing for a sustainable future

London • Washington, DC

Earthscan Ltd, Dunstan House, 14a St Cross Street, London EC1N 8XA, UK
Earthscan LLC, 1616 P Street, NW, Washington, DC 20036, USA
Earthscan publishes in association with the International Institute for Environment and Development

For more information on Earthscan publications, see www.earthscan.co.uk or write to earthinfo@earthscan.co.uk

ISBN: 978-1-84971-092-3 hardback
ISBN: 978-1-84971-093-0 paperback

Typeset by 4word Ltd, Bristol, UK
Cover design by Susanne Harris

A catalogue record for this book is available from the British Library

Library of Congress Cataloging-in-Publication Data

Leach, Melissa.
  Dynamic sustainabilities : technology, environment, social justice / Melissa Leach, Ian Scoones and Andy Stirling.
      p. cm.
  Includes bibliographical references and index.
  ISBN 978-1-84971-092-3 (hbk.) – ISBN 978-1-84971-093-0 (pbk.)
  1. Sustainable development. 2. Economic development–Environmental aspects.
  3. Poverty. 4. Social justice. I. Scoones, Ian. II. Stirling, Andy. III. Title.
  HC79.E5L393 2010
  338.9'27–dc22
                        2010000818

Contents

List of Figures, Tables and Boxes   *vii*
Preface and Acknowledgements   *ix*
List of Acronyms and Abbreviations   *xi*
Glossary   *xiii*

1 Sustainability Challenges in a Dynamic World   1

2 Dynamic Systems: Environment and Development Challenges   15

3 Pathways to Sustainability: Responding to Dynamic Contexts   37

4 Governance in a Dynamic World   65

5 Opening Up, Broadening Out: Empowering Designs for
   Sustainability   99

6 An Alternative Politics for Sustainability   125

7 Towards Pathways to Sustainability   155

Notes   *173*
References   *175*
Index   *205*

List of Figures, Tables and Boxes

Figures

3.1	Multiple framings	44
3.2	Variability in assessment of policy options for electricity supply	50
3.3	Variation in policy judgements on alternative agricultural policy options	52
3.4	Dimensions of incomplete knowledge	53
3.5	GM foods and crops: Dimensions of incomplete knowledge in African settings	56
3.6	Avian and human pandemic influenza: Dimensions of incomplete knowledge	58
3.7	Dynamic properties of sustainability	59
3.8	Combining dynamic properties of sustainability	62
4.1	Closing down towards risk	79
4.2	Closing down towards planned equilibrium	84
5.1	Characteristics of appraisal methods	106
5.2	Appraisal methods for addressing contrasting aspects of incomplete knowledge	109
5.3	Permutations of breadth and openness in appraisal	122
6.1	Three lenses on the policy process	130
6.2	Types of knowledge-making	152
7.1	Realizing pathways to sustainability	170

Tables

3.1	Creating narratives: Practices	46
4.1	Comparing adaptive, deliberative and reflexive approaches to governance	95
5.1	Examples of appraisal approaches	101
5.2	Framing effects in appraisal	112
5.3	Empowering designs: Five principles, two cases and some questions	121

6.1   Policy spaces – and strategies for opening them up   138
7.1   Water resources in dryland India: Dominant and alternative
       narratives   158
7.2   Seeds in Africa: Dominant and alternative narratives   160
7.3   Epidemics and health systems: Dominant and alternative
       narratives   163
7.4   Energy and climate: Dominant and alternative narratives   165

Boxes

3.1   Dimensions of framing   45

Preface and Acknowledgements

Linking environmental sustainability with poverty reduction and social justice, and making science and technology work for the poor, have become central practical, political and moral challenges of our times. These must be met in a world of rapid, interconnected change in environments, societies and economies, and globalized, fragmented governance arrangements. Yet despite growing international attention and investment, policy attempts often fail. Why is this, and what can be done about it? How might we understand and address emergent threats from epidemic disease, or the challenges of water scarcity in dryland India? In the context of climate change, how might seed systems help African farmers meet their needs, and how might appropriate energy strategies be developed?

This book offers a new 'pathways approach' to address sustainability challenges such as these, in today's dynamic world. It lays out a framework for understanding and action that embraces the dynamic interactions between social, technological and ecological processes; takes seriously the ways that different people and groups understand and value these; and recognizes the political choices and institutional and governance requirements for seeking out pathways to sustainability. And it suggests a series of ways forward – in tools and methods, forms of political engagement, and styles of knowledge-making and communication – to enable a more inclusive politics of sustainability, and support for alternative, progressive pathways.

This is the first book in the Pathways to Sustainability series, and it lays out some of the conceptual and practical concerns picked up in subsequent volumes. As such, the book is very much a collective effort which draws on thinking and debate among members and partners of the STEPS Centre during its first few years. Like the STEPS Centre itself, the book also builds on longer-term strands of work at IDS and SPRU. These include work on environmental policy processes based in the Knowledge, Technology and Society Team at IDS; work on science and citizenship conducted under the auspices of the IDS-based Citizenship Development Research Centre; and work on energy systems appraisal and policy within the Sussex Energy Group at SPRU. We would like to acknowledge the contributions to this book of the following STEPS Centre members, past and present: Gerald Bloom, Adrian Ely, Henry Lucas, Fiona Marshall, Lyla Mehta, Erik

Millstone, Synne Movik, Hayley MacGregor, Paul Nightingale, Esha Shah, Adrian Smith, Sigrid Stagl, John Thompson, Linda Waldman and William Wolmer. We would also like to thank the following colleagues for their insights and contributions, especially as part of various review processes: Robert Chambers, James Fairhead, Wim van Damme, Katherine Homewood, David Leonard, Gordon McKerron, Alan Nicol, Geoff Tansey, Steve Bass and Andrew Scott, as well as other members of the STEPS Centre Advisory Committee. Our grateful thanks are also due to Harriet Le Bris, Naomi Vernon and Julia Day for supporting the process of editing and production.

List of Acronyms and Abbreviations

BSE	bovine spongiform encephalopathy
CSERGE	Centre for Social and Economic Research on the Global Environment
DRC	Development Research Centre
ESRC	Economic and Social Research Council
FSR	Farming Systems Research
GM	genetically modified
GOARN	Global Outbreak Alert and Response Network
GRIP	(World Bank's) Grass Roots Immersion Programme
HPAI	highly pathogenic avian influenza
IAASTD	International Assessment of Knowledge, Agriculture, Science and Technology for Development
IDS	Institute of Development Studies
logframe	logical framework
MCM	multicriteria mapping
PRA	participatory rural appraisal
RRA	rapid rural appraisal
SARS	severe acute respiratory syndrome
SPRU	Science and Technology Policy Research
SSP	Sardar Sarovar Project
STEPS	Social, technological and environmental pathways to sustainability
TAC	Treatment Action Campaign
UNEP	United Nations Environment Programme

Glossary

(Italicized terms are cross-referenced to their own individual definitions)

ambiguity: a state of knowledge in which there are acknowledged to exist divergent, equally valid ways to *frame* different possible outcomes.

designs: deliberate configurings of *social appraisal*, which may include a variety of methods and processes, involving qualitative interpretation or quantitative analysis and specialist expertise as well as inclusive participation.

durability: a *dynamic property* of a *system* involving the ability to sustain structure or functional value by controlling sources of long-term *stress.*

dynamic property: a feature of the *dynamics* of a *system* or its behaviour or context, for instance in the face of *shocks* or *stresses.*

dynamics: patterns of complex interaction and change observed in the behaviour over time of social, technological and environmental systems.

environment (of a system):   those relevant parts of the external world which are seen in any given context to interact with a *system.*

framing: the different ways of understanding or representing a social, technological or natural *system* and its relevant *environment.* Among other aspects, this includes the ways system elements are bounded, characterized and prioritized, and meanings and *normative* values attached to each.

governance: political and institutional relationships including those of power and knowledge.

ignorance: a state of knowledge combining aspects both of *uncertainty* about probabilities and *ambiguity* over outcomes – in other words: exposure to the possibility of surprise.

incomplete knowledge: a general state of knowledge, which may take the form of various combinations of more specific conditions of *risk, uncertainty, ambiguity* or *ignorance.*

normative: relating to norms, standards, priorities, values and meanings as embodied in contrasting ways in different institutional interests or social perspectives.

pathways: the particular directions in which interacting social, technological and environmental *systems* co-evolve over time.

reflexivity: recognition that *framings* of a *system* are partly constituted by the observer's own circumstances and so are conditioned by (as well as inform) intended action.

resilience: a *dynamic property* of a *system* involving the ability to sustain structure or functional value by responding effectively to short-term episodic *shocks*.

risk: a state of knowledge in which possible outcomes are held to be well characterized and it is also possible confidently to determine the probabilities associated with each.

robustness: a *dynamic property* of a *system* involving the ability to sustain structure or functional value by responding effectively to long-term enduring *stress*.

social appraisal: social processes, including tools and methods, through which knowledges are gathered and produced, learning performed and meanings constructed in ways that inform decision making and wider institutional commitments.

stability: a dynamic *property* of a *system* involving the ability to sustain structure or functional value by controlling sources of short-term episodic *shocks*.

sustainability: a normatively explicit form of the general term, referring to the capability of maintaining over indefinite periods of time specified qualities of human well-being, social equity and environmental integrity.

shock: a short-term transient perturbation in conditions experienced by a *system*.

stress: a long-term secular shift in conditions experienced by a *system*.

system: a particular configuration of dynamic interacting social, technological and environmental elements.

uncertainty: a state of knowledge in which possibilities are held to be well characterized, but there is little basis for assigning probabilities.

Chapter 1

Sustainability Challenges in a Dynamic World

Today's world is highly complex and dynamic. Environmental conditions are changing fast as water, land and other ecological systems interact with climate change and new patterns of disease incidence. Developments in science and technology are proceeding faster than ever, with the spread of technologies shaped by new and often highly globalized patterns of investment and information. Social systems are changing rapidly too, linked to population growth, urbanization and market relationships. Such dynamics are, in turn, driven by shifting patterns of mobility – of people, practices, microbes, ideas and technologies – and globalized economic change, as some areas of the world transform, while others remain in deep poverty.

Yet the policies and institutions that have to deal with this new dynamic context are often premised on far more static views of the world. Where the rapidity of change is acknowledged, it is often seen to follow relatively clearly determined, single linear trajectories. Either way, assumptions of stability, equilibrium and predictable, controllable risks dominate. Yet the failures of such approaches to intervention and policy are everywhere to see. Simple blueprints, technological fixes or the transfer of technologies and regulations developed elsewhere frequently fail to work and create further problems. Standard approaches all too often betray their intended beneficiaries. Complex, dynamic contexts often undermine the neat assumptions of imported models. Emerging backlashes – from nature, from social movements, from politics – reveal this widening gap between standard policy approaches and dynamic systems.

Indeed, a major contradiction is emerging in contemporary responses to environment and development challenges. On the one hand, there is now a wide recognition of growing complexity and dynamism – evident across high science, popular media and the experiences of daily life. On the other hand, there appears to be an ever-more urgent search for big, technically driven managerial solutions – whether in the form of 'magic bullet' seeds and drugs, continent-wide roll-outs of high-impact solutions or top-down emergency-type responses aimed at shoring up stability and providing security. When such responses falter in the face of local dynamics and uncertainties, the response tends to be to implement with greater force or to blame locals or critics – rather than to question the underlying assumptions. The result can be a perpetuating cycle that narrows options, excludes alternative and dissenting voices, and fails to learn from mistakes and failures. This matters because it ultimately fails to tackle big problems of environment and development that affect us all, while often perpetuating inequalities and injustices.

All this raises some major policy and development challenges. For instance, how are shifting human–animal interactions and food production systems altering the likelihood of new global pandemics? How can the world respond to these interactions in ways that do not constrain poor people's livelihoods and freedom? What are the challenges of sustainability in rapidly growing Asian cities? As technology and economic growth bring wealth for some, how can the fall-out for those living on the margins – in overcrowding, pollution, ill-health and hazard – be addressed? How are farmers in dry parts of Africa coping with the challenges of climate change and disease? Can the potentials of new agricultural and health biotechnologies be harnessed to help, or will they provoke new uncertainties and missed opportunities to build on farmers' own adaptations? And how, in a world of rapidly advancing technologies and markets for drugs, seeds, energy and water use, can supply and regulatory arrangements be developed that suit the interests of the poor? How must global models of regulation be rethought to work in dynamic social and political settings? And how can these models respond to poorer and marginalized people's own perspectives on risk and uncertainty, grounded in their everyday lives and livelihoods?

Today, such questions are becoming ever more pressing. This book offers a way of thinking about these core relationships between ecology, technology, poverty and justice in a world of pervasive and growing inequality. Our starting point is that linking environmental sustainability with poverty reduction and social justice, and making science and technology work for people who are poor have become central practical, political and moral challenges of our times. We argue that meeting these challenges in a dynamic world requires an approach that embraces the dynamic interactions between social, technological and ecological processes; takes seriously the ways that diverse people and groups understand and value these; and acknowledges the role of economic and institutional power in shaping the resulting choices. In short, we need to recognize the essentially plural and political nature of our quest for pathways to sustainability.

Why are dynamics and complexity so important?

In meeting the challenges of sustainability, why is it so critical to take a perspective that treats dynamics and complexity seriously? Newspaper headlines across the world regularly highlight rapid rates of environmental and social change – and their threats and consequences. Even the World Bank acknowledges (Chen and Ravallion, 2008) that one and a half billion people are currently living 'without sufficient means for human survival' (Parsons, 2008). As disparities between rich and poor worsen (Worldwatch Institute, 2003), global environments are deteriorating (UNEP,[1] 2007). Carbon emissions are increasing (Met Office, 2009). Climate change is accelerating dangerously (Houghton, 2008). Multiple threats are posed to global food supplies (Beddington, 2009; Watson, 2009); and an array of other vulnerabilities are increasing (UNISDR, 2009).

Such reports and the dramatic statistics they cite can easily give the impression of impending catastrophe and disaster. While not diminishing the existence of serious environment and development problems, however, we argue that responding to these effectively requires a closer look at these dynamic systems and a deeper, more nuanced analytical approach that allows us to respond in effective ways. This requires looking at the interactions of different systems (social, ecological, technological) across multiple scales and as they play out in particular places with particular contexts. It also requires looking from the perspectives of different people with different views of these dynamics and their consequences. In particular this book argues that four major hurdles have to be addressed if more effective approaches to sustainable development are to be realized.

First, dynamics have often been ignored in conventional policy approaches for development and sustainability. Conventional approaches have often been rooted in standard equilibrium thinking, underlain by deeper-rooted notions of a 'balance' in nature. This tends to centre analyses – and so recommendations – on what are assumed to be aggregative, equilibrium patterns and on attempts to control variability, rather than adapt and respond to it. Equally, conventional methods often assume that models developed for one setting – usually the more controlled, managed contexts favoured by privileged interests – will work in others. This is so whether the export of models is from the developed to the developing world or from the laboratory or research station to the field. By contrast, this book recognizes the limits to planned intervention and argues for a more located, context-specific approach.

Second, governments and institutions are of course increasingly preoccupied with risk and with the insecurities that real and perceived threats seem to pose. However, as we argue in this book, dominant approaches involve a narrow focus on a particular (highly incomplete) notion of risk. This assumes that complex challenges can be calculated, controlled and managed – excluding other situations where understandings of possible future outcomes are more intractable. Some of these involve uncertainty, where the possible outcomes are known but there is no basis for assigning probabilities, and judgement must prevail. Other situations involve ambiguity, where there is disagreement over the nature of the outcomes, or different groups prioritize concerns that are incommensurable. Finally, some social, technological and ecological dynamics involve ignorance, where we don't know what we don't know, and the possibility of surprise is ever-present. Whereas conventional, expert-led approaches to analysis and policy are well-attuned to handling risk, they become highly inadequate in the increasingly common situations in which these other kinds of incomplete knowledge can be recognized to prevail. A wider appreciation of the dimensions of incomplete knowledge, this book argues, is essential if we are to avoid the dangers of creating illusory, control-based approaches to complex and dynamic realities.

Third, underlying such approaches are often wider assumptions about what constitutes the goals of 'development' or 'sustainability', often assuming a singular path to 'progress' and a singular, 'objective' view of what the problem might be. Yet of course different people and groups often understand system functions and dynamics in very different ways. They bring diverse kinds of knowledge and experience to bear – combining informal and more experiential ways of knowing with the disciplines and procedures associated with formal science. People also value particular goals and outcomes in very different ways. Rather than singular notions of 'progress' in relation to environment, technology or development, we can increasingly recognize situations in which there is a multiplicity of possible goals, which are often contested. Put another way, systems, and their goals and properties, are open to multiple 'framings'. Here, the concept of framing refers to the particular contextual assumptions, methods, forms of interpretation and values that different groups might bring to a problem, shaping how it is bounded and understood. In many situations, such understandings take the form of diverse narratives or storylines about a given problem: how it has arisen, why it matters and what to do about it. Paying serious attention to multiple, diverse framings and narratives, we argue, brings vital opportunities to advance debates about sustainability and connect them more firmly with questions of social justice.

Fourth, while debates about sustainability have become mainstream over the last two decades, they have also given rise to a great deal of confusion and fuzziness, in which easy rhetorical use masks lack of real change and commitment. In addition, ideas of sustainability have become co-opted into inappropriately managerial and bureaucratic attempts to 'solve' problems which are actually far more complex and political. This has led some to suggest abandoning the term 'sustainability' altogether. However, in this book we re-cast the notion of sustainability as a more explicitly normative (and so overtly political) concept. Rather than treat sustainability in a general, colloquial sense, implying the maintenance of (unspecified) features of systems over time, we are concerned with its specific normative implications. Thus sustainability refers to explicit qualities of human well-being, social equity and environmental integrity, and the particular system qualities that can sustain these. All these goals of sustainability are context-specific and inevitably contested. This makes it essential to recognize the roles of public deliberation and negotiation – both of the definition of what is to be sustained and of how to get there – in what must be seen as a highly political (rather than technical) process.

These are the reasons why we elaborate in this book an approach both to understanding sustainability and responding to challenges which we term a pathways approach. This addresses these four hurdles, highlighting the importance of 'dynamics', 'incomplete knowledge', 'multiple framings' and 'normativity'. Our pathways approach is thus explicitly normative, focused on reductions in poverty and social injustice as defined by/for particular people in diverse settings. Particular narratives are produced by particular actors and so co-construct particular pathways of response. Some are dominant; shaped by powerful institutions and substantial financial backing – these are the 'motorways' that channel current mainstream environment and development efforts. But these can often obscure and overrun alternatives; the smaller by-ways and bush paths that define and respond to different goals, values and forms of knowledge. This is what we mean by 'pathways': alternative possible trajectories for knowledge, intervention and change which prioritize different goals, values and functions. These pathways may in turn envisage different strategies to deal with dynamics – to control or respond to shocks or stresses. And they envisage different ways of dealing with incomplete knowledge, highlighting and responding to the different aspects of risk, uncertainty, ambiguity and ignorance in radically different ways.

We argue in this book that there is a pervasive tendency – supported by professional, institutional and political pressures – for powerful actors and institutions to 'close down' around particular framings, committing to particular pathways that emphasize maintaining stability and control. In so doing, these often create universalizing and generalizing approaches. These can in turn obscure or deny the reality of alternatives. Yet addressing the full implications of dynamics and incomplete knowledge requires, we argue, 'opening up' to methods and practices that involve flexibility, diversity, adaptation, learning and reflexivity, and an alternative politics of sustainability that highlights and supports alternative pathways.

Some examples

So how might such an approach respond to some of the major environment and development challenges of our times? In this section we introduce a series of examples, drawn from a range of research from the STEPS Centre and beyond, which we return to throughout the book. These include a focus on water in dryland India, seeds in Africa, policymaking on epidemic disease and energy systems as responses to climate change. Across the book, these cases illustrate both the contradictions between dominant approaches and dynamic realities and how a pathways approach helps to pose questions, unpack problems and identify alternative ways forward.

Water in dryland India[2]

Solutions to the problems of drought, climate change and agricultural development in dryland India often rest on two competing narratives about water. Perhaps the longest running and most heavily backed narrative, politically and financially, is centred on aggregated notions of water scarcity which need to be addressed through large-scale technical and infrastructural solutions, such as large dams, river diversions and massive irrigation schemes. This is often set in the context of an impending water crisis, where violence and conflict might be the result unless urgent action is taken at scale. A competing narrative contests this vision and focuses instead on small-scale, often community-based solutions responding to a similar scarcity and water crisis narrative. Yet both of these offer planning-based technological solutions which assume that the need is to fill a scarcity gap. Yet, for example, farmers in the dry zones of Kutch in Gujarat, India, approach the issue of water scarcity in a different way. There are multiple scarcities – it depends on the place, the time and the purpose to which the water is being used. Water carries multiple meanings, with cultural values and symbolic importance interplaying with people's material needs. There is huge uncertainty and a number of ways of responding to the situation, some of which involve living with and responding to uncertainty in a more flexible way, adjusting cropping, livestock-grazing and domestic practices accordingly. There is thus not one solution, but many. And the issue is not so much one about absolute amounts of water, but its distribution. Who gets access, and when? Here, as well as for the small-scale irrigation tanks of southern India (Mosse, 2003), the dynamics of gender, caste and power –

often deeply embedded in history and cultural context – shape patterns and inequalities in resource use in ways that confound comfortable assumptions that small-scale, community-based approaches will be sustainable, equitable or both. Hydrological solutions, at whatever scale, often fail to respond to inherent uncertainties and are not geared up to cope with surprises. Given the unfolding dynamics of climate change in dryland areas across the world, how might diverse pathways be built that respond to cross-scale water dynamics in ways that meet the needs and values of currently marginalized groups?

Seeds in Africa[3]

Debates about the global food crisis have re-energized green revolution narratives which were present in the 1960s and 1970s, which see technology-driven solutions as the core to any response. Thus investments in new seeds, genetic modification and breeding programmes, and associated packages of inputs (fertilizers etc) are seen by some advocates as the solution to Africa's food production problems and hunger more generally. Yet this supply-led, technology-push narrative is challenged by others. They argue that the challenge of hunger is less a question of production than of distribution and entitlement to food and that processes of market failure, social and power relations and the politics of access to resources influence who goes hungry. Others agree that production remains a challenge, but question both the appropriateness and efficacy of so-called modern seed technologies and systems. Instead, alternative technology pathways are suggested based on low external inputs, which are argued to be more ecologically and socially appropriate in the complex, diverse and uncertain settings in which farming happens. Another narrative focuses less on the technological end-products and more on the processes through which innovation occurs and who defines its proprieties. In particular, a 'farmer first' approach advocates a process of research and innovation in which farmers themselves are in the driving seat. Local social networks through which farmers exchange knowledge and seeds often enable them to respond to highly complex and embedded socio-ecological systems. Given the unfolding dynamics of environmental change, markets and politics that constitute the global food crisis, what pathways of innovation and mixes of technology make sense for poorer farmers as they live and work in diverse African settings?

Epidemics and health systems

Concerns about the emergence and re-emergence of infectious diseases and their capacity to spread rapidly in an interconnected world of mobile people

and microbes have defined at least two major narratives guiding health policy and practice in recent years. The first focuses on the control of outbreaks
through pervasive surveillance, rapid response, contingency planning and
the timely delivery of medical technologies in outbreak settings. For example
in recent years the response to highly pathogenic avian influenza has been
characterized by a massive global effort directed at controlling the avian disease at source and so reducing the potential of pandemic spread. Responses
to Ebola and other haemorrhagic fevers have focused on urgent control of
outbreaks of these rapid-killing diseases, using a standard package of exter-
nally led responses. The second narrative responds to widespread endemic
diseases of the poor (including malaria, HIV, tuberculosis and others)
through technological solutions to be rolled out and applied at scale. Thus
drugs, vaccines, bednets and associated therapeutic/educational/counselling
packages (voluntary counselling and testing, direct observation systems to
ensure drugs compliance, immunization information and education) are
promoted as part of grand challenges to which donors, philanthropic organizations and public–private partnerships are now devoting major resources
in the interests of global health. Yet other narratives point to the mixed
effects and sometimes local resistance that such interventions encounter
when they face the complex, diverse social, political and ecological settings
in the developing world. Standardized programmes, whether in outbreak
mode or technology roll-out mode, must confront highly diverse and
dynamic disease–ecological settings, where uncertainty and surprise may
rule – potentially confounding the best laid plans and models of health professionals. They confront diverse local social dynamics and cultural logics
regarding how diseases and their ecologies and technologies operate; logics
which alternative narratives see as valuable starting points for approaches to
health which work in context. And they confront a diversity of institutional,
political and market settings, involving diverse sources of authority and
bureaucratic control, as well as diverse suppliers of knowledge and technology in health systems. Alternative narratives highlight a blossoming of
innovative local governance arrangements and citizen responses which offer
the potential to bring access to appropriate health technologies and services
to poorer and marginalized people. Given the major health challenges, epidemic and endemic, facing the world, and given the particular disease
challenges of poorer people, what pathways of response would ensure good
health in an equitable, socially just and sustainable way?

Energy and climate

Debates about climate change have triggered a renewed series of debates
about energy for development. In the past, debates about energy were

framed in terms of narratives about energy 'gaps' (shortfalls and resources scarcity), whether of fossil fuel or woodfuel. Today attention has shifted to low-carbon alternatives as routes to achieving greenhouse gas reductions. However, approaches may still be centred on a single-fix technological solution to perceived energy security problems as dependence on fossil fuels is reduced. Thus for example, nuclear energy, biofuels and even some renewable sources are seen as the 'solution' to national energy requirements. Across the world, major controversies have arisen over the appropriateness of nuclear responses to energy problems, as in the case of India. Equally, biofuels have provoked controversy over the trade-offs around the use of land for food crops and the appropriation of land for large-scale biofuel plantations. Alternative narratives focus on the diverse energy needs of different people and places and the need to match these with a variety of technological and institutional options. They point out the way that energy technologies become part of socio-technical and political systems and thus transitions to low-carbon pathways must take account not only of technologies but also of broader social, political and governance settings. A shift is often advocated from a national energy planning and system mode to more decentralized approaches to technology and system design and the appraisal of different options, encompassing participatory, deliberative and community-based approaches. Given the imperative of a transition to a low-carbon economy, how might technological and energy system pathways emerge which respond to the diversity of both national and local demands?

Each of these cases thus generates a series of challenges and questions. We pick up on these throughout the book, exploring in more detail the particular examples and drawing in a variety of particular literatures on each. As we explore what a pathways approach means in practice, the cases are used to demonstrate and test the approach and the way it illuminates both the different implications of different narratives and the consequences of choices made on sustainability. In the concluding chapter, we return to the cases and revisit the challenges posed by each, asking how these might be addressed differently through the lens of a pathways approach. The pathways approach, as the book demonstrates, is not only a useful analytical tool, but one that highlights and makes clearer policy options and trade-offs and the real politics of sustainable development in ways that, we hope, will be useful to social movement activists as much as donor agencies and government policymakers.

Moving forward

The central questions of this book focus on how we might genuinely build pathways to sustainability in a complex, dynamic world – and the analytical, policy and appraisal approaches that can guide this. The chapters that follow combine an examination of existing approaches to understanding and intervention, addressing both their insights and shortcomings, with a forward-looking agenda that synthesizes elements of these into a new pathways approach.

This is an intrinsically collective and thoroughly interdisciplinary endeavour. Indeed, the book draws on and draws together a wide range of perspectives and analytical traditions that are rarely considered together – from development studies, science and technology studies, anthropology, political and policy sciences, to evolutionary economics, ecology and work on complexity in the natural sciences. Our aim is not to review any of these areas or their sub-fields comprehensively, but rather to distil key strands and convergences, including some unexpected and productive ones.

Drawing from this array of work, a core argument of this book is that we must define new ways of thinking and doing that take complex dynamics seriously. This is perhaps one of the major challenges for development in the 21st century. We are optimistic that there are new ways forward, however, and this optimism derives from three sources. First, that the failures of equilibrium approaches to intervention and policy are everywhere to see. The new dynamic contexts presented by a globalized, interconnected world make these all the more evident. There are emerging backlashes against the standard view which help encourage alternatives, opening up the chinks and spaces for a new politics of sustainability to flourish.

Second, despite the often confusing and contradictory debate about sustainability and sustainable development in particular, the broad, normative perspectives at the core of this discourse, highlighting the intersection of economic, social and environmental objectives, are now centre-stage and barely disputed across geographical location – North and South – and political persuasion – Left and Right. The widely recognized imperative of addressing climate change, for example, has brought global environmental change and development issues to the top of the political agenda internationally. This agenda – and the wider challenges of sustainability – are *par excellence* cases where social–ecological–economic–political dynamics must be at the core of any analysis. Public and political buy-in, it seems, has arrived and with it a more welcome context for what is currently lacking: clear thinking about how to conceptualize and address sustainability challenges in a dynamic world.

Third, there are many strands of work that can help in this thinking. There is an emergent yet rather remarkable convergence of thinking, across an array of fields of enquiry and disciplinary perspectives, which points towards the importance of dynamics, complexity, diversity, nonlinearity and uncertainty as critical to both understanding and, importantly, policy and practice. Such areas of work are often rather nascent and certainly remain largely peripheral to the core disciplines to which they refer. But there are some important common themes – as well as interesting divergences and dissonances – between them. This book is about drawing these strands together and relating them to real-world dilemmas.

Signposts towards pathways to sustainability

In subsequent chapters we elaborate on these issues and concerns, illustrating them in relation to the case examples introduced in this chapter. The chapters introduce a set of simple diagrams to facilitate thinking around key concepts and their application to real-world problems.

The next chapter focuses in on the question of dynamics and how they have – and have not – been addressed in debates around sustainability and development. The chapter begins by illustrating how each of our four examples involves highly dynamic, complex and interacting socio-ecological-technological systems. Nonlinear dynamics create thresholds and tipping points, often unleashing deep uncertainty and the possibility of surprise. Indeed wherever one looks – in biological, social, economic or political systems and particularly in their interactions – complex dynamics are important and have long been so. Yet dynamics – both old and new – have often been ignored in conventional approaches to development. The chapter identifies a number of reasons for this, adding up to a problematic political economy of equilibrium thinking and practice. It then briefly reviews five fields in which equilibrium views have been challenged. It addresses the science and economics of complexity, drawing on wider work on complexity sciences, before turning to perspectives from non-equilibrium thinking in the ecological sciences. The third field explored draws on recent thinking in science, technology and innovation studies to address the dynamics of technical change and socio-technical transitions. The fourth field turns to policy, organizational and management responses to dynamic settings, highlighting perspectives from soft-systems approaches to management, nonlinear perspectives on policy processes and the rethinking of the role of expertise in a 'post-normal' science responsive to conditions of uncertainty. The final subsection, in turn, begins to look forward to a new dynamic systems approach for development.

Chapter 3 begins to construct a more integrated framework for addressing sustainability challenges in the dynamic contexts discussed in Chapter 2. Following a discussion of the notion of sustainability, establishing the need to treat this in normative and political terms, we introduce a set of building blocks of a pathways approach, using simple diagrams to assist explanation and illustration of key concepts. First, we discuss system framing and how different actors come to construct narratives about problems and solutions. We then explore how narratives differ in addressing the incomplete knowledge that pervades dynamic settings: whether narrow notions of risk are emphasized or whether uncertainty, ambiguity and ignorance/surprise are acknowledged. We go on to explore the kinds of intervention envisaged to address shocks and stresses – whether emphasizing stability or durability, resilience or robustness. The chapter argues that pathways to sustainability are thus constructed through decisions which must explicitly address contestation and trade-offs between such different dynamic system properties as seen under different framings and narratives. Negotiating pathways to sustainability is therefore necessarily a political process.

Then follow three chapters which, in different ways, explore the political processes around negotiating pathways to sustainability and offer ways forward. Chapter 4 focuses on governance. Which narratives come to prominence and which remain hidden, and which become powerful pathways and which remain marginalized depends heavily on governance, which we define here in a broad sense as political processes and institutions. The chapter begins by reviewing briefly a range of processes, styles and practices of governance in the contemporary world. These include an emphasis on networked, multi-scale governance processes, interacting with state institutions in various ways. Increasingly evident, too, are participatory processes and the power relations of these: the realities of politics and governance in practice, involving messy, day-to-day interactions and the locatedness of unfolding governance arrangements in particular cultural and historical contexts. Politics is today very much the politics of nature and technology, and the politics of knowledge. In the context of these aspects of governance, the chapter explores and illustrates how institutional, political and power/knowledge processes often interact to 'close down' around narrow notions of risk and stability. Other important dimensions of incomplete knowledge and of sustainability are thus ignored. Exposing the problems with this, the chapter also argues that it does not have to be this way. We consider how processes of networked, multi-level governance might enable alternative narratives and pathways to prevail, and how adaptive, deliberative and reflexive governance approaches offer prospects for addressing multiple dynamic properties of sustainability and multiple dimensions of incomplete knowledge.

Chapters 5 and 6 turn explicitly to ways of 'opening up' and 'broadening out' analysis and action. This, we argue, is essential if the narratives and potential pathways that attend to the full range of dynamic properties of sustainability, and to goals around reducing poverty and promoting social justice, are to be pursued. The focus in Chapter 5 is on 'designs', or approaches and methods for appraisal. We explore what we term 'empowering designs': diverse ways of consciously engaging with the challenges of sustainability through broadening out the inputs to appraisal and opening up the outputs to decision-making and policy. Empowering designs aim at eliciting and exposing hidden narratives and pathways, and getting all potential pathways on the table – by being inclusive. Empowering designs also aim at facilitating processes of negotiation among narratives and potential pathways, through deliberation. The chapter focuses in on a potential array of methods and tools that can be used in the appraisal of sustainability issues. Following a discussion of what is meant by social appraisal, we examine a range of approaches which offer good prospects for broadening out and opening up complexity and addressing the diverse dimensions of incomplete knowledge and sustainability. The chapter then returns to the discussion of framing and looks in particular at the interaction between different methodological approaches and framing effects. In this context, it outlines four elements of effective appraisal for pathways to sustainability.

Chapter 6 asks what would it take for governance processes themselves to broaden out and open up – to receive and act on the outputs of appraisal, incorporating them into pathways to sustainability? What is taken up and acted upon is clearly influenced by power, politics and interests. In this chapter, we pursue further the argument that there are chinks and spaces in existing governance arrangements which, if opened up, might enable alternative narratives to be acknowledged, appreciated and become pathways; and for the adaptive and reflexive approaches needed to cope with dynamics and uncertainty to become real. The chapter outlines two key arenas and forms of engagement which offer prospects for opening up governance processes. First, we look at understanding and influencing policy processes. Second, we move to an exploration of the way citizen action and social movements can affect change. Finally, we address roles for researchers, public intellectuals and the media in seeking out and supporting pathways to sustainability.

In the concluding chapter, we summarize the book's argument. We revisit the major contradiction it started with – the growing gulf between complex dynamics and approaches premised on a stable, manageable world – in this light. We return to the four case examples – of epidemics and health systems, water in dryland India, seeds in Africa, and energy and climate – and to the specific questions being asked by policymakers now. Systematically, the chapter considers how these might be addressed differently through the pathways approach. Finally, we draw together the potential ways forward outlined in earlier chapters and consider how these add up to a new agenda for thinking and action towards pathways to sustainability and social justice.

Chapter 2

Dynamic Systems: Environment and Development Challenges

Introduction

As Chapter 1 outlined, dynamism, uncertainty and complexity dominate today's world. We know intuitively that dynamics are central to understanding complex, interacting systems; we must negotiate these every day. No one can deny the complexity of most developing world agricultural systems or the interactions between livelihoods and health and disease or the multi-level uncertainties arising in the management of water or energy.

Each of the four examples introduced in Chapter 1 are characterized by highly dynamic, nonlinear and complex socio–ecological–technology systems, as explored in a series of background papers that contributed to this book (Bloom et al, 2007; Mehta et al, 2007; Thompson et al, 2007). Nonlinear dynamics create thresholds and tipping points, often unleashing deep uncertainty and the possibility of surprise. Thus, in the case of water resources in India, climate change compounds the highly variable inter-annual and spatial patterns of rainfall. As these dynamics, complex and uncertain in themselves, interact with variable soils, land use and landscapes, so surface and ground water resources respond in ways characterized by non-equilibrium patterns. In the case of seeds in African settings, genetics interacts with highly diverse and dynamic agro-ecological and social contexts and practices. Particular crop varieties perform very differently, depending on where and how they are grown, and may respond unpredictably to rapid environmental shifts.

Epidemics and so-called emerging infectious diseases illustrate such rapid, inter-coupled social–ecological–technological system dynamics clearly. The intimate relationships between human societies, ecosystems and potential pathogens have, throughout history, given rise to complex challenges to human health. Yet the acceleration of a range of biological, social, ecological and technological processes during the last half-century has contributed to the emergence of new infectious disease challenges – whether the introduction of HIV to the ecosystem or the fear of a pandemic of highly pathogenic influenza. The processes involved include the evolutionary dynamics of pathogens, as viruses and vectors exploit niches that become available through environmental, demographic and livelihood change. They include interactions between pathogens and technology, for instance as microbes develop resistance to drug treatments; and they include demographic change and rapid growth in the numbers of both humans and domestic animals. Human–animal demography also affects zoonosis, the process whereby disease passes to humans from other species, now widely acknowledged as critical in the emergence and re-emergence of infectious disease. Most new infectious diseases of human beings to emerge in the past 20 years have had an animal source, while more than 60 per cent of emerging infectious disease events since 1940 involve zoonoses, 72 per cent of these with wildlife origins (Jones et al, 2008).

Finally, addressing the challenge of climate change and the transition to low-carbon energy systems will require confronting highly uncertain dynamics – both in environmental and technological trajectories. Uncertainty around future climate scenarios results in widely differing visions for the development of low-carbon energy options. Planning for transitions to 'sustainable' energy systems is far from straightforward, with multiple contending goals and a variety of different possible pathways (WEA, 2000). These may alternatively centre on: distributed renewable energy systems; efficient use and smart grids; fossil fuels with carbon capture; nuclear fission followed by fusion; or trans-continental infrastructures for centralized renewable energy systems (Scrase and MacKerron, 2009). Although there will always be some diversity, we cannot simultaneously organize future pathways equally around all these conflicting possibilities (Stirling, 2009b). The political dimensions are as important as the technical and environmental performance. Each alternative path in its own way runs counter to established practice. The realization of any particular pathway depends strongly on a feedback between expectations and unfolding dynamic realities (Brown and Michael, 2003). Yet incumbent energy infrastructures have a powerful momentum of their own, militating against agility, flexibility and diversity – and rendering it extremely difficult to move beyond rhetorical invocations to tangible change (Hughes, 1983). Despite the recognition of the need for a dynamic, nonlinear approach to energy policymaking given the challenges of climate change and the urgent need for a transition to a low-carbon energy system, processes of technological 'lock-in' and 'path dependence' are prevalent, making any shifts difficult (Unruh, 2006). As with the other cases, then, dynamic complexities compound interactions between social, ecological, economic and technological systems. Building pathways to energy sustainability must, despite the obstacles, treat these issues explicitly and seriously.

At one level, then, issues of complex dynamics appear to be widely recognized. Yet many policy interventions ignore this understanding and so often fail. What is often missing is a rigorous and systematic approach to addressing these issues, one that encompasses an understanding of complex system dynamics and provides a useable guide to action. This and the following chapters offer an approach to addressing complex system dynamics in the quest for pathways to sustainability.

Why dynamics?[4]

There are plenty of statistics to show that there are accelerated rates of change in the world today. In natural systems, the impacts of climate change, land-use shifts, hydrological pressures and pollution, for instance, are well documented. They link with changes in demographic pressures, disease incidence and technological advance, driven by changing patterns of mobility – of people, microbes, ideas and technologies. But we have to go beyond simply describing such change, towards real understandings of the underlying patterns and processes at play. What are the rates of change of different elements of socio-ecological systems in different places? How do these interact? Over what temporal and spatial scales? Addressing such questions of system dynamics is critical to contemporary policymaking and intervention strategies for sustainability but is so often missed.

However, an appreciation of dynamic systems is not a new phenomenon. As ecologists have long described, nonlinear interactions in very simple systems can result in highly dynamic patterns over time (May, 1976, 1981). In recent years, research ranging from the study of economic change to sub-cellular gene-protein functions has revealed that dynamic systems – characterized by complexity and uncertainty – are the norm, rather than the exception. For example, at the macro level, an examination of the histories of economies shows patterns which are much more effectively explained by models emphasizing non-equilibrium, sometimes chaotic dynamics, rather than conventional linear, general equilibrium approaches (Puu, 1993). At the very micro scale, molecular biology increasingly demonstrates how genes do not simply map onto function in a neat, linear way as perhaps hoped in the high-profile genome-mapping projects of the recent past. Post-genomic biology reveals how cross-genome interactions result in different pathways to expression depending on genome ecology and context (Brookfield, 2005).

Thus wherever one looks – in biological, social, economic or political systems and particularly in their interactions – complex dynamics are important and indeed have been so forever. Yet dynamics – both old and new – have often been ignored in conventional approaches to policy and development. Why is this? A number of reasons can be identified.

First, approaches which we now recognize as disciplines usually start with a descriptive phase, where detailed observation and basic categorization dominate over the modelling of generalizable patterns and regularities. Thus, for example, modern biology was preceded by a natural history approach that only with time gave rise to theories of natural selection and evolution or ecological systems and population biology. In some disciplinary areas – and biology is a good example – such generalized models and aggregate statistics are critiqued, finessed and elaborated and complex dynamics become part of the disciplinary terrain. In recent years this has been massively enhanced by the capacity for sophisticated modelling work due to exponentially increasing computing power. In other disciplinary areas, however – and particularly those associated with applied policy advice – the simple, generalized, often equilibrium-based models, and aggregative statistical approaches remain resistant to such developments, as they become locked in with particular institutional and policy frameworks and associated professionalized practices. In the context of development, applied sciences such as range management, forestry and agriculture have been dominated by such equilibrium thinking, ignoring complex dynamics, despite the fact that in the wider science of ecology, for example, such ideas have become mainstream.

In applied policy arenas, then, the last century has seen the emergence of certain ways of thinking which have defined 'good' science (both social and natural) and so guided policy thinking and intervention. Such thinking is often rooted in standard equilibrium ideas and practices, where the work of modellers and statisticians often defers a treatment of complexity, uncertainty and variability in favour of a focus on what are assumed to be underlying aggregative, equilibrium patterns. Thus in economics, the macro-economic techniques of general equilibrium modelling have been the *sine qua non* of economic planning for development (Starr, 1997). In the same way, epidemiological models of disease transmission, based on often highly simplified understandings of interactions between disease organisms, hosts and the wider ecology have guided many public health interventions (Gerstman, 2006). Clearly, such analyses are only one part of a wider array of methodologies and approaches within these very broad disciplinary areas, and many professional economists, ecologists, engineers and epidemiologists are exploring non-equilibrium perspectives that grapple with complex, dynamic systems. The point, however, is that in the application of ideas in the practice of development and policy more broadly, it is often the more simple, equilibrium perspectives that hold sway, very often reinforcing professional biases, funding streams and disciplinary hierarchies in favour of such approaches.

A focus on equilibrium perspectives of course echoes much longer, deep-rooted cultural understandings in the West about the relationships between people and nature. The somehow elemental, natural 'balance of nature' has become so deeply accepted that it guides both public discourse and policy thinking, informing in turn the way academic debates are framed.[5] Notions of balance or equilibrium in nature have a long tradition in Western thought, traceable to Greek, medieval Christian and 18th-century rationalist ideas (Worster, 1977). Ecology, a term first coined by Haekel in 1866 (Goodland, 1975), not surprisingly drew on such concepts as a way of explaining the structure and functioning of the natural world.

This tradition of equilibrium thinking can be traced to the present in much popular environmentalist discourse, as well as more academic strands of social science thought. Yet the debate in ecology that disputes this view has also spanned the last 80 years. Charles Elton in his famous textbook of 1930 noted: 'The balance of nature does not exist and perhaps never has existed' (Elton, 1930). Connell and Sousa (1983) came to a similar conclusion 50 years later: 'If a balance of nature exists, it has proved exceedingly difficult to demonstrate.' But despite such commentaries, the science of ecology over much of this century has been built on equilibrium notions, ones that assume stasis, homeostatic regulation, density dependence and stable equilibrium points or cycles.

Such embedded styles of thinking have had profound influences on the way contemporary debates have been constructed around discourses of conservation, preservation and maintaining balance. Divergences from what is assumed to be the norm are seen as necessarily negative and in need of rectification, thus ignoring the potential alternative interpretations that systems are not 'naturally' in equilibrium at all, and shifts between stable states or continuous variability are in fact the norm around which responses must be constructed.

With neo-classical economics by far the most dominant influence in the development field, a long-running resistance to addressing the dynamics of 'real markets' can be identified. From the classic work of Joan Robinson (1974) to more recent debates within economics (see Axelrod, 1997; Lawson, 2005), especially as a response to the financial crisis, and as applied to developing country settings (De Alcantara, 1993), this has been an ongoing debate. The focus on equilibrium understandings can in part be understood in relation to the disciplinary commitment to modelling economic processes primarily in terms of rational utility-maximizing individuals. These foundational assumptions thus result in divergences from pure market functioning being seen in terms of 'imperfections' or 'distortions', rather than the core of the issue.

Of course standard equilibrium models do have their merits. One clear advantage of a simple model is that its limitations are there for all to see. In principle – though unfortunately often not in reality – this allows them to be debated, challenged and revised by diverse groups of (sometimes non-professional) stakeholders. By contrast, highly complex dynamic models may end up describing complexity and other dynamic character-istics more completely, but hiding from view the critical assumptions in a welter of complex equations. Thus, as a heuristic device, the equilibrium models of economics and epidemiology, for example, are a useful way of thinking about what might happen if certain aggregate conditions hold. In some settings such conditions do indeed hold (more or less), and the models have some important utility for planning and policy. But in other contexts models developed for one setting – usually a more controlled, managed one – are found seriously wanting in others. This is particularly the case when models are exported from the developed to the developing world, or from the laboratory or research station to the field. It is therefore not just dynamics that matter, but it is dynamics-in-context which are particularly critical.

This is the second reason why dynamic perspectives have often been ignored in development. Much of the history of development – from colo-nial times to the present – can be read as a history of the export of inappropriate, doctrinal models (Cowen and Shenton, 1996). In all our four cases, whether in technology policy around energy systems, the manage-ment of water resources, the design of health systems or seed breeding programmes, we see, time and time again, the confident assumption that a particular model developed for one part of the world can be applied in others, or the idea that 'one-size-fits-all' technological solutions can be applied and rolled out unproblematically at scale. Too often we see such models failing the intended beneficiaries.

Yet such failures do not seem to offer a deterrent. When dynamic con-texts result in the model prescriptions failing, the response is usually not to blame the model and its assumptions. Rather, it is either to see this as 'implementation failure', urging reapplication of the model with greater force, or to blame the context – or the critics. There often appears to be a blindness to the basic adage that 'context matters', and, because it does, contexts can undermine the neat assumptions of imported models, however worthily applied and argued for. This lack of reflexivity is, we argue, at the heart of the problem. How we understand the world is deeply intertwined with cultural, disciplinary, political and social norms and worldviews. Development efforts exist at this interface, and a failure to reflect on the framing assumptions behind models – most critically the understanding of the system's functioning and the normative objectives for system outcomes

– too often means failure in well-meaning development activities (Pieterse, 1996).

The reasons why simplistic, blueprint-driven, managerialist development fails are well known (Chambers, 1982, 1997). But it still persists. This requires us to look at the wider institutional and political context for development and its underlying framings. Mainstream debates about development in the 'South' are often couched – implicitly if not explicitly – in terms of notions of 'progress' (Esteva, 1992; Crush, 1995). The assumption is often that such progress is achieved through the transfer of ideas, models, technologies and practices from the 'developed' North to the South. Within this framing are often embedded ideas about how development occurs in stages – from backward to modern, from old to new, from under-developed to developed. A social Darwinist vision of evolution often lurks not far beneath the surface (Scoones and Wolmer, 2002). There is often assumed to be a singular path to progress, any questioning of which is taken to indicate an 'anti-innovation', 'anti-technology' or 'anti-development' stance (Stirling, 2007a). While there are of course a variety of critiques to this mainstream perspective on development – coming from an array of populist and political economy stances from different scholars and activists from both North and South (see Sachs, 1992) – the fact is that such views remain, despite such challenges, accepted parts of the mainstream.

Thus the denial of alternative, multiple pathways towards a broader goal of poverty reduction, social justice and environmental sustainability is very common in mainstream development discourse. In considering the multiple pathways to such ends, there is a need to accept that there is no single pathway to progress; and, as Goran Hyden (1983) cautioned, no short-cuts either. Accepting dynamic contexts, interacting with dynamic systems over time and space, means that inevitably – indeed from first principles – there will be multiple, possible routes available. Which one is chosen and with what results is of course a wider political choice – discussed in more depth in Chapters 4, 5 and 6 – but one that must take into account underlying dynamic conditions in particular contexts.

Why is it that conventional bureaucratic, administrative and policymaking institutions and routines find dealing with dynamic systems so difficult? This is a near universal problem, but one that has particular characteristics in the developing world. The export of models for development since colonial times was of course accompanied by the export of professional practices and associated institutions. These took on particular characteristics, often in more extreme versions than their originators (Leach and Mearns, 1996). Thus, across much of the developing world, forestry departments, ministries of agriculture, energy ministries or water boards were populated with professionals trained by the colonial powers in institutions steeped in a particular way of thinking and doing. The new departments, ministries and boards that were set up – and continue to be set up or reformed at the margins – were of course modelled on their counterparts in the North; and this despite the fact that they were dealing with very different issues, in very different contexts, with very different resources and capacities. As such they became professionalized gatekeepers, controlling knowledge and managing access, and exercising the power to include and exclude, as Chapter 4 discusses.

The patterns established over the past century continue to be reinforced. In a globalized world where the professional and practical signals for 'good science' and 'effective performance' are taken from outside the developing world, the opportunities to question ways of doing things are highly constrained in most bureaucratic and policy settings (Keeley and Scoones, 2003). The 'room for manoeuvre' (Clay and Schaffer, 1984), the potential to look outside the box and to imagine alternatives, is restricted by the way the development enterprise is both conceived and constructed. Instrumentalist, managerial visions of development thus dominate and continue to be co-constructed through the interactions of development agencies, national governments and indeed many NGOs. James Scott (1998) eloquently describes the ways of 'seeing like a state' that reinforce the predilection for what he terms 'high modernist' planning approaches which offer a limited, restricted vision of what is possible, excluding dynamics and politics in the process (Agrawal, 2005).

Challenges to equilibrium thinking

How have different academic communities responded to these challenges? How has an equilibrium view been challenged, and how does this provide the basis for a new science of sustainability? What follows is a very partial and necessarily highly contracted review of a huge array of different perspectives presented across diverse literatures. It is therefore inevitably somewhat dense, but the ideas and associated references allow a starting point for further exploration of these important concepts. The brevity also certainly does violence to some of the more nuanced and specific debates within such areas of work. Our aim here, however, is not to cover every dimension of each sub-debate, but to generate a general basis from which – in Chapter 3 – we can draw out key elements and begin to construct a more integrated, heuristic framework for addressing these issues.

Our review is grouped into five sub-sections. The first two look at the science and economics of complexity, drawing on wider work on complexity sciences and at perspectives from non-equilibrium thinking in the ecological sciences. The third section explores dynamic perspectives in the understanding of transitions in industrial and technological systems. The fourth section looks at policy, organizational and management responses to dynamic settings, including soft-systems approaches to management, nonlinear perspectives on policy processes and perspectives on so-called post-normal science. In the final section, we begin to look forward to a new dynamic systems approach for development.

The science of complexity

Over the past century a wide field known as 'complexity science', with a variety of strands, has evolved. This began with the early recognition of intractabilities in the dynamics of simple deterministic systems, such as the famous 'three body problem' in celestial mechanics addressed by Poincaré (Peterson, 1995). Facilitated by progress in recursive differential and complex number calculus, a rich variety of nonlinear properties have since been recognized. Sophisticated new concepts have been developed to explain and explore them, including the notion of strange attractors in the study of stability (Ruelle, 1989), the idea of fractional dimensionality in topology and geometry (Mandelbrot, 1967), and new understandings of phenomena of bifurcation in system dynamics (Feigenbaum, 1979). This process has inspired – and been informed by – parallel developments in experimentation, which have revealed the highly unexpected behaviour of dissipative structures in chemistry (Prigogine, 1980) and yielded refined understandings of common features in material phase transitions (Anderson, 1997). Perhaps most importantly, progress in the understanding of complexity has been accelerated by radical enhancements of computational capabilities and capacities to process large datasets, which have revealed pervasive new statistical structures such as scale invariance (Zinn-Justin, 2002) and power law distributions (Newman, 2005). Improvements in computer processing power have also enhanced capabilities for visualizing complex, multidimensional phenomena such as catastrophe curves (Thom, 1989) and fractal geometry (Mandelbrot, 1982).

Together, these developments contribute to a growing appreciation of the importance of dynamic (rather than static) perspectives, based on holistic (rather than reductive) analysis, acknowledging context-dependence and the conditioning effects of structure. In short, they point to the inevitability of uncertainty even in some of the most deterministic of systems. Of course, such concerns over reductionism, determinism and spurious quantification have been long established in other disciplines (Koestler, 1967; Bertalanffy, 1968; Bateson, 1972; Rose, 1982; Goodwin,

2001). Yet – largely eschewing quantitative approaches themselves – these have hitherto failed to gain much purchase in the more positivistic areas of scientific enquiry. The new complexity sciences are, however, succeeding in sustaining a cautious qualification of positivism, without resorting to a pessimistic subjectivism.

Over the past two decades, insights from complexity studies have become increasingly influential across a range of different disciplines – as well as in wider social and policy discourse. An apparently insatiable market has developed for (sometimes rather breathless) popular science writing on these themes. Lurid accounts of catastrophe theory (Woodcock and Davis, 1978) join glossy expositions of chaos (Gleick, 1988; Lewin, 2000) and enthusiastic advocacy of complexity studies (Casti, 1995; Kaufmann, 1995). These jostle on the shelves with competing volumes proclaiming the importance of emergence (Fromm, 2004) and (confusingly) simplicity (Cohen and Stewart, 1994; Gribbin, 2004). Centres of activity in these areas – notably the Santa Fe Institute in New Mexico – have achieved almost cult status (Horgan, 1995). Indeed, so intense has been the intellectual energy and exposure in this area, that some key ideas from these literatures have achieved globally iconic status. Examples include the evocative image of the 'butterfly effect' (Lorenz, 1963; Hilborn, 2004), the influential notion of the 'tipping point' (Schelling, 1978; Gladwell, 2000) and the transcendent, graphic beauty of the Mandelbrot set (Barnsley, 1993).

Alongside this intrinsic importance as background themes in contemporary scientific, policy and wider social discourse, 'complexity science' (in its broadest sense) has – despite the hype – begun to make significant contributions to the current thinking on the relationships between society, technology and the environment. Drawing on different permutations of the concepts and insights referred to above, these may be organized under a variety of aspiring new disciplinary labels.

Non-equilibrium thermodynamics, for example, explores the generation of structure in open nonlinear physical systems (Nicolis and Prigogine, 1977), encouraging new approaches to entropic (Georgescu-Roegen, 1976), evolutionary (Nelson and Winter, 1982), co-evolutionary (Gowdy, 1994), institutional (Hodgson, 2000) and ecological economic theory (Stagl and Common, 2005). As a distinct offshoot, chaos theory illuminates the conditions under which apparently simple systems can generate surprisingly complex outcomes (Stewart, 1989). Catastrophe theory, in turn, preceded the rise of chaos theory and focuses on discontinuities and exponential episodes in the dynamics of otherwise continuous processes (Zeeman, 1977), with significant implications for the modelling of economic (Rosser, 2006), environmental (Diamond, 2005), technological (Fagerberg et al, 2005) and social (Tainter, 1988) change.

Arising to prominence more recently, complexity theory addresses the ways in which multiple interactions in complex, inter-coupled systems can give rise to relatively simple emerging structures (Kauffman, 1993). These are issues now explored in the rapidly growing field of agent-based modelling (Gilbert and Troitzsch, 2005) and in the study of emergent structures (Sawyer, 2005), diverse behaviours (Page, 2007) and structures (Stirling, 2007d), plural institutions (Ostrom, 2005) and power law distributions in social phenomena (Ball, 2005).

As a distinct aspect of (or alternative vocabulary for) complexity, general notions of self-organization in evolutionary studies focus on the ways in which the emergence of order need not always be seen as a consequence of hierarchical causal relationships (Bak, 1996) – an insight applied in some branches of economics (Krugman, 1996) and geography (Allen, 1997). Finally, and related closely to the study of self-organization, the more specific concept of autopoiesis has arisen in systems theory applications to molecular and evolutionary cellular biology (Varela et al, 1974). This has inspired newly intensified attention to the implications of reflexivity in general social theory (Luhmann, 1995; see also the discussion of 'soft systems' below).

New perspectives in ecology

For many years, both in scientific and popular discourse, the dynamics of ecological systems were thought of in terms of 'balance' and 'equilibrium' (Botkin, 1990; Zimmerer, 1994; Scoones, 1999), with disturbance from stable states seen as a divergence from a 'natural' condition. In popular discussions these understandings led to notions of the 'balance of nature' and framed understandings of how human interventions in ecosystems should be understood. In applied management applications, an equilibrium view led to ideas such as 'carrying capacity' or 'stable state succession', where limits were imposed on use and harvesting to avoid shifts from an assumed stable state.

While some ecosystems of course demonstrate stable, equilibrium-type properties, many do not. Both theoretical and empirical studies in ecology over the last 30 years have demonstrated how it is important to understand systems in terms of multiple stable states and shifts between stability domains (DeAngelis and Waterhouse, 1987). Other systems are truly non-equilibrial, where dynamics are dominated by external drivers (such as rainfall) which are highly variable. In these, the population dynamics (of, say, grasslands and animals) are not primarily governed by the classic density-dependent feedback mechanisms assumed for homeostatically controlled equilibrium systems (Ellis and Swift, 1988; Behnke et al, 1993).

Understanding complex ecosystems in terms of the sum of networks of interactions with food webs or nutrient cycles, for example, suggests a particular perspective on nonlinear dynamics (DeAngelis, 1992; Pimm, 2002). Even relatively simple, deterministic model systems, based on a few interactions of relatively few components, can of course result in chaotic, nonlinear dynamics (May, 1989), so it is hardly surprising that studies of real ecosystems show a high degree of stochasticity resulting from nonlinear interactions. A challenge in the ecological sciences, then, has been to develop understandings – and in turn predictive models – which reflect such dynamics and move away from misleading understandings based on too rigid an acceptance of equilibrium perspectives (Holling, 1973; Chesson and Case, 1986).

Such a non-equilibrium view of ecosystem dynamics has many important applied management implications. Thus the 'new' rangeland ecology has rejected the simplistic application of carrying capacity approaches to rangeland management, shifting to a more spatially and temporally attuned approach. A spatial approach highlights the importance of differences in patch dynamics in different parts of a rangeland landscape, contrasting 'key resource' areas, where more equilibrium properties are evident, with large areas of dry rangeland, where rainfall variations dominate dynamics. Different management responses are needed in each area and over time, with an approach to 'opportunistic' management that tracks available resources over space and time seen as the most appropriate. Thus in dry, pastoral areas in Africa, it is argued that the most efficient and effective response to high levels of spatial and inter-annual variability in rangeland productivity is mobility, combined with rapid-response disposal and restocking of animals to track fodder availability (Sandford, 1982; Behnke et al, 1993; Scoones, 1995; Homewood, 2008).

In forest management, critiques of simple succession models of vegetation change have highlighted how shifts between different forest types and savannah vegetation are driven by variations in soil, fire regimes and rainfall over time and space. There is thus no one 'natural' forest type to be protected or conserved, or against which human use might be judged as 'disturbance'. Rather, forest management must respond to ecological dynamics and their interaction with use practices in relation to different objectives for management, whether production forestry, biodiversity conservation or supporting local livelihoods (Shugart and West, 1981; Sprugel, 1991; Fairhead and Leach, 1998). Appreciation of dynamic ecologies has also had an impact on other areas of management, including fisheries (Hilborn and Gunderson, 1996), soils (Scoones, 2001), pest control (Walters and Holling, 1990) and restoration ecology (Suding et al, 2004); each suggesting wider implications for resource management under conditions of uncertainty (Ludwig et al, 1993).

Such non-equilibrium thinking also applies to disease ecologies and the way disease control and management takes place. Simple epidemiological models of transmission and disease spread may not be appropriate, as disease organisms interact in nonlinear ways with both the wider environment and the organisms that any disease virus or bacterium infects (Anderson, 1994). Instead, more sophisticated understandings of disease–host–environment interactions are needed, requiring different modelling approaches (Ahmed and Hashish, 2006), as well as more located understanding of disease contexts through approaches such as participatory epidemiology (Catley, 2006).

Thus, drawing on ideas from the wider field of complexity science, non-equilibrium perspectives in the diverse applications of ecology and epidemiology provide a challenge to the first-approximation static, equilibrium models that dominated early work in these fields. New approaches – while by no means being dominant in the applied contexts of development policy and practice – draw on non-equilibrium and complexity thinking, offering new approaches to analysis and in turn new perspectives on management and policy.

Dynamics of technological change

Similarly enhanced appreciations of complexity, dynamism and diversity are also transforming our understandings of technological change. Not all directions for technological change are intrinsically feasible or contextually viable (Freeman, 1974; Perez, 2002). Yet, at any given point for any specific artefact, as for entire infrastructures, there are typically a number of contrasting trajectories along which technologies may progress (Dosi and Labini, 2007). At each stage, only a restricted subset is realized (Williams and Edge, 1996). In this way – whether deliberately, blindly or unconsciously – societies choose certain orientations for technology change rather than others (Collingridge, 1982).

There is a multitude of specific processes through which such commitments are made (Geels, 2002). Complex historic contingencies play a crucial role (Mokyr, 1992), but many more systematic mechanisms exist through which developments are channelled (Kemp et al, 1998; Elzen et al, 2005). For instance, though they may originate in essentially random patterns, the simple positive-feedback dynamics of market lock-in may direct the course of change (Arthur, 1989). Here, the ubiquitous dysfunctionality of the QWERTY keyboard (David, 1985) is an iconic example of the path-dependent consolidation of an initial accident (Liebowitz and Margolis, 1995). Similar mechanisms of path-dependency and lock-in may also serve to reinforce less arbitrary or politically innocent patterns. The social forces shaping early configurations of nuclear power (Cowan, 1991), chemicals production (Stringer and Johnson, 2001) and weapons systems (Kaldor, 1981) can all be recognized to reflect the needs, preferences, values and interests of restricted social groups (Pool, 1999). This is also true of the routines and practices and paradigmatic ways of thinking in the most influential of successfully innovating organizations (Nelson, 2008). These also become imprinted in the resulting technologies and their subsequently institutionalized trajectories (Von Tunzelmann et al, 2008).

More distributed pressures – such as those exerted by cultural expectations – may further assert the interests of relatively privileged social actors such as entrepreneurs, investors, regulators and opinion formers (Brown and Michael, 2003). Once established in these ways, technological configurations can be seen as 'socio-technical regimes' (Rip and Kemp, 1998), acquiring their own 'momentum, at the expense of alternative, less privileged configurations' (Hughes, 1983). Under this richer understanding, incumbent interests can be seen to exercise a degree of 'autonomy' (Winner, 1977) in their capacity to condition their own 'selection environments' (Nelson, 1993). This can involve various kinds of 'capture' (Sabatier, 1975) and 'entrapment' (Walker, 2000) of ostensibly neutral or even supposedly contending social actors.

These kinds of processes have repeatedly been shown to shape the direction taken by innovation – for instance in energy systems. Here in areas such as electricity systems (Hughes, 1983), nuclear infrastructures (Walker, 1999), fossil fuel infrastructures (Unruh, 2000) and automobile manufacture (Geels, 2007), we find the direction of technological change to be as dependent on institutional and social dynamics as on the progressive unfolding of scientific or technological understandings. Although nature imposes crucial constraints on what is possible, it typically accommodates a range of mutually exclusive possibilities and so fails uniquely to determine the realization of any particular socio-technical configuration. Large-scale centralized electricity systems might as readily have developed around DC as AC power transmission – with important implications for specific technologies (Patterson, 1999). Likewise, the light-water reactor designs into which nuclear power remains seemingly irreversibly locked were well optimized for the confined spaces of ballistic missile submarines in the 1950s, but are poorly adapted to the requirements of safe, economical civilian power production in the 21st century (Cowan, 1990). Even the ubiquitous petroleum-driven automobile engine displays tell-tale signs of contingency, which might have yielded fundamentally different outcomes if history had unfolded differently (Arthur, 1989).

It is against this background of an increasing recognition of complexity and diversity in the dynamics of technological change that the new policy imperatives of sustainability are being considered. How can society deliberately shape 'transitions' to more 'sustainable' (healthy, empowering or fair) socio-technical regimes (Kemp et al, 1998)? Such approaches highlight the significance of influencing the visions of entrepreneurs, the expectations of financiers and the preferences of users which are often not closely reflected in existing markets, as well as recognizing wider diversities in livelihoods and lifestyles (Bijker, 1997). Also influential are the specific routines, practices and cultures associated with scientific disciplines and professional groups, the strategic intentions of market institutions and the interests and incentives represented in wider governance structures (Nelson and Winter, 1982; Dosi et al, 1988). This recognition of 'socio-technical regimes' helps policymaking escape from simplistic mainstream linear and deterministic notions of scientific and technological progress and address the diverse complexities of the real dynamics of technology in society.

In seeking to steer socio-technical regimes through transitions towards sustainability, the focus shifts from innovation of individual products or single business practices (Berkhout, 2002) to interventions addressing lifestyle expectations, consumption patterns, user preferences, regulations, infrastructures and the cultures of associated institutions (Hoogma et al, 2002). These are obviously very ambitious aims. One relatively manageable way to achieve them is to create new 'niches', protected from prevailing power structures, priorities and interests in existing markets. In this way, business, policymakers and social movements (or new partnerships and alliances) can experiment with novel applications, innovations or demonstration programmes (Schot, 1998). These provide space for development of new ideas, artefacts and practices, free from the pressures imposed by the interests of the incumbent regime (Geels, 2004). Socio-technical niches exist as part of a complex, multi-level system, which includes the existing socio-technical regimes, as well as the wider socio-technical landscape (Geels, 2004). If transitions are to be successful, then these higher-level structures and processes must also be addressed (Elzen et al, 2005). This raises important questions about how different contexts lead to different kinds of transition pathway (Berkhout et al, 2004), about the nature of relationships between different scales (Smith and Stirling, 2007) and about the fundamental political dynamics of agency and power (Smith et al, 2005). In sum, the complex, multi-dimensional nature of technology change is not about a linear dynamic or singular progress; instead, it is about grappling with multi-scale, complex dynamics of competing options and transitions (Smith and Stirling, 2009).

Policies, organizations and management responses in dynamic settings

Given such dynamic complexity in ecological, economic, social and technological systems, and the array of challenges that arise, how should policies, organizations and management systems respond? This question has been at the centre of a number of areas of enquiry, which offer some important pointers to ways forward.

Nearly all organizations are complex systems, particularly those associated with the complex and dynamic challenges of sustainable development. What are the organizational and management requirements in such settings? Ray Ison and colleagues (Ison et al, 1997, p262) point out that there are two different, possible ways of responding to complexity. Complexity can be seen as 'something that exists as a property of some thing or situation; and that, therefore, can be discovered, measured and possibly modelled, manipulated, maintained or predicted'; or, by contrast, 'as something we construct, design, or experience in relationship to some thing or event'. These two perspectives have very different implications for management and organizational change. With the first 'descriptive' approach to complexity, the challenge is first to describe, then to model and finally to respond prescriptively. By contrast, the second 'constructed' approach 'entails engaging in situations of complexity and using systems or complexity thinking to learn our way towards purposeful action that is situation improving' (Ison, 2004). This latter perspective implies a soft-systems approach (Checkland, 1981; Forester, 1994; Bawden, 1995) to management and organizational change. Soft-systems approaches evolved in response to the limitations of 'hard systems' analysis, based on cybernetics, structural modelling and mechanistic thinking. This latter engineering approach was seen to be inadequate for the types of complexity found in organizational and management issues.

Such approaches put the practitioner and analyst at the centre, for understanding the world from a soft-systems perspective is critically based on the positionality and subjectivity of the observer. As Schlindwein and Ison (2004, p30) emphasize:

> *Making a choice of one epistemological position or another in a given context is not an act of discarding or deciding against the other position – it is an act of being aware of the choice being made and taking responsibility for it... Being epistemologically aware opens up more choices for action.*

This negotiated, reflexive understanding of complexity, from a variety of different frames, echoes Donald Schön's perspective on the 'reflective practitioner' (Schön, 1995). To be effective, practitioners must engage with different system and problem framings and negotiate solutions. Such a practice-based perspective accommodates uncertainty, complexity and competing versions and does not seek to define a single model. Indeed, a critical process, particularly when confronted by controversy, is that of 'frame reflection' (Schön and Rein, 1994), whereby competing frames are examined at higher (meta) levels in order to seek routes for common understanding and moving forward.

Such perspectives overlap with the idea of the 'learning organization' (Senge, 1990, Argyris and Schön, 1978) and with critiques of 'stable' states (Schön, 1973) committed to technically driven, blueprint-based modernist development (Scott, 1998). Learning organizations are thus effective where incremental change in the face of complexity and uncertainty is based on sequential action, reflection and cumulative learning (Kolb, 1984). A number of analysts and many practitioners observe how large organizations very often fail to respond effectively to dynamic complexity (Mosse et al, 1998; Mehta et al, 1999; Pimbert, 2004). Thus, for example, Chapman (2002) observes 'system failure' in the UK National Health Service, while Uphoff (1996), Thompson (1995) and Korten (1980) comment on similar dynamics in irrigation systems and rural development in Asia.

Thus these different organizational change and management perspectives – whether soft-systems, reflective-practitioner or 'organizational learning' approaches – respond to dynamic complexity, within organizational systems and in relation to shocks and stresses from outside, through processes centred on reflective practice and experiential learning.

Towards dynamic systems approaches: The case of agricultural development and natural resource management

How then do all these emerging perspectives, focused on dynamic understandings of complex systems, contribute to thinking in development? Taking one of the case examples that run through this book, that of seed systems in Africa and the broader processes of agriculture and natural resource management in which they are embedded, we can see how a dynamic systems-oriented approach has emerged in debates in the field of agricultural development.

Systems perspectives in this case have a long tradition. But these are often based on hard-systems analyses and so fail to address the dynamic complexities arising from 'constructed' or soft systems. For example, in agriculture, systems approaches date back to classic descriptions and typologies of farming systems (Ruthenberg, 1971). Farming Systems

Research (FSR) evolved in the 1970s (Gilbert et al, 1980) as a response to earlier simplistic, technical approaches which focused only on single system elements – such as seeds and inputs – as part of technical transformation and transfer. This classic Green Revolution model did not take much account of complex system dynamics and worked best in areas where sources of variability and uncertainty were reduced. But in the vast majority of agricultural settings in the developing world, a more complex, diverse and risky context existed (Chambers, 1982; Chambers et al, 1989). Here a more interactive, systems-oriented analysis was required which was more holistic and integrative, and in particular addressed the wider social and economic issues together with technical questions.

However, much farming systems practice was little more than adaptive on-farm research which extended the linear, technical model to wider contexts. Agro-ecosystems analysis, which emerged through work in northern Thailand in the early 1980s (Conway, 1985), was an attempt to move beyond this restricted frame and develop a systematic approach to examining system properties in agricultural settings. Drawing inspiration from dynamic ecology and the work of Holling (1978) and others, the framework developed by Conway (1987) highlighted different system properties and their trade-offs. The approach asked, for example, whether increasing the productivity of a particular cropping system resulted in decreased stability (that is, increased variation in yields and so exposure to risk) and compromised sustainability (for example whether such productivity increases were to be achieved by the application of increased pesticides or fertilizer, both potentially resulting in long-term stresses on the system). Agro-ecosystems analysis, as originally practised, was largely expert-led field analysis, pushing technical experts as part of farming systems research teams to look at these wider questions, not normally part of the frame of agronomists or plant breeders.

However, the methodological innovation that became part of agro-ecosystems analysis – particularly the visualization and mapping of systems and farm landscapes – provided a focus for interaction with another emerging approach to analysing agricultural and rural development settings at that time: rapid rural appraisal (Howes and Chambers, 1979; Chambers, 1981) and participatory 'farmer first' approaches (Chambers et al, 1989; Thompson and Scoones, 2009). Such approaches increasingly emphasized participation as central to diagnosis and design in rural development and, drawing on long traditions in social anthropology, emphasized local understandings and 'indigenous technical knowledge' (Richards, 1985; Warren, 1990) as central to any analysis. However, in the more populist versions of such approaches in development – and particularly in the many applications of what came to be labelled 'participatory rural appraisal' (Chambers,

1994) – the politics and dynamics of such knowledge construction in participatory approaches was often not acknowledged (Mosse, 1994; Cooke and Kothari, 2001). Very often 'indigenous knowledge' was seen as a helpful adjunct to a technical, expert-led process of systems analysis and design, and not fundamental to the wider politics of framing and negotiation of systems, their functioning and purpose (Scoones and Thompson, 1994).

Some of these issues are central to what has been labelled 'adaptive management', linked to wider debates about the science of resilience and sustainability derived from non-equilibrium ecological thinking. These perspectives too have become important in debates about agricultural development (Ericksen, 2008; Thompson and Scoones, 2009). In the opening editorial of the journal *Conservation Ecology* (now *Ecology and Society*), Holling laid out a prospectus for a new applied ecology which took dynamics and complexity seriously (Holling, 1998). This emphasized integration, holism, uncertainty and surprise as key elements for effective management of complex ecosystems, with ideas of system resilience being central to meeting the challenges of sustainability. The work of the Resilience Alliance (www.resalliance.org) has elaborated these ideas over a number of years, exploring both ecological and social dimensions of dynamic systems in diverse settings – from dry rangelands (Janssen et al, 2004), to forest pest outbreaks (Ludwig et al, 2002), to coral reefs (Bellwood et al, 2004), to lakes (Carpenter et al, 1999), to wetlands (Gunderson, 2001) and marine systems (Hughes et al, 2005).

This work has emerged from the practical challenges of managing ecosystems where dynamic ecologies undermined attempts derived from conventional approaches due to the existence of multiple stable states, non-linear dynamics and uncertainty (Ludwig et al, 1993). Thus, for example, the 'maximum sustained yield' approach to fisheries management was found wanting (Larkin, 1977), as was conventional forest management in the face of episodic and uncertain pest outbreaks of spruce budworm (Holling, 1978). Approaches to adaptive management – based on experimentation and incremental learning about system dynamics – were seen as more effective than conventional blueprint management models in such complex systems (Walters and Hilborn, 1978).

These approaches to the management of resilience in complex ecosystems emphasize in particular how system scales and hierarchies (Allen and Starr, 1982; O'Neill et al, 1989) interact with multi-level system dynamics, with 'cascade effects' (Folke et al, 2004), 'scale mismatches' (Cumming et al, 2006) and networks potentially emerging and affecting resilience properties (Janssen et al, 2006). Resilience is thus seen as an emergent property, linked to processes of adaptation and transformation (Walker et al, 2004). This moves beyond 'engineering' focused definitions where resilience is seen in relation to return times to previous stable states (see Pimm, 1991), to assessments of 'ecological' resilience through measures of how far a system could be perturbed before shifting to a wholly different system regime (Holling and Meffe, 1996). In recent years there has been an increasing emphasis on linked social–ecological systems in this body of work (Berkes et al, 2003), associated with ideas of 'panarchy' (Gunderson and Holling, 2002), where understandings of resilience emerge from nested and interacting social and ecological systems. As discussed in more depth in Chapter 4, this leads in turn to questions of system governance and the principles of learning, participation, networks, trust and leadership this requires (Walker et al, 2006).

Emerging from similar concerns, but from different starting points and disciplinary perspectives, an overlapping set of issues has been raised in attempts to define a new 'sustainability science' (Kates et al, 2001; Clark and Dickson, 2003; Turner et al, 2003). Geographers in particular have highlighted the need for an integrative science of sustainability, linking natural and social sciences, to address the challenges of global change and 'regions at risk' from natural hazards and disasters (Kates and Kasperson, 1983; Wisner et al, 2004). Here again questions of scale interactions – across both time and space – and uncertainties resulting from complex system dynamics are highlighted. A regional, place-based approach is advocated, allowing such integrative approaches to environment and development problems to be pursued in located ways.

Dynamics, complexity and development

In this chapter we have introduced a somewhat bewildering variety of diverse areas of enquiry, all emphasizing the importance of dynamics and complexity. Across these areas, a number of common threads can be identified. There is, for instance, a common recognition of the need to move away from the analytical assumptions of equilibrium thinking, centred on linearity, predictability, homogeneity and simplification, to ones that encompass nonlinearity, complexity, heterogeneity, uncertainty, ambiguity and surprise. There is also a repeated identification of scale interactions as critical. No longer is it adequate to separate off disciplinary foci into 'the micro' and 'the macro', the 'local' and the 'global', but it is the interactions across scales, with dynamics operating at different rates across them, that key. This requires an openness to concepts of hierarchy and cross-scale analysis, with a focus on the implications of divergent framings and on interaction and integration in analyses and responses. These perspectives on key drivers and system functioning suggest, too, different ways of approaching the complex questions that dominate management and policy issues. The narrow and closed equilibrium models that have dominated past perspectives must be used with extreme caution, with multiple health warnings attached. And yet we continue to see institutions geared towards working with these models and associated perspectives. A non-equilibrium perspective, by contrast, requires a more experimental approach to learning and an incremental approach to developing understanding under conditions of uncertainty, where surprises are always around the corner.

A core challenge is to go beyond narrow modelling approaches that close down options and obscure or factor out variability (Stirling, 2008). This applies too to our statistical routines, suggesting the need to question our assumptions about normal distributions rooted in standard statistical tests of proof. Dealing with outliers, contingent events and complex combinations requires new ways of judging and appraising outcomes (Riley and Fielding, 2001). Nevertheless, there are some cautions. A key lesson is to avoid going down the route of describing everything and learning little. Adaptive experimentation, double-loop learning and an open-ended perspective on research and appraisal are key attributes, as Chapter 5 explores. As discussed at greater length in subsequent chapters on governance questions, all this has important implications for the design of institutions and governance arrangements capable of working in this way (Ostrom et al, 1993).

The subsequent chapters of this book therefore pick up on these themes and apply them to some concrete issues and contexts. The next chapter tries to distil some of the key features and offers a framework for responding to dynamic contexts in the quest for sustainability.

Chapter 3

Pathways to Sustainability: Responding to Dynamic Contexts

Debating sustainability

How does an understanding of complexity and dynamics influence our understanding of sustainability? The incorporation of an explicitly normative stance, as discussed in Chapter 1, together with a dynamic complexity perspective, discussed in Chapter 2, contrasts strikingly with more technocratic, managerial and equilibrium approaches to sustainability. An emphasis on pathways implies debates about politically contested goals and objectives. Given the way such pathways are constructed in highly dynamic, uncertain and complex settings, there is also a need for reflexivity in path-building, whereby destination, routes and directions are continuously reconsidered by multiple participants.

As discussed in Chapter 1, sustainability has become one of the most debated and contested terms of recent times.[6] But, like all such terms, sustainability has a history. It did not always have such significant connotations. Several hundred years ago the term was first coined in an environmental context by a German forester, Hans Carl von Carlowitz in his 1712 text *Sylvicultura Oeconomica*, to prescribe how forests should be managed on a long-term basis. It was, however, not until the 1980s that 'sustainability' came into much wider currency. With the birth of the contemporary environmental movement in the late 1960s and 1970s, and debates about the 'limits to growth' (Meadows, 1972), environmentalists were keen to show how environmental issues could be linked to mainstream questions of development. The commission chaired by Gro Brundtland, former prime minister of Norway, became the focal point for this debate in the mid-1980s, culminating in the landmark report 'Our Common Future' in 1987 (Brundtland, 1987). This offered the now classic modern definition of sustainable development:

> *Sustainable development is development that meets the needs of the present without compromising the ability of future generations to meet their own needs (Brundtland, 1987, p43).*

The term 'sustainability', and more particularly 'sustainable development', drew on longer intellectual debates across disciplines (Scoones, 2007). From the 1980s there was an explosion of academic debate about these issues, as the terms were projected onto the centre stage of policy debates globally, particularly in the run-up to the World Conference on Environment and Development held in Rio in 1992.

As Chapter 2 has already discussed, ecologists have long been concerned with how ecosystems respond to shocks and stresses. In particular, mathematical ecology had blossomed through the 1980s, with important work on this issue from the likes of Buzz Holling and Robert May on the stability and resilience properties of both model and real biological systems (May, 1977; Holling, 1978). Sustainability could thus be defined in these terms as the ability of a system to bounce back from such shocks and stresses and adopt stable states (Holling, 1993; Ludwig et al, 1997; Folke et al, 2002). Neo-classical economists drew on theories of substitutable capital to define (weak) sustainability in terms of the constancy of human and natural capital in delivering constant consumption goods over time, with market failures due to externalities corrected. Within economics, debates raged over whether such a 'weak' definition of sustainability was adequate or whether a stronger definition highlighting the lack of substitutability of 'critical natural capital' was needed (Turner, 1992; Pearce and Atkinson, 1993; Goodland, 1995; Goodland and Daly, 1996).[7] Ecological economics traces more concrete links with ecological systems, generating such fields as life-cycle analysis, ecological-footprint assessment and alternative national accounting systems (Common and Perrings, 1992; Common and Stagl, 2005). Building on these different debates, Herman Daly and others developed an economic vision of sustainable development which challenged standard growth models (Lele, 1991; Daly 1991, 1996). Elements of this were picked up by the business community and notions of the 'triple bottom line' emerged, where sustainability was seen as one among other more conventional business objectives, resulting in a whole plethora of new accounting and auditing measures which brought sustainability concerns into business planning and accounting practice (Welford, 1995; Elkington, 1997). The World Business Council for Sustainable Development was launched with much fanfare (Schmidheiny, 1992; Holliday et al, 2002), bringing on board some big corporate players. Drawing on wider popular political concerns about the relationships between environment, well-being and struggles for social justice, political scientists such as Andrew Dobson (1999) delineated political theories that incorporated a 'green' politics perspective and where sustainability concerns were put at the centre of a normative understanding of social and political change. Others offered integrative syntheses, linking the economic, environmental and socio-political goals of sustainability into what Robert Kates and colleagues dubbed a 'sustainability science' (Kates et al, 2001).

By the 1990s, then, we had multiple versions of sustainability: broad and narrow, strong and weak, and more. Different technical meanings were constructed alongside different visions of how the wider project of sustainable development should be conceived. Each competed with each other in a vibrant, if confusing, debate. But how would all this intense debate translate into practical policy and action on the ground? The 1992 Rio conference, convened by the United Nations and attended by 178 governments, numerous heads of states and a veritable army of over a thousand NGOs, civil society and campaign groups, was perhaps the high point – the coming of age of sustainability and sustainable development. This was the moment when many hoped that sustainability would find its way to the top of the global political agenda and would become a permanent feature of the way development, both North and South, would be done (Holmberg et al, 1991).

The Rio conference launched a number of high-level convention processes – on climate change, biodiversity and desertification – all with the aim of realizing sustainable development ideals on key global environmental issues (Young, 1997, 1999). Commissions were established and national action planning processes set in train for a global reporting system against agreed objectives (Dalal-Clayton et al, 1994), and a whole plethora of economic valuation, indicator measurement and auditing/accounting techniques were elaborated. For example, David Pearce, Kerry Turner and colleagues at the ESRC Centre for Social and Economic Research on the Global Environment (CSERGE) developed approaches to environmental valuation as a means to ensure that environmental issues were taken into account in economic accounting and appraisal (Barbier et al, 1990; Pearce and Turner, 1990; Pearce and Warford, 1993; Turner et al, 1994),[8] while others joined the growth industry in producing sustainable development indicators (Pearce et al, 1996; Rennings and Wiggering, 1997; Bell and Morse, 1999; Bossel, 1999; Pannell and Glenn, 2000). At the same time a more local-level, community-led process was conceived – Agenda 21 – which envisaged sustainability being built from the bottom up through local initiatives by local governments, community groups and citizens (Lafferty and Eckerberg, 1998; Selman, 1998). These were heady days indeed. But what did implementing sustainability mean? The result was an exponential growth in planning approaches, analysis frameworks, measurement indicators, audit systems and evaluation protocols which were to help governments, businesses, communities and individuals make sustainability real.

However, the simplistic managerialism of many initiatives labelled 'sustainable development' left much to be desired (Berkhout et al, 2003;

Scoones, 2007; Jordan and Adger, 2009). Critiques focused on the lack of progress on major targets set in 1992, the endless repackaging of old initiatives as 'sustainable' this or that, and the lack of capacity and commitment within governments and international organizations genuinely to make the ideals of sustainability real in day-to-day practice (Vogler and Jordan, 2003). With the default bureaucratic mode of managerialism dominating – and its focus on action plans, indicators and the rest – the wider political economy of sustainable development was being ignored, with key elements of the sustainability debate being captured by powerful interest groups (Redclift, 1987, 1992; Meadowcroft, 1999). With mainstreaming and bureaucratization, the urgency and political vibrancy was lost, and with this came a dilution and loss of dynamism in a previously energetic and committed debate.

But all was not lost. Debates in recent years have refocused on some big issues which hit the headlines internationally, substituting for the emblematic issues – of the ozone hole, acidification, biodiversity loss and desertification – that dominated the run up to Rio. These have resulted in both public and, usually later, political reactions. For example, the controversy around genetically modified (GM) crops, which peaked in Europe in the late 1990s/early 2000s, had many political and policy reverberations internationally (GEC, 1999). This was a debate about, inter alia, the sustainability of farming systems, the future of food, human health and biodiversity and corporate control of the agri-food system (Thompson et al, 2007). In the same way, the climate change debate really only began to be taken seriously post-2000. No longer was this a discussion on the arcane specifics of global climate models but, as became clear, a real political and economic issue, which people and governments had to take seriously (Munasinghe and Swart, 2005; Roberts and Parks, 2007; Giddens, 2009). Concerns about the environment and development drivers of new global diseases and pandemics were also pitched into the public and political realm, first with severe acute respiratory syndrome (SARS) and then avian and H1N1 influenzas (Abraham, 2005; Greger, 2006; Bloom et al, 2007; Dry, 2008; Scoones and Forster, 2008). All of these issues – and the list could go on – are centred around classic 'sustainability' questions: they each involve complex and changing environmental dynamics having an impact on human livelihoods and well-being; they all have intersecting ecological, economic and socio-political dimensions; and, as with an increasing array of environment–development issues, they have both local and global dimensions.

But what is equally sure is that the existing 'sustainable development' institutional and policy machinery is incapable of dealing with them effectively. Options for a post-Kyoto climate change agreement, which involves the USA, China and India, have yet to be elaborated. Questions of biosafety surrounding GM crops have not been resolved and nor does the UN Biosafety Protocol necessarily deal with these effectively. Also, recent disease scares have shown that neither global institutions nor local health systems are able to deal with a global pandemic.

So what of the future? Will sustainability become the unifying concept of the 21st century as many so boldly proclaimed just a few years ago? Certainly the 1990s managerialism and routinized bureaucratization has been shown to have its limits. While sustainability-related commissions, committees and processes persist in various guises, they have perhaps less political hold than before. But with climate change in particular – and wider risks associated with environmental change, whether in disease, biodiversity loss or water scarcity – now being seen as central to economic strategy and planning, there are clear opportunities for the insertion of sustainability agendas into policy discourse and practice in new ways.

What is required, this book argues, is a more concrete clarification of what is meant by 'sustainability'. For example, the classic Brundtland definition of 'sustainable development' highlights notions of needs and limitations. Explaining these concepts, it defines 'needs' as 'in particular the essential needs of the world's poor, to which overriding priority should be given', and limitations are seen in relation to 'the state of technology and social organization on the environment's ability to meet present and future needs' (Brundtland, 1987, p43). However, we must ask whether, given the complex, uncertain and dynamic contexts in which negotiations of sustainability must take place, such static notions of needs and limits are appropriate. Colloquial usage of the term 'sustainability' simply refers to the general quality of being 'capable of being maintained at a certain rate or level' (OED, 1989) and is inherently conservative and not dynamic. What exactly is to be maintained is often not specified.

Towards a normative, politicized perspective on sustainability

In the post-Brundtland, post-Agenda 21 policy debates on sustainability, however, the usage is explicitly normative. Sustainability refers to a broadly identifiable, but often poorly specified, set of social, environmental and economic values. Although the details are often ambiguous, contested and context-dependent, the functions concerned include the securing of particular standards of social equity, economic well-being or environmental quality. In this policy context, then, structures – such as particular laws, technologies, infrastructures or institutions – are not ends

in themselves, but means to the ends of delivering on these broad normative aims.

We share this spirit, but go further. We argue that it is useful to distinguish between different normative views of sustainability, recognizing that
there are multiple sustainabilities which need to be defined quite precisely
for particular issues and groups. Thus sustainability neither carries its colloquial connotations, implying the maintenance of system properties in a
general sense, nor its broad normative connotations, in Brundtland's terms.
Rather, we need to specify versions of sustainability in terms of the particular properties and flows of goods and services valued by particular social
groups or in the pursuit of particular goals. Rhetorical appeals to sustainability can be, and often are, used to obscure complex or contested
interpretations and interests around such particular versions of sustainability. Digging beneath such rhetoric and uncovering particular interpretations
and their links with particular goals and interests is a key task.

It follows from this that the sustainability debate must shed its managerial pretensions. Rather, sustainability must become recognized as a
contested, discursive resource – a boundary object (Gieryn, 1983) – that
facilitates argument about diverse pathways to different futures. This
brings sustainability firmly into the realm of the political, where debates
around 'justice', 'democracy' and 'citizenship' have been for centuries.

Across our four case studies, it is thus not surprising that we find highly
contested versions of sustainability. For example, in dryland India sustainable water management may be defined in relation to the sustained
provision of urban water supply or the sustainability of irrigated farming –
which might both be served through the building of large dams. In contrast,
sustainability may be defined in relation to sustaining rain-fed farming
livelihoods in particular dryland areas and the provision of groundwater-
based village water supplies there. In the case of debates about the
sustainability of seed systems, the focus may be on their contribution to
national food security goals and sustaining overall aggregate production.
Alternatively, the focus may be the ability to sustain the livelihoods of
poorer farmers in the face of increasing shocks and stresses. Even within
such a small-farmer focus, men and women, or elders and youth, might prioritize the sustainability of different crops or varieties. In the case of
epidemics, the sustainability of the response system may be defined in
terms of its ability to protect global populations from disease outbreaks. Yet
in other versions sustainability may mean responding to the specific vulnerabilities and livelihood contexts of those confronting diseases on a
day-to-day basis. In the case of energy systems, sustainability is routinely
restricted – and not just in the industrialized world – to the single question
of carbon intensity. Yet many of the alternatives to fossil fuels present their

own sustainability challenges, suggesting different versions of sustainability centred on, for instance, the toxicity and risks associated with nuclear materials, the resource implications of certain renewable strategies or the agronomic and land-use implications of wholesale shifts to biomass.

Across the cases, these versions – and indeed many others – are not just different, but are the subject of highly politicized contestation. This may occur at all scales, from disputes within and between households and communities to those between local, national and global priorities. Therefore what is defined as sustainable (or otherwise) and the indicators that are used must be subject to deliberation, with a clear and careful unpicking of the particular goals and their trade-offs.

A systems perspective

Although the world is endlessly complex and dynamic, it is useful for analytical and practical purposes to think in terms of particular systems. Systems, as we consider them in this book, consist of social, institutional, ecological and technological elements interacting in dynamic ways.

Such systems need to be understood in relation to both their structures and their functions. Structures concern the ways in which the system and its boundaries are constituted, its internal and external relationships and the patterns in which its processes unfold. System functions, on the other hand, concern things such as services, outputs and consequences. These are the 'outcomes' that are held to be delivered by the system, as well as associated notions of purpose and meaning.

How these structures and functions are understood and prioritized can vary markedly, as the examples above indicate. Thus the 'water management system' of interest may be bounded at the regional or national level in relation to fulfilling water supply functions for irrigators or urban populations. Or it may be bounded and understood as a local water-agro-ecological system with very different functional qualities in terms of contributing to a flow of livelihood benefits. As in this example, systems might be bounded at very different scales, with different consequences for how structures and functions are defined. System-bounding can, however, also involve the same scale, but with different priority given to particular elements, relationships and functions. Thus, in the case of seed systems, a national system for research, innovation and supply of new seeds might be geared to high-value crops for high potential zones, or to crops and varieties suited to the circumstances of poorer farmers.

The ways that system structures and boundaries are understood and functions prioritized constitute central dimensions of what we term 'framing'.

This concern with framing, or the different ways of understanding or representing a system – drawing from the insights of methodological constructivism in the social sciences – is a central building block of our pathways approach. Thus we recognize that system boundaries, dynamics, functions and outcomes are always open to multiple, particular, contextual, positioned and subjective assumptions, methods, forms of interpretation, values and goals. These might be held, for instance, by diverse international organizations, technical agencies, sectoral ministries, professional disciplines, civil society or local actors, different community members or networks which connect members of these different groups (see Figure 3.1 and Box 3.1).

So whereas much systems thinking – including in debates about sustainability – seeks to reflect comprehensively a full range and diversity of elements, linkages and dynamics in a system and its environment, our pathways approach adds a reflexive dimension. This recognizes that all analysis of a system – whether by researchers, policy actors or different local people – involves framing. All framing involves not just choices about which elements to highlight, but also subjective and value judgements. Such framings are produced by particular actors and co-constituted with their particular institutional, political and life settings. Attention to the

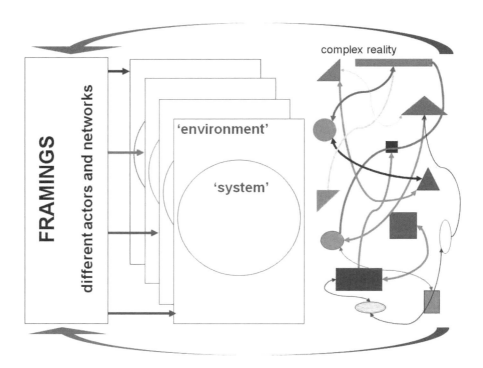

Figure 3.1 Multiple framings

Box 3.1 *Dimensions of framing*

Choice of elements:	*Subjective judgements:*
• Scale	• Perspectives
• Boundaries	• Interests
• Key elements and relationships	• Values
• Dynamics in play	• Notions of relevant experience
• Outputs	• Goals

ways in which particular actors and networks produce – and sometimes seek to promote – particular framings is an important addition to systems perspectives which otherwise have a tendency to downplay the roles of particular actors and their agency.

Framing and narratives

Particular system-framings often become part of narratives about a problem or issue. These are simple stories with beginnings defining the problem, middles elaborating its consequences and ends outlining the solutions (Roe, 1994). Narratives often start with a particular framing of a system and its dynamics and suggest particular ways in which these should develop or transform to bring about a particular set of outcomes. Thus, in relation to the case of water in dryland India, an example of a mainstream policy narrative might be: 'Major water scarcities are developing and undermining economic development; therefore the construction of large dams and investment in the infrastructure for water delivery must take place.' In the case of epidemics, a frequently heard narrative holds that 'the global threat of a pandemic and its consequences for massive mortalities and economic costs require substantial investments in surveillance, drug stockpiling and intervention in areas of the world where outbreaks originate, in order to protect us all.' In the case of seeds in Africa, we often hear a narrative that 'growing food deficits require massive boosts to agricultural productivity and only GM crops will provide the answer.' In the case of energy, we often hear the narrative that 'the challenges of dealing with climate change and energy security can only be dealt with through a centralized system including nuclear power generation.'

Table 3.1 highlights a number of ways by which narratives are formed, involving value judgements about what and who is included and excluded and what issues, questions and solutions are prioritized.

Table 3.1 *Creating narratives: Practices*

Stating goals	Defining problems	Including disciplines
Setting agendas	Prioritizing issues	Interpreting results
Posing questions	Setting baselines	Highlighting values
Deciding context	Choosing methods	Drawing boundaries
Discounting time	Recruiting expertise	Formulating criteria
Handling uncertainties	Characterizing options	
Constituting 'proof'	Exploring sensitivities	

Let us work through narratives related to two of our case examples in more detail, to consider how a system is framed, identify which actors are involved and consider the elements of system framing, as well as how these aspects are drawn into a particular narrative, through some of the practices highlighted in Table 3.1.

In the case of pandemic threats, an 'outbreak narrative' is often pushed by international agencies and governments in northern settings. As Wald (2008, p2) puts it:

> *[This] begins with the identification of an emerging infection, includes discussion of the global networks throughout which it travels, and chronicles the epidemiological work that ends with its containment. As epidemiologists trace the routes of the microbes, they catalogue the spaces and interactions of global modernity. Microbes, spaces and interactions blend together as they animate the landscape and motivate the plot of the outbreak narrative: a contradictory but compelling story of the perils of human interdependence and the triumph of human connection and co-operation, scientific authority and the evolutionary advantages of the microbe, ecological balance and impending disaster.*

The narrative therefore defines and bounds the system in global terms. In terms of objective elements of system framing, it focuses on a particular interpretation of disease dynamics (sudden emergence, speedy, far-reaching, often global spread) and a particular version of response (universalized, generic emergency-oriented control, at source, aimed at eradication). More subjective dimensions include the value placed on protecting global populations, which often implies protecting particular populations in richer countries. Goals are defined in terms of impacts on human mortality and national economies and business viability. This narrative calls upon particular kinds of knowledge and expertise – notably formal science and epidemiology – in diagnosing and solving the problem.

Such an overall outbreak narrative has been typical of the international responses to highly pathogenic avian influenza (HPAI), for example, with distinct versions associated with veterinary, human public health and pandemic preparedness strands of the response. The HPAI outbreak narrative in particular has been framed in terms of a globalized version of 'health security' (WHO, 2007; Scoones and Forster, 2008; Scoones, 2010). This, in turn, has given rise to a plethora of initiatives and associated institutional arrangements focused on early warning, risk assessment, intensive surveillance, outbreak monitoring, pandemic-preparedness planning, rapid response teams, contingency plans and so on. With disease-specific variations, dominant narratives around SARS and Ebola similarly emphasize short-term, acute outbreaks requiring rapid identification and control – to 'stamp out' the outbreak and prevent dangerous spread ultimately to global populations (Heymann et al, 1999; Crawford, 2007; Leach, 2008; Dry and Leach, 2010). Specific elements of the institutional response have included the creation by the WHO of a revised set of International Health Regulations in 2005 (WHO, 2005) and of the Global Outbreak Alert and Response Network (GOARN) (WHO, 2009) which mobilizes multiple agencies to respond to epidemic shocks as they arise.

Yet there are alternative narratives produced by different actors which frame the system in different ways. One alternative narrative, for instance, promoted by certain researchers, technical agencies and non-governmental organizations, emphasizes a local intervention model focused on reducing disease risk and exposure in a particular area. The system is thus bounded here in more local or regional terms. Relevant dynamics include the social, political and ecological processes which result in disease outbreaks and make particular people vulnerable to them. Variants of this narrative therefore embrace attention to long-term changes in human–animal–environment interactions (for example, trends in farming, livelihoods and land use in the context of climate change) as a focus for development and adaptation. These might include, for instance, land-use and ecosystem interventions such as integrated vector management, or the restructuring of market chains – for example in the poultry industry (Parkes et al, 2004; Waltner-Toews and Wall, 1997). In some versions, dynamic disease ecology comes to the fore, with attention to the often-unpredictable ways that viruses, social and environmental dynamics co-evolve in particular settings such as to render particular people and places vulnerable (Slingenbergh et al, 2004). Thus deforestation through agriculture and logging, and its political, economic and poverty-related causes, has been argued to contribute to viral haemorrhagic fevers, by bringing populations closer to their forest animal viral reservoirs and secondary vectors. Outbreaks of haemorrhagic fevers have often centred on the forest–savannah boundary zone, suggesting interactions with nonlinear forest–savannah dynamics and land use (Fairhead and Leach, 1998), and with agricultural and bushmeat-trading livelihoods

(Hardin, 2008), which may themselves be influenced by the uncertain effects of climate change. Subjective goals and values in this alternative narrative focus more on addressing the underlying structural causes of inequity and disease vulnerability among particular populations (Farmer, 2003), and addressing the longer-term social justice and livelihood implications of disease and response.

In a related alternative narrative, advocated by some field practitioners with long experience of engagement with local populations, infectious diseases are seen as more endemic than epidemic; long present among local populations who have developed culturally embedded ways to live and deal with them, as with haemorrhagic fevers for example (Hewlett and Hewlett, 2008). Like the previous alternative narrative, the system is bounded in local terms. But here, the system relationships highlighted include local knowledge and social protocols which can, so this narrative argues, inform and be integrated into participatory surveillance and response strategies, helping to make these more context-specific, locally appropriate and acceptable.

Thus different actors and networks, framing system dynamics, boundaries and goals in different ways, produce very different narratives about what a response should be and what might make it effective. A similar array of contrasting narratives can be found across all our case examples. To take another, let us look at water in Western India.

The case of water-scarce Kutch, a region of Gujarat in Western India, has become iconic in the debate about water scarcity in India, particularly around the controversial Sardar Sarovar Project (SSP) (Mehta, 2005). Those promoting large-dam building as a solution to regional water scarcity, including certain state planners, water engineers and elite land owners with potential access to irrigation water, promote a narrative which sees the creation of a massive dam across the Narmada river as necessary to supply downstream irrigation and urban water needs. The system is bounded as a large, regional watershed, linking water supplies to a range of users. System dynamics are characterized in terms of declining water availability, portraying scarcity as natural – attributed to low and ever-decreasing rainfall and perennial droughts. As research by Mehta (2005) has shown, there is a widespread view in Kutch that due to the harsh climate, erratic water supply, declining groundwater sources and frequent droughts, the only solution is to get water from the rivers of Gujarat, with hopes pinned on the ambitious dam project SSP. These arguments have become incorporated into popular and media discourses, which have also become a way of expressing concerns about the political marginalization of the region. Kutchi identity is moulded around water or the lack of it. Villagers across the length and breadth of the district say in certain contexts that the lack of water is the cause of their misery, the depopulated villages and mass migration out of Kutch (Mehta, 2005). Thus the subjective values and goals in this narrative include not just increasing physical water availability, but also the rescuing of the region from political marginality.

In contrast, farmers and pastoralists living in Kutch express in their everyday lives and practices a highly contrasting narrative. Their framings of the system focus on local dryland livelihoods and on the knowledge and livelihood strategies that allow them to adapt to the unpredictability and temporary scarcity of water. This narrative also draws attention to distributional issues and the social and political dynamics which enable some to access water while others do not. The water 'crisis' in Kutch in this view is largely human-induced and intensely political, and not simply 'natural' (Mehta, 2005). Emphasis is placed on the culpability of large farmers, bad water-management practices, misuse of water and the circumventing of legislation. Activists and researchers allied with this narrative, in turn, take a different view on the SSP. They argue that much of the water made available downstream will either be utilized by the industrial complex in southern Kutch or be diverted to meet the needs of big irrigation farmers whose use of water is neither economic nor judicious. They argue that, following present plans, SSP water will not help to recharge the groundwater aquifers of Kutch or reduce soil salinity; neither will it meet the water needs of poor dryland cultivators, women and pastoralists. Therefore with different subjective values and goals, as well as a different understanding of dynamics, the narrative emphasizes different solutions. These focus on learning lessons from history. In the past, even though rainfall was precarious and scanty, the region's water resources were managed either by local people or by the Raos of Bhuj, using principles and practices compatible with Kutch's needs: for example, earthen dams, tanks and other water-harvesting methods.

Thus, for any given issue, it is possible to identify a range of different narratives which link different system framings to particular goals and values. While narratives are produced by particular actors and networks, the same people may become allied with different narratives at different times and in different contexts. Thus, in the case of debates about water in Kutch, farmers may represent water scarcity as natural when they speak in popular, politicized terms about the region's marginalization, yet express very different perspectives as they live with water uncertainty in their day-to-day farming livelihoods.

As we see in these examples, different narratives lead to radically different assessments of policy options. Even among different actors in the policy field, different system framings are important and often lead to very different narratives around intervention and action. In the energy sector, for instance, great efforts have been expended to conduct comprehensive comparative assessments across a full range of policy options (CEC, 2004). Results have been influential in areas of policymaking such as climate change, nuclear power and utility regulation.

Figure 3.2 shows the results obtained across 63 international cost-benefit studies, looking at the adverse effects caused by a range of different electricity-generating options – from coal to biomass. Each study was conducted according to comparably stringent disciplinary principles and subject to similarly rigorous processes of expert accreditation or peer review. Not every study reviews every energy option, which is why the values of *n* on the right-hand side do not add up to 63. The impacts of energy technologies are expressed in this literature as 'economic externalities'. This involves taking all the different kinds of environmental, health and wider social pros and cons of each energy option and calculating a monetary value to represent the relative magnitude of each. In Figure 3.2, the results are represented as the additional 'external cost' (in US cents at 1998 prices) that would have to be added to the existing market price of one unit of electricity (a kilowatt-hour, kWh) if this were to reflect the full 'social cost' of electricity production

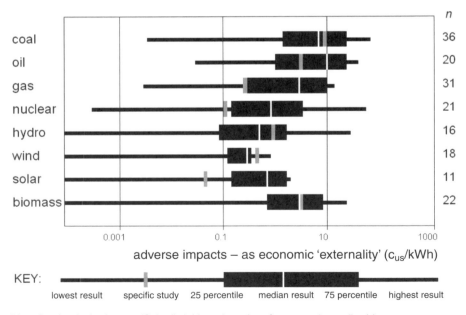

Note: Results obtained across 63 detailed risk- and cost-benefit comparative studies (*n*).
Source: Adapted from Sundqvist et al, 2004

Figure 3.2 Variability in assessment of policy options for electricity supply

by each means (Sundqvist et al, 2004). Although the expression of these results in terms of monetary values is controversial (Stirling, 1997), it is standard procedure in this energy-assessment literature, as across other areas of technology assessment such as chemicals, agriculture and transport (Amendola, 1992; Saltelli, 2008). Whereas individual studies typically express their results as very precise, there is enormous variability in the literature as a whole, extending to several orders of magnitude around the median values for each range in Figure 3.2. Thus, depending which result is chosen from within the range associated with each option, contending energy supply technologies could be ranked very differently. These contrasts between the results obtained by different studies are due to the divergent framings of their analyses. Although privately well known to analysts, this importance of subjective judgement is rarely reflected in the presentation of results, let alone policy discussions, which routinely refer to this kind of 'science based' analysis as offering clear prescription for choice among alternative technology options (Stirling, 2008).

In the same way, Figure 3.3 displays the variety of judgements exercised by different experts involved in advising the UK government on the regulation of GM crops in the late 1990s. Using an elicitation method called 'multicriteria mapping' (MCM) (Stirling, 1997; Stirling and Mayer, 1999), each individual expert explored their own understandings of the options, evaluation criteria, policy priorities and technical uncertainties. The result in each case included an individual picture of the relative performance rankings for a series of different agricultural strategies. Each chart in Figure 3.3 summarizes these individual pictures for six agricultural strategies that were comparable across all experts. The results reveal large uncertainties within individual views (shown by the lengths of the bars) and stark ambiguities across different perspectives (shown by the contrasting rankings across individual charts). The detailed picture of the underlying framings provided by MCM contrasts strongly with the typically quite precise prescriptive collective findings expressed by the advisory committees on which these same experts sit. Each framing is similarly 'expert' and 'legitimate', yet yields radically divergent implications for policymaking. Conventional unified recommendations 'close down' these uncertainties and ambiguities and obscure the importance for policymaking of divergent 'expert' framings.

The reason that expert assessment procedures such as these can yield such contrasting pictures is that the answers that are derived typically depend on the framing of analysis (Goffman, 1975). As Chapter 5 illustrates further, framing effects such as these shape the application of appraisal tools, methods and procedures of all kinds.

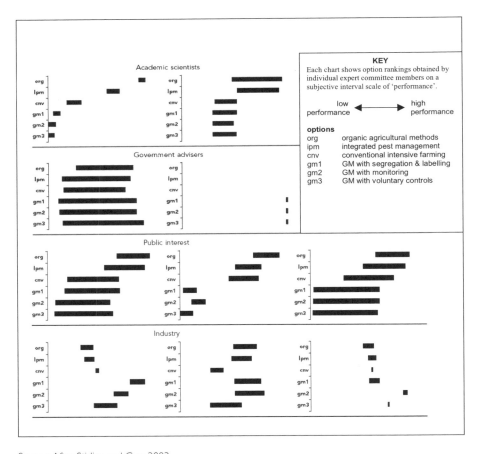

Source: After Stirling and Gee, 2003

Figure 3.3 Variation in policy judgements on alternative
agricultural policy options

As we now go on to explore, narratives differ not just in how they frame systems and prioritize particular goals, they also differ in how they address risk and uncertainty, and in the particular dynamic properties of sustainability that they emphasize. We now deal with these themes in turn.

Addressing risk and uncertainty

As seen from these examples from the field energy policy and agriculture, the world involves both complex dynamics and radical differences in framings of them. For our understandings (and policymaking) to be as effective as possible, attention must therefore focus very directly on the risks, uncertainties and ambiguities which result.

Yet there are many ways of thinking about risk and uncertainty. These can be illustrated by building on the two basic dimensions that constitute the mainstream policy concept of 'risk'. First, there are the things that might happen: 'hazards', 'possibilities', 'benefits' or 'costs' – which can be referred to as 'outcomes'. A second dimension is the likelihood of each outcome happening – conventionally represented as a numerical probability between zero and one. Routine economic and policy analysis represents 'risk' as the simple product of these two parameters. But what is neglected in this kind of approach is that either of these dimensions may itself be subject to variously incomplete or problematic knowledge.

As Figure 3.4 shows, this conventional definition of 'risk' actually implies three other idealized possible states of knowledge about likelihoods and outcomes (Stirling, 1999). In naming these, Figure 3.4 employs terms in a sense that reflects both their colloquial meanings and their strict (and original) technical definitions. The crucial point here, however, lies not in terminology or taxonomy. The four distinguished aspects of incomplete knowledge are 'ideal types', reflecting different facets of incomplete knowledge that typically occur together in varying degrees. The value of this

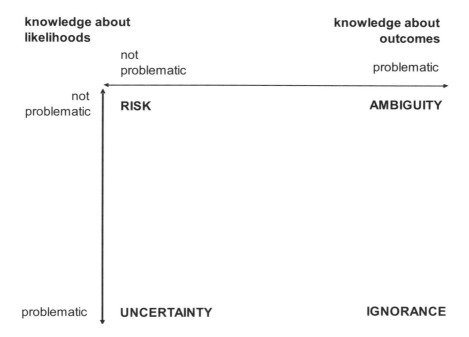

Figure 3.4 Dimensions of incomplete knowledge

picture lies rather in the substance of the distinctions, highlighting their very different implications for practical and policy responses. By recognizing the different properties of these contrasting states of knowledge, we can gain important insights into the challenges for sustainability.

The top left-hand quadrant defines risk in the strict sense of the term. This refers to a situation where there is confidence that probabilities can be calculated across a range of known outcomes. However, the three other dimensions of incomplete knowledge are situations where these conditions do not apply: uncertainty, ambiguity and ignorance. These describe a range of circumstances under which reductive, analytic methods – such as risk assessment – are, even in their own terms, quite simply not applicable.

Under the strict definition of uncertainty in Figure 3.4 (lower left quadrant), we can be confident in our characterization of the different possible outcomes, but the available empirical information or analytical models do not present a definitive basis for assigning probabilities (Keynes, 1921; Knight, 1921; Rowe, 1994). It is under these conditions – in the words of the celebrated probability theorist de Finetti – that 'probability does not exist' (1974). Of course, we can still exercise subjective judgements and treat these as a basis for systematic analysis (Luce and Raiffa, 1957; Morgan et al, 1990). However, the challenge of uncertainty is that such judgements may take a number of different – equally plausible – forms (Wynne, 1992). Rather than reducing these to a single expected value or prescriptive recommendation, the rigorous approach is therefore to acknowledge the open nature of a variety of possible interpretations.

Under the condition of ambiguity (upper right quadrant), it is not the probabilities but the characterization of the outcomes themselves that is problematic. This may be the case even for events that are certain or have occurred already. Disagreements may exist, for instance, over the selection, partitioning, bounding, measurement, prioritization or interpretation of outcomes (Wynne, 2002; Stirling, 2003). Examples may be found in decisions over the right questions to pose in regulation: 'Is this safe?', 'sustainable?', 'sustainable enough?', 'acceptable?' or 'the most sustainable option?'. For instance, in the regulation of genetically modified seeds, ambiguities arise over contending ecological, agronomic, safety, economic or social criteria of harm (Grove-White et al, 1997; Levidow et al, 1998; Stirling and Mayer, 1999). Similar ambiguities emerge when we are forced to compare 'apples and oranges'. These might be qualitatively different forms of damage; impacts on different people (e.g. workers or the public; children or adults); consequences over different time-frames (e.g. present or future generations) or on different life-forms (e.g. humans or nonhumans). When faced with such questions over 'contradictory certainties' (Thompson and Warburton, 1985), Nobel prize-winning work in rational choice theory has shown that analysis alone is unable to guarantee definitive answers (Arrow, 1963; Kelly, 1978; MacKay, 1980). Where there is ambiguity, then, reductions to a single 'sound scientific' picture are also neither rigorous nor rational (Collingridge, 1982; Bonner, 1986).

Finally, there is the condition of ignorance (lower right quadrant). Here, neither probabilities nor outcomes can be fully characterized (Keynes, 1921; Loasby, 1976; Collingridge, 1980). Where 'we don't know what we don't know' (Wynne, 1992, 2002), we face the ever-present prospect of 'surprise' (Brooks, 1986; Rosenberg, 1996). This differs from uncertainty, which focuses on agreed known parameters (such as carcinogenicity or flood damage). It differs from ambiguity, in that the parameters are not just contestable but are acknowledged to be at least partly unknown. Some of the most important challenges of sustainability involve issues that were – at least at their outset – of just this kind (Funtowicz and Ravetz, 1990). In the early histories of stratospheric ozone depletion (Farman, 2001), novel zoonotic diseases such as bovine spongiform encephalopathy (BSE) (van Zwanenberg and Millstone, 2001) or highly pathogenic avian influenza (Stirling and Scoones, 2010), and the recognition of new mechanisms of chemical toxicity such as endocrine disruption (Thornton, 2000), for instance, the initial problem was not so much divergent expert views or mistakes over probability; rather, it was straightforward ignorance over the possibilities themselves.

Returning to the case example of seed systems in Africa, one of the hottest debates of recent years has been over the potential role of GM food crops. At the heart of this has been an intense discussion about multiple dimensions of risk and uncertainty, with different actors articulating different narratives with different emphases. Perhaps the most dominant of these has focused on the classic, narrow definition of risk. Here the potential toxicity or biosafety risks of GM food and crops are assessed in controlled conditions or through extrapolating from experiences in the USA and Europe. Principles such as 'substantial equivalence' (Millstone et al, 1999) are deployed, which not only assume the appropriateness and completeness of risk assessment, but seek to elevate these assumptions to the status of a global regulatory principle. On this basis, it becomes an institutional imperative to confine attention to 'risk based' assessments of the probabilities of a set of specific forms of harm to people and environments. However, both potential consequences and associated probabilities may be viewed very differently. Take the emergence of 'superweeds' or the toxic effects of GM food, for instance. The consequences of superweeds depend on assumptions about the efficacy, accessibility and affordability of management techniques, which can look very different for different groups. Toxic effects appear differently depending on whether they are understood as aggregate statistical effects over large populations or as specific impacts on genetically susceptible sub-populations. In either case, the probabilities of such outcomes occurring in particular places or conditions are typically deeply uncertain. This applies in particular to agro-ecological and social settings in Africa, for example, where standard experimental models designed for other contexts may not apply. In many situations, furthermore, conditions of ignorance may arise – where we simply don't know what we don't know. The synergistic impacts of GM foods on immune-suppressed populations, for example, may result in very different and wholly unforeseen toxicity reactions. Or the impacts of shifts in climate and agro-ecology may interact with crop weed genetic dynamics in ways that cannot be foreseen, particularly in biodiverse areas. Finally, the GM debate has been fraught with conditions of ambiguity, where different views on potential outcomes and why they matter prevail. Thus for example, GM may be discussed in terms of its potential for boosting crop productivity, disease and pest resistance and nutritional value. However, it may also be discussed in quite different terms in relation to the political economy of corporate control of agriculture and the implications this has for autonomy, dependence and livelihood options for the future (Scoones, 2005; Glover, 2009). Such different categories of incomplete knowledge in relation to GM crops are illustrated in Figure 3.5.

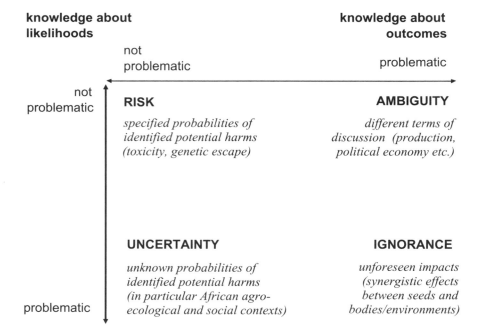

Figure 3.5 GM foods and crops: Dimensions of incomplete knowledge in African settings

Let us take another of our examples and look at how different dimensions of incomplete knowledge are invoked in the debate on avian influenza (Figure 3.6). Much of the debate has been dominated by quantitative probabilistic models of risk which sometimes present information about outcomes and likelihoods in far more definitive terms than is warranted. In 2005, for example, two models were presented in the journals *Nature* (Ferguson et al, 2005) and *Science* (Longini et al, 2005) which together had a huge influence in framing the response as one that needed to be focused on containment at the source of the outbreak. But of course a wide range of uncertainties exist – from the big uncertainty (will a devastating pandemic happen at all, and if so when?) to more specific uncertainties (about the impacts of veterinary control measures, about vaccination and drug efficacy, about behaviour change in situations of crisis and so on) (Scoones and Forster, 2008; Scoones, 2010). Thus, for example, the interplay between viral ecology and genetics (such as patterns of antigenic shift and drift), transmission mechanisms (such as the role of wild birds or poultry, backyard chickens or large factory units) and impacts (such as the consequences in immuno-compromised individuals and populations) are highly complex and contingent. There are also ambiguities: How do we define an 'outbreak'? What different perspectives are there on the potential distributional consequences and associated implications for the 'fairness' of different possible interventions? Outcomes can be defined, for example, in terms of potential impacts of pandemic influenza on human mortality. Up to 150 million deaths may occur in a major global pandemic according to some estimates (although there are huge variations in the numbers quoted). Human mortality impacts may also be more tightly defined, in relation to particular groups at risk – for example, women or children handling poultry. Potential economic impacts of a global pandemic are also quoted, with some estimating the cost at US$3 trillion. Yet cast in a different way, outcomes may be seen in terms of lost livelihoods and impacts on poverty and well-being. These outcomes may emerge from the response itself, as culling campaigns have resulted in around two billion chickens being slaughtered, many of which were backyard birds owned by poor families in developing countries (Scoones and Forster, 2008).

The condition of ignorance has also characterized debates over avian and pandemic influenza. The possible importance of hitherto unknown further mutations means that no one knows whether sustained human–human transmission will arise from the H5N1 virus or not. The possibility of as-yet undocumented transmission mechanisms and vectors means, further, that no one knows whether (if this occurs) it will result in rapid, global transmission with huge mortalities or not. And the possible importance of unexplored determinants of efficacy and wider consequences of response

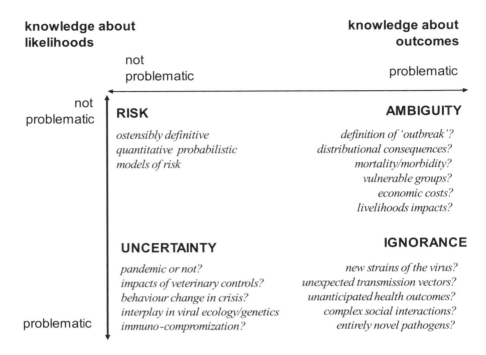

Figure 3.6 Avian and human pandemic influenza: Dimensions of incomplete knowledge

measures (e.g. containment, anti-viral drugs, vaccination) further com-pound the unknown implications for the spread of a pandemic. Of course, it is inherent in the nature of surprise that it is difficult to give possible examples of ignorance *ex ante*. However, possible surprises may plausibly be anticipated around the emergence of radically new strains of the virus (such as new combinations of avian and swine flu viruses), unexpected transmission mechanisms or unanticipated health outcomes, including those arising in complex interactions with other health/social conditions. Beyond this, there is always the broader possibility of the emergence of entirely novel pathogens; indeed more than 70 per cent of new infectious diseases affecting humans that have emerged over the last 30 years have emerged unexpectedly from non-human animal populations (Woolhouse and Gaunt, 2007; Jones et al, 2008).

Addressing dynamic properties of sustainability

Narratives about actions aiming to promote sustainability also involve assumptions about the nature, or 'temporalities', of the changes these actions are intended to counter. Are changes seen as short-term shocks or long-term stresses? And these narratives also differ strongly in terms of the styles of actions that are envisaged. Is the aim to control the causes or drivers of change, or to respond to them? These are important practical distinctions that are often elided or ignored in existing analysis for policy-making on sustainability. Figure 3.7 maps out these further distinctions and the dynamic properties of sustainability associated with them. The vertical axis rests on a distinction between temporalities of change – the dynamics of the system in question. If changes are characterized mainly as shocks, then disruptions are seen as transient under otherwise continuous trajectories. On the other hand, if changes are seen as stresses, then we are talking of enduring, long-run shifts to the directions of the trajectories themselves. The horizontal axis rests on the distinction between different kinds of strategic action or intervention. If sources or drivers of disruption are seen as tractable to control, then relatively ambitious measures of control may be held justifiable. If the driving causes of change are more intractable, then it may be that only relatively modest forms of response are appropriate. Such styles of action reflect the distinction between more conventional, control-oriented management and responsive, adaptive management.

Thus we might ask, within any given policy narrative: Are intervention strategies aimed at exercising control in order to resist disturbance or shocks to what is otherwise assumed to be an essentially unchanging trajectory

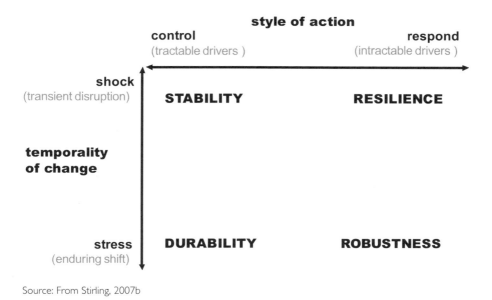

Source: From Stirling, 2007b

Figure 3.7 Dynamic properties of sustainability

(stability)? Or is there an acknowledgement that there may be limits to control, and thus that interventions should resist shocks in a more responsive fashion (resilience)? In other circumstances, the system may be subject to important stresses, driving long-run shifts. In this case, interventions might attempt to control the potential changes – aiming at durability. Alternatively, embracing both the limits to control and an openness to enduring shifts would suggest strategies aimed at robustness.

In dealing with epidemics, an emphasis on stability is the case for many outbreak narratives, which, as we have seen, emphasize 'stamping out' short-term disease shocks to return to a previous status quo. Thus control-oriented responses to outbreaks of Ebola in East and Central Africa, involving rapid response, containment and public health measures to limit contact and spread, have often proved highly effective (Heymann et al, 1999). This is a classic case of a control response to a short-term shock, with the aim of ensuring stability. However, in thinking about a sustainable disease response system over wider areas and longer time frames, there is a need to respond to outbreaks as they arise in a more flexible manner. A flexible response network that can be mobilized as and when needed can, in this context, be seen as a strategy for resilience. The WHO's Global Outbreak Alert and Response Network (GOARN) (WHO, 2009) is a potential example, although most of its activities focus on control responses to immediate shocks. The responses thus mobilized emphasize one-off, short-term disease-eradication efforts, often with little attention to longer-term stresses. For instance, in the case of Ebola, there are questions over how response infrastructures might respond to longer-term evolutionary changes in viruses and their ecological interactions (Pinzon et al, 2004; Walsh et al, 2005). Yet existing strategies are conventionally built on assumptions of internal stability, in which the fundamental dynamics are assumed to stay the same. In this way the property of durability is downplayed at the expense of stability.

Finally, there is the property of robustness – a conjunction of challenges both of intervention and change as represented in the bottom right of Figure 3.7. Like durability, this requires consideration of possible stresses towards secular long run shifts in conditions. But in this case these are recognized to lie beyond the ready reach of control. In dealing with Ebola, there exist numerous examples which point to this latter challenge of robustness (Leach, 2008): changes in viral susceptibility in different populations; long-term shifts in forest–savannah dynamics and their effects on the populations of rats that are the main vectors for the disease (Denys et al, 2005); ecological shifts and stresses resulting in more human–animal contact and the effects of climate change on these. These issues have not been addressed at a fundamental level in mainstream policy narratives.

There is an argument (usually geared to funders), that investment in epidemic responses and infrastructure networks at a global level will proof the system against future outbreaks by improving capacity (surveillance, diagnosis and so on) – and so ensuring, in our language, durability and robustness. Yet there is very little attention to the specific challenges presented by long-term, external changes which are not amenable to prediction and control.

In the case of water management – in India as elsewhere – short-term shocks creating variability in water supply have been responded to through engineering systems with an emphasis on water control through dams, pipes and pumps. The definition of sustainability therefore is centred on the maintenance of stability of supply. However, increasingly, water supply engineers and managers are having to confront long-term secular shifts in rainfall and hydrological patterns as a result of climate change. Again, control-oriented strategies are linking engineering solutions to long-term predictions of climate-related stresses. So, for example, dam infrastructures are built with margins to accommodate extra water or to operate with less. Thus, conceptions of sustainability extend from stability to durability, but still remain within a control-oriented paradigm.

In many instances, though, the tractability of the drivers of future environmental shocks and stresses affecting water supply and hydrology is understood to be limited. Here, more response-oriented strategies are essential in assuring sustainability. Thus, in cases of short-term shocks such as droughts or sharp, high rainfall episodes leading to floods, strategies for resilience are required. This involves moving beyond a control-oriented engineering approach to consider a diversity of response strategies and management interventions. In the Indian case, this might include building on local understandings, techniques and technologies – such as tank systems, water harvesting and so on, or strategies for pastoral mobility or inter-annual shifts in crop mixes. Water engineering for resilience requires inbuilt flexibility and an ability to manage flows in a responsive and adaptive manner.

However, given long-term stresses associated with climate change in places such as Kutch in Western India, acting in conjunction with other long-term stresses linked to population shifts, economic change and alterations of land use, adaptation to short-term shocks may be insufficient. Strategies to ensure robustness of water supply for users would need to respond not just to inter-annual variability or episodes of infrastructure failure, but to long-term changes in water supply and its use. This might involve longer-term shifts in land use, in agricultural practices, in crop types and varieties, and in the overall dependence on rain-fed agriculture in people's livelihoods. The suite of technologies and management practices required for sustainability focused on robustness will look different. Again, engineering solutions will be important but might, for instance, focus on a variegated system of smaller dams which can be adjusted more flexibly in response to long-term shifts in water availability. There are no simple answers; indeed debate and experimentation around strategies for responding to shocks, stresses and their less tractable causes in the Indian context, as elsewhere in South Asia, is live and ongoing (Moench and Dixit, 2004).

Sustainability is about the maintenance of qualities of human well-being, social equity and environmental integrity over time. This inherently encompasses both shocks and shifts (as the kinds of change against which qualities are maintained) and control and response actions (as the kinds of intervention that might be adopted to achieve these ends). The four properties mapped out in Figure 3.7 may therefore be seen as individually necessary and collectively sufficient elements of sustainability (see Figure 3.8). 'Sustainable solutions' are thus those that offer stability, durability, resilience and robustness in specified qualities of human well-being, social equity and environmental quality. Defined in this way, these dynamic properties of sustainability relate to benefits and flows delivered in any particular system, as framed in a particular way.

These quite fundamental conceptual distinctions give rise to some very practical policy implications. For instance, rather than speaking about some particular policy aim in terms of undifferentiated 'strategies for sustainability', we cannot assume that particular strategies fostering one aspect of the dynamics of sustainability will necessarily promote others. Thus, in the case of an epidemic response system, a sustainable system would combine not

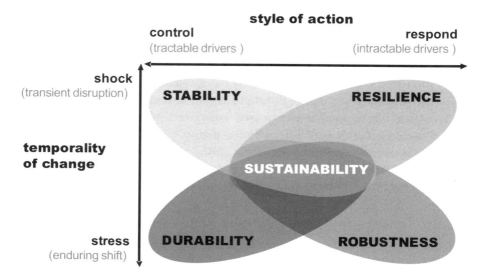

Figure 3.8 Combining dynamic properties of sustainability

only measures to control outbreaks at source as they arise, but also be positioned to respond adaptively to emergent outbreaks, thus conferring resilience and to identify, track and respond to longer-term shifts in disease incidence linked to changes in ecological and demographic conditions – both those that can be relatively easily controlled (durability) and those that require more adaptive responses (robustness). The relative emphasis on each of these dynamic properties of sustainability will depend on how the system is framed (its structures, elements and relationships) and on the associated policy goals and objectives. Thus narratives aimed at controlling global outbreaks of avian influenza, and those focused on more localized livelihood goals of Asian farmers affected by this as a long-term poultry disease, would highlight different dynamic properties and different goals of sustainability.

A new science for sustainability?

Following the discussion above, the task faced in thinking about and appraising issues of sustainability involves more than just a technical assessment of the dynamic properties of stability, durability, resilience and robustness. We must ask: What is the system? What are its purposes, functions and meanings? What is to be sustained and for whom? Who is to define each of these things and how? All such aspects are inevitably contested.

Drawing together the various sets of distinctions discussed above, for any issue we might therefore identify an array of narratives – different stories about the nature of a problem and potential solution. For each particular narrative we might ask:

- Who are the actors and networks articulating the narrative?
- What is the specific framing of 'the system' and its dynamics – including the treatment of different notions of bounding and spatial and temporal scale, and the goals and values prioritized for system change (Figure 3.1)?
- How is incomplete knowledge dealt with? To what extent does the narrative address the issue in terms of risk, uncertainty, ambiguity or ignorance (Figure 3.4)?
- Which dynamic properties of sustainability are prioritized? In particular, to what extent is the narrative focused on shocks or stresses, control or response (Figures 3.7 and 3.8)?

Narratives are important not just as stories about the world. Some of them, at least, justify and become entwined with particular pathways of intervention and system change. As we have discussed above, for any particular issue it is often possible to identify multiple narratives, each suggesting different pathways to different sustainabilities. Some exist, some are hidden and some are, currently, only imagined. But all must be subject to analysis, consideration and debate.

Pathways to sustainability are thus constructed through decisions which must explicitly address contestation and trade-offs between different dynamic system properties as seen under different framings and narratives. Critically, this requires a reflexive process, whereby assessments become necessarily positioned and partial, constructed in relation to the social–economic–political subjectivities of the analyst.

A new science for sustainability thus requires a joining together of now well elaborated non-equilibrium perspectives from the natural sciences (see Chapter 2) with social science perspectives which take the issue of framing seriously in an integrated manner. With Holling (1998) we agree that a positivist, sometimes reductionist analytic is needed alongside more integrative, holistic sciences. This requires greater dialogue and interaction across disciplines, sectors and policy debates. As Holling (1998, p5) notes, even 'Those more comfortable in exercising only one of these have the responsibility to understand the other.'

Central to the approach that we have developed in this chapter is what we might call a 'reflexive turn', by which we mean taking account of how analysis and understanding always depend on the position and assumptions of the analyst. This derives from a position on understanding systems, their structures, properties and functions, in relation to particular, normative goals and values. Any negotiation of pathways to sustainability in dynamic, complex systems must therefore be centrally about focusing on framings of systems and their properties – recognizing divergent epistemological (ways of knowing) and ontological (ways of being) positions, associated with different actors and interests. It must also involve negotiating the trade-offs across diverse pathways (actual, potential and imagined) in relation to the political-normative positions, goals and values of diverse actors.

Negotiating pathways to sustainability is therefore necessarily a political process. It can be informed by scientific analyses of contexts, systems and their properties but fundamentally requires an opening up of debate, through a diversification of knowledge bases and processes of inclusive deliberation at all steps. This needs to be supported by reflexive institutional frameworks and governance systems – and perhaps above all an increased humility and attention to power relations in processes of appraisal and decision-making. Just how this might come about – and often why it does not – both in terms of wider governance issues and particular appraisal designs – is the subject of the next three chapters.

Chapter 4

Governance in a
Dynamic World

Introduction

This book has posed a fundamental question: How can dynamic, intertwined social, technological and ecological change contribute to processes
and outcomes that are more sustainable – stable, durable, resilient and
robust – with respect to the functions, goals and values that are important
to poorer people in particular settings? Realizing this is in large part a question of 'governance', which we define here in a broad sense to refer to the
intersection of power, politics and institutions. This includes both private
and public institutions – and the market, political and civil processes in
which these are embedded, as well as relationships around knowledge and
power.

The nature of governance and pathways to sustainability are intimately
intertwined in at least two ways. First, as we saw in the last chapter, issues
and problems in today's world – whether concerning food and seeds, water,
energy or health, as in our case examples – are open to a variety of different
narratives about problems and potential solutions, each suggesting potential
response pathways. Such narratives are promoted by particular actors in
specific contexts; they embody different system-framings and goals, and
they attend, to varying degrees and in different ways, to issues of risk,
uncertainty, ambiguity and ignorance and different dynamic properties of
sustainability. But questions remain as to which narratives and pathways
come to dominate and which remain marginal or even hidden – present
perhaps only in the imaginations of marginalized groups in a given situation. Which pathways are pursued and which are not is in large part a
question of governance: a politics of narratives and pathways shaped by
power relations and institutions.

The second inherent interlinkage between governance processes and
pathways to sustainability is that political and institutional processes are
often themselves key factors implicated within the narratives and pathways
themselves. For instance, narratives are at least partly (and often deeply)
about social relationships and political and institutional power; about who is

responsible for a problem and who has the power to deal with it. Thus narratives about Africa's food crisis often locate the problem in farmers' poor agricultural and seed-selection practices and consider solutions to lie in the import of 'green revolution' technologies developed by biotechnology firms and global public–private partnerships (Paarlberg, 2008). Through such assertions, these narratives contain and reinforce assumptions about the power of the private sector and global institutions. In contrast, narratives which value and validate farmers' own seed and varietal selection practices, and the local social networks through which they develop and apply them (Richards, 2009; Rubyogo and Sperling, 2009), embody very different assumptions. These can suggest instead the empowerment of local and informal institutions. Acts of blaming are also acts of power, and in these contrasting narratives blame and responsibility are placed very differently – the first blaming the farmers or 'anti-GM' NGOs from Europe; and the second, perhaps, wider market or environmental factors which render local agricultural practices less successful.

In practice these two dimensions of the interrelationship between governance, narratives and associated pathways often merge. Thus we often see a process by which particular narratives giving rise to different pathways are promoted by powerful actors and institutions, upholding the status of their institutions and their power to intervene, manage or at least avoid blame for the situation. The orientations of pathways thus interlock with the nature of governance, so that pathways become, in effect, self-reinforcing and reinforcing of existing power relations. In contrast, other narratives – often those of more marginal actors, and supporting their political and institutional interests – remain marginalized. The point here is not that all existing or possible narratives necessarily each entail some practically realizable pathway. The issue is rather that particular narratives play an essential role in justifying and constituting those pathways that do come to be followed – and suppressing those that (even if technically and socially possible) remain unrealized in practice. It is in this way – as well as through the mobilization of more tangible power, resources and interventions – that the storylines favoured by powerful interests so often come to occlude the alternative narratives and associated pathways favoured by poorer and more marginal groups.

But does it have to be this way? Governance processes are certainly neither a seamless whole, nor set in stone. In this chapter we explore a range of processes, styles and practices of governance in the contemporary world, especially in relation to the social–ecological–technological systems which are our central concern. We argue that, while some processes and practices reinforce narrow, power-laden narratives and pathways, others offer prospects for incorporating more effectively the goals and perspectives of marginalized groups and the full range of dynamic properties of sustainability. In short, we begin in this chapter to address the question: What kinds of political relationships and institutions are needed to respond effectively to contemporary dynamics, and so help shape pathways towards sustainability for particular groups of people struggling to escape from poverty and marginalization?

Understanding contemporary governance

How then should we conceptualize politics, institutions and governance? Approaches are of course as varied and deeply rooted as the traditions of social and political science in which they are embedded. Diverse philosophical and ideological positions, as well as fundamental distinctions between different strands of social theory, have spawned a huge variety of concepts and emphases, as an earlier STEPS Working Paper explored (Leach et al, 2007). Across this large literature, what themes emerge? What in turn do these suggest for our understanding of how pathways to sustainability might be constructed? What dimensions of power, politics and institutional arrangements are important? In the next sections, we identify six contemporary trends in the wider debates about governance. These offer necessarily brief overviews of large literatures, but point to some of the key issues and questions. These themes reflect shifting trends in the real world, as well as shifting emphases in analytical attention. Together, they point to some central characteristics of political and institutional arrangements in today's world, and indicate styles and practices which – as we argue later – have important implications for whether and how pathways to sustainability are pursued.

From government to networked, multi-levelled governance

First and fundamentally, recent debates about political processes move beyond a narrow focus on the state to recognize the relevance of interactions and networks between multiple actors and institutions. This is, in effect, the move from 'government' to 'governance'. Thus conventional approaches to understanding government often focused largely on the power of sovereign states to make policy and influence firms and members of the public (Stoker, 1998). Such approaches often conceived of the state in fairly monolithic terms, as leading prescriptive, all-encompassing, top-down solutions. States were seen to lead linear policy processes in which agenda-setting, decision-making and implementation followed each other in an orderly way (Easton, 1965; Hogwood and Gunn, 1984). Yet in the last few decades these simple models of government have been under-mined. Much evidence has shown that top-down, state-led plans rarely work out as intended (Scott, 1998). Equally a far wider range of actors and organizations is, in practice, involved with policymaking, management and regulation. These do not comprise monolithic, bounded entities; rather interactions within and across them are key, creating networks and blurred boundaries. Furthermore, many issues involve multi-level action across multiple geographical, social and time scales.

These changing understandings have been linked with lively debates about the role and capacities of the state, from all sides of the political spectrum. Dominant models of state-led policy and regulation have variously been critiqued for constraining individual rights and for failing to address inequalities (Kymlicka and Norman, 1994). Critiques of state-led development also interplayed with the economic reform agendas of the 1990s led by the World Bank and International Monetary Fund, with their emphasis on 'rolling back' the state, privatization of public services and wider neo-liberal agendas. A broad and vociferous critique of neoliberalism has emphasized its negative effects on the poor and tendency to increase inequalities (Chomsky, 1998; Stiglitz, 2002). For some, the term 'governance' thus has particular politicized origins, traceable to the 1980s and the emergence of neo-liberalism and the so-called New Public Management. While it is important to recognize these ideological underpinnings, however, we – along with many others – treat the term in a broader way, to capture the multiple political processes and relationships through which state and non-state actors do and might engage – with a variety of possible political implications. In this sense:

> *Governance is a descriptive label that is used to highlight the changing nature of the policy process in recent decades. In particular, it sensitizes us to the ever-increasing variety of terrains and actors involved in the making of public policy. Thus, governance demands that we consider all the actors and locations beyond the [central government] 'core executive' involved in the policymaking process (Richards and Smith, 2002).*

Within a large literature on networked governance, emphasis is therefore placed on 'unpacking' the state to recognize the interaction of different actors within it, amongst themselves and with wider networks (Stoker, 1998; Hajer and Wagenaar, 2003). Thus networks may build up around the government ministries formally responsible for a policy sector – an agriculture, health or energy ministry, for example – so it is through these networks that policy gets formulated and implemented (Marsh and Rhodes, 1992;

Smith, 2000; Rhodes, 1997). Networks may involve market actors and institutions (Rhodes, 1997; Jessop, 1998; Kooiman, 2003), as well as those of civil society. Thus since the 1990s substantial literatures have documented such processes of networking and interaction between actors in citizens' groups, donor agencies and the state in dealing with health, agricultural, water and energy issues. Interactions between ministries of agriculture, seed companies, agro-dealers and NGOs have, for example, emerged as central to the delivery of seeds in many African settings. Equally, emergent networks linking electricity supply companies with government agencies and consumer groups have helped steer policy in the energy sector.

These networked governance arrangements also operate across social, spatial and temporal scales. Thus the last few decades have seen the emergence both of an array of local and decentralized networks and governance arrangements and of regional and global ones – and these interact in complex ways. Literature on multi-level governance (Bache and Flinders, 2004) moves beyond a concern just with inter-governmental relations, to explore how governance arrangements at different territorial levels interrelate and interpenetrate with one another. It is argued both that multiple levels are involved in how governance actually plays out in practice – and, more normatively, that multi-level arrangements are needed to address contemporary problems. Thus multi-level governance has been seen as particularly important for environmental problems whose causes and manifestations frequently cross-cut local and global scales (Vogler and Jordan, 2003; Jasanoff and Martello, 2004).

The climate and energy field exemplifies an area where multi-level governance arrangements have emerged fast and are argued to be essential (Giddens, 2009). Climate policy and politics now encompass international architectures (Aldy and Stavins, 2007), carbon market arrangements, non-governmental, civic and business groups (Newell, 2006), and a large variety of grassroots movements and actions. In shaping decisions about energy systems and supplies in any national or local setting, these influences interact in complex ways with national ministries, technical agencies and supply forms, and with both formal and informal institutions which represent and articulate consumer demands.

In the health field, the rise of multi-level and global forms of governance has been associated with understanding of certain health benefits – including protection from epidemic disease spread – as global public goods (Kaul et al, 1999). Thus it is argued that agreements based solely on national interest are no longer adequate to the rapid emergence of health challenges that are truly global in nature (Fidler, 1998). Indeed the health field illustrates well the multiplicity and complexity of actors and networks now involved in governance across scales, including large private corporations, NGOs, advocacy groups, civil society organizations and large charitable foundations, as well as national and international public agencies (Global Health Watch, 2008). One highly visible model is the so-called public–private partnerships – such as the Global Fund to fight AIDS, TB and Malaria – which have been constructed with mandates to address specific health problems, often with ambitious short-term targets for developing new technologies and spreading them rapidly around the world. These actors are establishing new forms of relationship with governments and with each other, with strong political dimensions (Kickbusch, 2003). Powerful philanthropic and business actors are now playing a role in the reshaping of global and national institutional arrangements, often with rather little accountability (Global Health Watch, 2008).

Thus it is increasingly recognized that the networks involved in governance extend far beyond the nation state. The implications of globalization serve to exacerbate, deepen and extend complex interdependencies between state and non-state actors across multiple territorial levels (Bache and Flinders, 2004). Thus work highlights the emergence and politics of citizen action in global arenas (Edwards and Gaventa, 2001) and the emergence of a so-called global civil society (Clark, 2003; Keane, 2003). Recent work on new social movements emphasizes the breadth and diffuseness of their spatial context, involving multi-layered forms of networking and alliance (Appadurai, 2000; Edelman, 2001). Social movements around environment, science and technology frequently link participants in diverse local sites across global spaces, constituting forms of 'globalization from below' (Falk, 1993; Appadurai, 2002; Leach and Scoones, 2007).

Participatory governance

A wide stream of literature has been concerned with popular participation in processes of governance and the power relations it involves. This includes a now vast set of experiences and reflections on participation in development projects and programmes – including around agriculture, water, energy and health (Chambers, 1997). This has shown the potential of project-based participation to improve both effectiveness and alignment with participants' goals and values. However, experiences have also revealed how power relations – among participants and between them and planners – strongly shape whether and how such potentials are realized (Cornwall and Gaventa, 2000; Cooke and Kothari, 2001). Others have widened the debate to address broader processes of participation in policy and political forums, building on longstanding interest in participatory democracy and its diverse relationships with other democratic forms – such as representation through voting (Pateman, 1970; Habermas, 1996). In a contemporary context in which 'including the public' in decision-making processes has become an expected part of 'good practice' in many arenas across the world, discussions address the roles of and power relations involved with direct, participatory forms of democracy (Cornwall and Schattan Coelho, 2006).

Moving beyond liberal notions of citizenship that consider people as individuals with rights and claims in relation to a nation state, debates increasingly recognize other ways in which members of the public partici-pate in contemporary political processes. This may be as interest or identity-based groupings (Melucci, 1989; Young, 1990), or temporary sol-idarities formed around specific issues (Mouffe, 1995; Ellison, 1997). It may be in 'invited', claimed or 'raided' spaces and in relation to national or global institutions (Cornwall and Schattan Coelho, 2006). Such citizen-based, participatory engagements with contemporary sustainability issues involve a range of styles and practices, from direct activism to uses of the media and Internet, to pursuing issues through legal forums (Leach and Scoones, 2007).

Governance in practice

The messiness of politics-in-practice is also increasingly recognized. In relation to the state, this is a longstanding insight in political science (Lindblom, 1959). Recasting conventional distinctions between politics and bureaucracy, it is emphasized that 'bureaucratic politics' is a messy process in which different actors within the state define, negotiate and secure their interests in a diversity of ways. Another important and related strand in the bureaucratic politics literature emphasizes the roles of street-level bureaucrats, and the discretion they often exercise, for instance in dealing with clients – becoming de facto policymakers as well as rule-followers (Lipsky, 1980; Long and Long, 1992). More broadly, insights from 'actor-oriented' approaches to institutions and governance suggest that it is not just a matter of following rules – whether these are the formal rules and codes of organizations or regulatory procedures, or the less for-mal norms and 'rules of the game' that characterize institutions (North, 1990). Rather, people interpret, negotiate, accede to or may subvert rules in ways that fit their intentions or circumstances. This recognition of peo-ple's agency applies whether one is talking about bureaucrats within a state organization, members of a citizens' group or NGO, or field-level health workers or agricultural extension agents. Equally, as people and groups interact with each other in processes of management or governance, their encounters involve negotiations and sometimes mutual exchange and shaping of interests and perspectives (Long, 2001). Such perspectives help to explain why, in practice, plans and regulations often fail to have their intended outcomes, as they are 'diverted' by the realities of bureaucratic politics and interactions with assumed policy beneficiaries. Rather than governance procedures following predictable, often linear, processes towards a clear set of outcomes, the reality is a more messy and unpredictable set of interactions in which unintended consequences are inevitable (Jessop, 2003).

Politics of nature and technology

As work across the fields of political ecology and science and technology studies has emphasized, nature, technology and their dynamics also need to find a place in the analysis of governance (Forsyth, 2003; Latour, 2004). Political and institutional relationships around issues concerning agriculture, water, health and energy involve not just relationships between people and each other. Implicated also are people's relationships with things and processes in the natural and material worlds. Thus, for instance, the very liquidity of water – and its flows and dynamics in the landscape – may help to shape the kinds of institutional arrangements which emerge and which are possible (Mehta, 2007). Actor-network theory in science and technology studies points to the ways in which entities in 'nature' or technological artefacts can themselves become 'actants', enrolled in governance networks (Callon et al, 1986; Latour, 1993). Coalitions of common concern that drive and become involved in politics may thus include non-human entities. Going beyond earlier approaches that understood the relationships between institutions and nature in largely harmonious terms, as mutually adapted to each other, the broad field of political ecology has fused the analysis of ecology (and in some cases, disease ecology) with the analysis of power. Thus attention is drawn to inequality, hierarchy and (material) power in people–environment relationships. This relates both to large-scale political–economic processes (Blaikie and Brookfield, 1987; Vogel, 1995) and micro scale and everyday forms of struggle, community rights, participation and resistance to ecological destruction (Peet and Watts, 2004; Raymond and Bailey, 1997).

An important strand of political ecology literature has critically explored how 'nature' is represented, whether among local communities or in scientific and policy worlds (Fairhead and Leach, 1996; Forsyth, 2003). Converging with debates in other fields such as science and technology studies (Latour, 1993, 2004) and anthropology (Descola and Palsson, 1996), this work draws attention to the social construction of natural and material processes. How different people or groups understand or represent these depends on their social positions, knowledge and experiences. This has led to a strand of work that examines representations and explanations of ecological processes and problems and identifies a politics in how actors' different representations engage and compete.

Political culture and context

Unfolding governance processes cannot be separated from their contexts: political history and culture matter (Wilson, 2000). Thus in many settings, assumptions that standardized (often Western) governance models would emerge or could be developed unproblematically have proved wrong, while arrangements that were put in place have often unravelled. Similarly, in countries that have experienced transition from command to market economies, experiences have been highly divergent but have frequently challenged the assumption that Western governance models work unproblematically. Instead, emergent institutional and political arrangements often reflect deeply embedded principles and cultural styles. Particular governance arrangements emerge in the context of particular political histories, whether locally, nationally or globally (Diamond, 1993). As comparative studies have emphasized, the influence of historical legacies and historically contingent interactions is key in shaping what kinds of interactions between actors emerge in policy processes or regulation (Wilks and Wright, 1987). The very different trajectories in different places also suggest that understanding emergent governance processes needs an approach that is embedded in history and context. As long-established perspectives in historical institutionalism emphasize, emergent political processes reflect both the agency of current actors and the influence of historically embedded structures, practices and legacies. Governance practices thus emerge and transform in path-dependent ways. These sometimes combine periods of consolidation with conjunctures when rapid change occurs (Pierson, 2000; Pierson and Skocpol, 2002; Thelen, 2003; Fukuyama, 2004).

Diverse histories can lead to diverse forms of political culture which shape the ways scientific or policy issues are approached (Wynne, 1989; Jasanoff, 1990, 2004). Particular notions of patrimonialism and patron-clientage, for instance, have proved key to the ways that seed systems have developed in some African settings (Richards, 1986, 2009). Particular, culturally embedded notions of trust have been key to the ways that political–economic and institutional arrangements have emerged in a number of Asian transitional economies. Even within the USA and Europe, national regulatory cultures and styles for dealing with biotechnology issues, for example, have been shown to differ starkly (Jasanoff, 2005).

Politics of knowledge

Finally, the politics of knowledge have assumed greater relevance in governance debates. Some would argue that knowledge politics have always been significant; others that they are becoming more so as the world reconfigures as a global knowledge society (Castells, 1996; Jasanoff, 2005). Such views move well beyond assumptions that knowledge and political processes are separate and related in a linear way ('truth speaks to power'). They also firmly question the ideas that so-called 'objective evidence' and 'sound science' are the only legitimate sources of knowledge in governance. Instead, diverse kinds of expertise are acknowledged (Collins and Evans, 2007). The role and limits of expertise in policymaking have, for instance, been discussed at length by scholars aiming to understand the ways in which power acts on scientific advisors (Collingridge and Reeve, 1986; Jasanoff, 1990). The importance of various dimensions and forms of knowledge politics has emerged. Thus constructivist perspectives connect forms of knowledge (whether of scientists, policymakers, or diverse farmers, health service users or others) with their underlying social, political and institutional commitments (Wynne, 1992; Jasanoff, 2004). Insights from work in science studies help illuminate how knowledge claims derived from particular instances and sites are spread and consolidated by enrolling other actors and institutions into knowledge/power networks (Latour, 1987, 1999, 2005). Highlighted, too, are how particular events, forums and practices shape the co-production of scientific and social, political or policy positions (Jasanoff and Wynne, 1997; Fairhead and Leach, 2003; Keeley and Scoones, 2003).

Recent work highlights the interrelations between particular ways of knowing (epistemologies) and governance processes. Thus at the national scale, for example, Jasanoff's study of European and US approaches to the regulation of biotechnology has coined the term 'civic epistemologies' to describe the ways in which political culture affects the production of knowledge in modern nation states (Jasanoff, 2005, p15). Many studies have examined how forms of grounded local knowledge are linked to political and material claims – to resource control, to particular rights and ways of life – and how people seek to press such claims in national or global arenas, for instance in social and environmental movements (Peet and Watts, 2004). Whether around environment, agriculture or health, work on rural people's knowledge, for instance (Richards, 1985; Scoones and Thompson, 1994; Rocheleau et al, 1996), draws attention to the embeddedness of forms of knowledge in experiences of ecological and technological processes; and the intertwining of knowledge with social, material and political claims. Some consider the politics of knowledge as part of national and global networks.

Shared knowledge and beliefs can be central in holding together 'advocacy coalitions' around particular issues (Sabatier and Jenkins-Smith, 1993) or in creating and sustaining broad epistemic communities (Haas, 1992) which may variously coincide with or cross-cut other political allegiances. Other streams of work have highlighted citizen engagement in the politics of knowledge around issues involving science, technology and health (see Epstein, 1996; Fischer, 2000; Leach et al, 2005).

A key strand of work on knowledge and governance has followed Foucault's lead in conceptualizing power and knowledge as inseparable; and mutually constituted as discourse (Burchell et al, 1991). Thus particular ensembles of power, institutions, language and practices are seen to construct issues in certain ways and to act on them to produce particular material effects. In this way, the politics of knowledge become part and parcel of political and institutional relationships more generally.

Towards an integrated approach

Looking across these vast literatures, then, recent conceptualizations of governance highlight some key processes, styles and practices. In sum, these include an emphasis on networked, multi-scale governance processes, interacting with state institutions in various ways; on participatory processes and the power relations of these; on politics and governance in practice, involving messy, day-to-day interactions; on the locatedness of unfolding governance arrangements, in particular cultural and historical contexts; on the politics of nature and technology; and on the politics of knowledge. The recent emphasis on such processes and dimensions of governance partly reflects tendencies in the real world, as political and institutional processes, it is argued, become more complex. At the same time, these emerging realities are becoming more visible as the analytical lenses used to study governance themselves shift – moving beyond the conventional, state-oriented perspectives in political science and international relations which might once have blinkered analysis, to incorporate insights from other fields and disciplines.

Thus, across these six areas, different elements speak to the core concerns of this book. For example, an emphasis on networked and multi-level governance arrangements highlights the need to develop institutional arrangements across scales in highly dynamic settings. Participatory governance highlights the importance of diverse voices, including those of people directly affected by environmental and technological change, and of citizen engagement and deliberation. An emphasis on governance in practice highlights how politics and institutions must respond to day-to-day realities, in fast-changing contexts often subject to surprise. A focus on the politics of nature and technology is essential when dealing with complex social–technological–ecological systems. Political cultures and contexts influence the way problems are framed and solutions are defined within different governance settings, while attention to the politics of knowledge highlights the importance of the ways understandings are generated through diverse forms of knowledge and expertise. As Chapter 3 showed, the bounding of the system and the goals for system change are all affected by these various dimensions of governance, involving: diverse framings and narratives by multiple actors; intractable issues of incomplete knowledge; divergent forms of action envisaged to deal with contrasting dynamic system properties in different settings. Together, these all affect which narratives come to prevail in the building of pathways.

Therefore addressing the politics of sustainability – conceptualizing the governance processes that are relevant to contemporary agricultural, health, water and energy issues – necessarily requires drawing together insights across these various literatures. It requires tracking how these processes and tensions are unfolding for particular issues, in particular contexts. And given our central concerns in this book, it requires doing so with several core questions in mind: Which particular narratives and pathways are promoted by, and become interlocked with, governance processes? How do emerging processes, styles and practices of governance deal with a highly dynamic world – and the resulting challenges of incomplete knowledge, and of multiple dimensions and dynamics of sustainability? And what are the implications for poorer and marginalized people?

Governing pathways to sustainability?

Considering these questions brings us back to the major contradiction that we noted at the beginning of this book and explored further in Chapter 1. On the one hand, social–ecological–technological systems in today's world are highly complex and dynamic, perhaps more so than ever. As the discussion above emphasizes, political realities are also complex, multiple and fast-changing. Human ambitions to govern the world are increasing. Yet the challenges of governance are often addressed as if the relevant factors were relatively straightforward, uniform and stable. Political and institutional processes often ignore or underplay complex dynamics and their implications.

To consider how and why this happens, we need first to return to the discussion of system-framing, narratives and pathways of the last chapter. There we argued that particular actors-in-context produce and promote narratives which frame systems and their dynamics in particular ways, linked to particular goals. Powerful narratives often justify and promote what become pathways of intervention and change. In the light of the discussion of institutions, power and knowledge above, we can now see how these different dimensions of governance often work together to shape which particular narratives and pathways come to prevail, and to sustain them; to make them into powerful 'motorways'. Particular pathways may become interlocked with the political interests of locally incumbent interests, or with the sustaining of more globally powerful institutions or networks.

Pathways also become interlocked with particular kinds of power/ knowledge. Through the process that Foucault termed 'governmentality', the 'technologies and rationalities' of government (Burchell et al, 1991, p2) intertwine knowledge – including particular system-framings – and power. This may involve processes of categorization and simplification that render social and environmental processes 'legible' for governance – whether by the state (Scott, 1998) or other institutions. It may involve biopower – whereby human and biological sciences become instruments of governance, put to use in sorting and classifying people and things (Rose, 2006). As Hacking argues, scientific disciplines and techniques such as statistics are in this way an integral 'part of the technology of power in a modern state' (1991, p181). Through such techniques, institutions (whether of the state, corporations or civil society) are able both to articulate particular system-framings, goals and narratives, and – importantly – to discipline people into accepting such framings and narratives as part of the natural order of things. Thus the institutionalization of particular strategies of governance involves transformations of subjectivities or changes in conceptions of the self. As Arun Agrawal put it in his study of local forest governance in northern India, 'Governmental strategies achieve their effects, to the extent they do so, by becoming anchors for processes that reshape the individuals who are a part and the object of governmental regulation' (Agrawal, 2005, p219). Through such processes of disciplining and governmentality, people may come to internalize the positions that particular narratives suggest for them. Thus knowledge, institutions, power relations and people's senses of themselves may come to interlock, mutually reinforcing each other.

Thus, in our concern with how pathways to sustainability (or otherwise) are shaped, we are concerned with what Foucault termed 'the conduct of conduct', or forms of 'activity aiming to shape, guide or affect the conduct of some person or persons' (Burchell et al, 1991, p2). Such perspectives allow recognition that political processes are present throughout society, not just in formal government structures. Indeed, while the term 'governmentality' might imply a focus on state action, it has been expanded – for instance in Arun Agrawal's (2005) notion of 'environmentality' and Debal

Deb's (2008) notion of 'developmentality' – to encompass the interactions of a range of disciplining relations including the actions of NGOs, corporate players and the wider environment and development industry. A governmentality optic thus enables recognition of political processes and power relations that become institutionalized, embodied in rules and practices that acquire predictability and staying power. In these ways, governance often becomes associated with 'lock-in' to a single powerful narrative and associated pathway, to the exclusion of others.

As we argue below, all too often the resulting powerful narratives and pathways neglect key dimensions of incomplete knowledge and key dynamic properties of sustainability.

Closing down: The politics of incomplete knowledge

To consider how governance processes shape how incomplete knowledge is dealt with, let us return to Figure 3.4, introduced in the last chapter. To recall, this highlighted four dimensions of incomplete knowledge which arise when dealing with complex, dynamic systems. In the top left-hand corner is risk in the strict sense, where probabilities are deemed calculable for a range of known outcomes. Yet, very often, complex system dynamics also throw up uncertainties, where outcomes may be known but their relative likelihoods are not amenable to calculation; ambiguities, where disagreements exist over the relevant outcomes and how to prioritize them; and ignorance, where 'we don't know what we don't know' and there is an ever-present possibility of surprise.

What follows from the discussion above is that these contrasting representations of the completeness or quality of knowledge are not politically symmetrical. Powerful imperatives to deploy knowledge as a means to justify, persuade and legitimate very often force a process of 'closing down' towards this top left-hand corner. As a result, system dynamics and their implications come to be treated in terms of 'risk', neglecting or underplaying these other dimensions of incomplete knowledge (Stirling, 2009c). Put another way, it is often risk-based narratives (and the pathways they justify) that come to dominate, over and above narratives that appreciate uncertainty, ambiguity, ignorance and their implications.

How does this happen? As shown in Figure 4.1, these processes of closure do not arise by chance. A number of quite concrete political, procedural and institutional pressures are in play. Obviously, the nature of these forces and constraints varies hugely according to the issue and context. In any given instance various pressures will be at work, representing knowledge and incomplete knowledge in contending ways. But, as indicated in Figure 4.1, the general net aggregate effect of power is often to lead ignorance to be recast more as uncertainty or ambiguity, and ambiguity or uncertainty to be recast more as risk.

The pressures summarized in Figure 4.1 are all aspects of governance (political and institutional processes) that entwine power, knowledge and governmentality. Thus the institutional remits of organizations may encourage a move from ignorance to uncertainty: ruling out surprise and defining the range of outcomes that the institution deals with. Liability law may reinforce this, by excluding responsibility for anticipating entire categories and mechanisms of harm. The use of particular indicators and definitions, and the use of particular legal frameworks, may further assist this. Other governance processes in turn may lead uncertainty to be re-defined and treated as risk. These range from bureaucratic and planning procedures that rely on (and thus reinforce) an image of a calculable, manageable world, to particular techniques of modelling, reasoning and categorization that render the world legible and apparently tractable in risk-based terms. Insurance contracts further enact probabilistic conceptions of the world, by excluding many contexts and aggregating what is left. Moving up the right-hand side of the diagram, governance processes may be used seemingly to 'tame' ignorance and surprise into a more manageable range of possibilities, even if these end up as non-congruent 'apples and oranges'. Practices such as reliance on (trans-disciplinary) expertise, and setting agendas and defining organizational mandates may be significant here. However, further pressures may act to narrow a range of possible outcomes (ambiguity) further, creating a set which can be clearly defined and dealt with as risk. Political

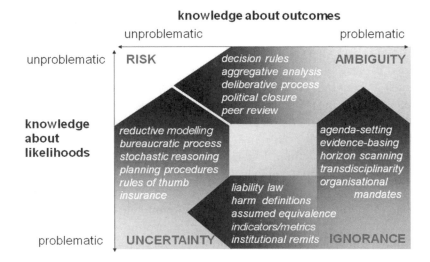

Figure 4.1 'Closing down' towards risk

closure, strategies of ordering and exclusion, and processes of subjectification whereby people – whether supposed policy beneficiaries, or workers
within an organization or agency, or others – come to internalize this possible range of outcomes as the appropriate set for consideration. All these
processes – and a host of others – have the effect of closing down understandings of more open appreciations of incomplete knowledge and
rendering them instead as the narrow concept of 'risk'.

But how do such governance pressures operate in practice? Let us consider a few examples.

Epidemics

In the last chapter we looked at the various dimensions of incomplete
knowledge given the dynamics of avian influenza. Different narratives, we
showed, prioritize different dimensions. In the case of the governance of
epidemics, however, in practice we often see narratives which cast the
problem predominantly in terms of risk; these are the ones which are
articulated by the major international agencies and which drive outbreak-
focused policy responses. Other dimensions of incomplete knowledge –
despite their relevance to the problem, as the last chapter discussed –
receive far less attention. Governance processes involved in this drift to the
top left-hand corner of Figure 4.1 in the case of avian influenza include,
fundamentally, the institutional remits and organizational mandates of
international agencies such as the WHO and FAO. These are not geared
up to deal with ignorance and surprise; the very existence and status of the
agencies is interlocked with the idea that outbreaks and their effects can be
known about and thus rendered amenable to management. In these
circumstances, planning procedures that are oriented towards risk management through outbreak containment at source are appealing and come
to dominate. Bureaucratic procedures – in the way that outbreak alert and
response programmes are organized – interlock with and support such
framings. Meanwhile the need for established procedures to deal with the
possible impacts on businesses have encouraged a focus on insurance
mechanisms, which themselves cast incomplete knowledge in terms of
quantifiable, calculable risk.

On the right-hand side of Figure 4.1, we can also observe a drift to risk-
oriented narratives at the expense of those which might highlight ambiguity.
Political–economic interests in garnering support for a massive global
response, and the funding flows from governments and donor agencies
required to sustain this, have required closure around a clear and dramatic
set of potential outcomes. The definition of outcomes in terms of massive
human mortality resulting from a major global pandemic of influenza has, in
this context, come to be emphasized – at the expense of other perspectives,

for instance on the damage to livelihoods that the response itself might cause. Aggregative forms of analysis that add up outcomes contribute to this closure. Claims about particular sorts of vulnerability, either to avian influenza or response campaigns, perhaps associated with the livelihoods or social positions of particular local groups, disappear as mere noise amidst the dramatic figures about aggregate risk that garner public, political and media attention. Thus, through a cluster of interlocking political, institutional and knowledge–power processes, the problem of avian influenza is treated in terms of risk, at the expense of uncertainty, ambiguity and ignorance.

Seeds

Taking the case of seeds in African settings, a similar governance-influenced drift towards risk-based framings is evident in dominant policy narratives around GM crops. Along with narratives that emphasize genetically engineered seeds as solutions to problems of hunger have come pressures from the international community, government actors and civil society alike to take seriously the areas of incomplete knowledge surrounding these technologies, their application and potential impacts. The creation and adoption of national biosafety regulations has been a key response. Yet in many cases these frame the issue in terms of narrow notions of risk (to ecology or human health), at the expense of uncertainty, ambiguity and ignorance. This is encouraged by the expectation of alignment with the international Cartagena protocol on biosafety, which itself emphasizes risks. The organizational mandates of ministries of agriculture emphasize the promotion of effective agricultural systems and managing risks to them, working against an openness to surprise. The use of particular kinds of scientific evidence in defining outcomes and then aggregating them in ordered ways which can translate into clear regulations works against appreciation of ambiguities. These might include diverse perspectives on the nature of outcomes and why they matter – for instance emphasizing how bio-engineered seeds might interact with particular agro-ecological settings and livelihood priorities.

Moving up the left-hand side of Figure 4.1, governance pressures in the construction of national biosafety regulations tend also to address uncertainties as if they were manageable risks. The very notion of regulation encourages a view that outcomes are calculable and regulable. The top-down planning procedures that characterize many African ministries of agriculture, along with the entrenched bureaucratic routines and hierarchies that they have developed, reinforce this view. Meanwhile, established processes of planning, ordering and hierarchy work against the incorporation of field-level knowledge – that of local extension workers or farmers themselves. The diversity of farmers' fields and livelihood dynamics throw up a range of areas of uncertainty and ambiguity in the possible impacts of GM seeds, as they intersect with these complexities. Yet the governance processes through which biosafety regulations are created and implemented are not geared up to incorporate such perspectives. Instead, regulatory processes often contribute to the construction of farmers in particular ways – as ignorant or risk-averse, for example. And through processes of subjectification, farmers may themselves come to represent themselves in such ways, at least in contexts in which they interact with authority. Again, then, we see political, institutional and knowledge-related processes interacting to push policy narratives towards framing GM safety issues in terms of risk.

Energy

In the energy sector, nuclear power provides a further example of the kinds of closure described in Figure 4.1. A range of governance processes push the issues to be treated in narrow, risk-based terms. Thus risk-assessment procedures reduce ambiguity to narrower notions of risk, for instance by focusing on parameters, scenarios and 'event trees'. Routinely excluded, for instance, are the complex and creative behaviours which featured so prominently in the unauthorized experiments leading to the Chernobyl disaster in 1986 or the desperate, last-minute operator interventions that compounded the Three Mile Island accident in 1979 (Mosey, 2006). Despite a history peppered with instances of sabotage, military targeting and planned terrorist attack, overtly malign motives are also typically exempt from attention. Moving up the left-hand axis of Figure 4.1, conventional nuclear regulation depends on the quantification of probabilities – reducing uncertainty to risk. Here, the role of insurance is crucial, with domestic policies worldwide routinely excluding the scenarios discussed above – denying compensation in the event of many kinds of 'acts of god' (such as earthquakes, storm or flood) or other 'forces majeure' (such as acts of war or insurrection). Actuarial or probabilistic representations of nuclear risk are thus quite systematically structured such as to restrict the depth and scope of the underlying realities and so reduce the exposure of powerful interests.

Behind these institutional processes there lies a series of further mechanisms which close down the representation of incomplete knowledge over nuclear power from ignorance to uncertainty. These range from the structure of international nuclear liability law, which effectively denies recourse by potential victims to those forms of legal support that are least readily controlled (such as customary international law). Instead, strictly codified international frameworks are binding even on governments: imposing limits on the types of victim or kinds of damage that might legitimately sustain claims; placing restrictions on the channelling of compensation from shareholders, financiers, suppliers or manufacturers; and setting ceilings to the overall amount of compensation that the industry must plan to provide (Sands, 1988). Similar institutional structures also condition the reduction of ignorance to ambiguity on the right-hand side of Figure 4.1. Here, restricted regulatory mandates typically marginalize the least powerful groups, such as communities affected by mining or waste management beyond the jurisdictions of leading nuclear countries. Apparently reasonable strictures of 'evidence-based policy' further confine attention to mechanisms or end-points of harm that are scientifically well established. But this reduces attention to 'type II errors', with the result that 'lack of evidence of harm' is routinely formally misinterpreted as 'evidence of lack of harm' (Gee et al, 2002). In the nuclear field, as in other areas then, these kinds of institution close down representations of incomplete knowledge and so externalize the responsibilities of incumbent interests at the expense of the more marginal groups who stand to be affected by their activities.

Closing down: Pressures towards planned equilibrium

Just as there are political pressures on the framing of incomplete knowledge, leading to a tendency to emphasize risk, so there are similar pressures affecting the way sustainability is thought about.

Here we can again return to one of the diagrams introduced in the last chapter. Figure 3.7 introduced four dynamic properties of sustainability. It asked: Within any given policy narrative, are intervention strategies aimed at exercising control to resist shocks (stability) or at resisting shocks in a more responsive fashion (resilience)? Do interventions aim to control the drivers of long-run shifts (durability)? Alternatively, do strategies aim to respond to long-run shifts whose drivers are seen as less tractable to control (robustness)?

In many situations, it is stability that comes to be emphasized in policy narratives. Thus – again – we see what can be characterized as a drift to the top left-hand corner of the diagram as indicated in Figure 4.2, whereby the problem and possible solutions come to be seen in terms of controlling shocks to maintain a stable situation. Other dynamic properties of sustainability – attending to longer-term shifts or to shocks or stresses which cannot be controlled – are often downplayed or neglected.

Again, a range of institutional and political–economic pressures are involved in encouraging this drift. Perhaps most fundamentally, power dynamics inevitably encourage and enable power-holding institutions to pursue strategies that maintain the status quo. In effect, their power and status – and sometimes an entrenched political economy of money and resource flows – is interlocked with such stability, deterring acknowledgement of other possibilities. Building on this basic observation, as we discussed in Chapter 2,

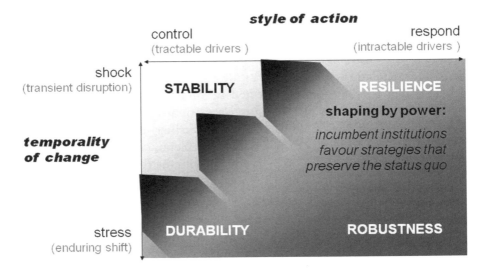

Figure 4.2 Closing down to planned equilibrium

there are a number of reasons why a focus on planned equilibrium, emphasizing stability, is so evident. These include deeply rooted styles of thinking and cultural assumptions about 'balance' in human–nature relations as a normal and desirable state. Divergences from what is assumed to be the norm are thus seen as necessarily negative, and in need of 'putting right', to restore equilibrium. Particular professional and disciplinary discourses have been built around and elaborated on such notions, marginalizing alternative interpretations and theories in the process. These include perspectives which recognize that the systems in question are not 'naturally' in equilibrium at all and that shifts between stable states or continuous variability are in fact the norm to which responses must be geared.

Yet it is the ways in which ideas and discourses about stability and equilibrium become cemented into bureaucratic, administrative and institutional practices and routines that make them so sticky. This, as Chapter 2 documented, is partly a matter of institutional history: government and international agencies and departments often originated at a time when equilibrial notions of the world dominated and were constructed around these. These legacies have proved hard to overcome. They have been reinforced by the professional styles and bureaucratic routines of ministries, planning departments and agencies. Routine responses in turn become the 'repeated practices and behaviours' that constitute institutions (following North, 1990). In many contexts, such institutionalization has served to uphold highly managerial, control-oriented approaches to planning, regulation and development. Thus forms of knowledge – of defining, measuring and categorizing human and natural processes – have often gone along with what Scott (1998) describes as 'high modernist' planning approaches which rest on, and are justified by, a limited and restricted vision of a manageable, controllable world.

Such interlocking governance pressures towards emphasizing a planned equilibrium are evident in each of our case examples. In the case of water in India, for instance, narratives around large dams as a way to control – and so maintain stability in – water supplies very much exemplify planning for equilibrium. Governance pressures towards such approaches and away from appreciating less equilibrial and longer-term dynamics, include particular technical and disciplinary understandings among engineers and hydrologists, and reliance on their expertise. They include the institutionalized practices and routines of state planning departments. And they include a powerful political economy which links dam-building industrialists, politicians and the particular elite farmers who stand to benefit from such water control-oriented approaches. As Mehta (2005) describes vividly for the Kutch area, these processes interplay powerfully with social processes among residents of dryland Kutch, who have embraced the litany of a water scarce region that will be 'saved' by a dam as a means of expressing their sense of the area's political marginalization.

In the field of energy policy, policymaking on 'energy security' frequently aims at the property of stability (emphasizing control of tractable shocks), rather than at resilience or robustness (emphasizing response to intractable shocks and stresses, respectively). Here, national governments and private corporations alike tend to highlight market equilibrium, coordination and planning, reliable infrastructures, incremental innovation, the enforcing of contracts, preventive actions, international force projection and domestic self-reliance. Much less prominent are strategies aiming at vigilance and foresight, supple infrastructures, adaptive institutions, agile management or system-level innovation (Stirling, 2009d). When pushed to promote transitions to sustainable energy, incumbent electricity-industry interests focus on options that assume the persistence of established centralized supply-driven generating trajectories, interpreting challenges simply as requiring the 'control' of 'shocks'. In this way, attention is focused on stability- or durability-based strategies, involving options such as nuclear power, carbon capture and storage and – more marginally – large-scale renewables such as offshore wind (Patterson, 1999). Alternative pathways around smart grids, energy service companies and distributed microgeneration all involve a loss of control and a long-term shift of trajectory, focused on robustness, and thus receive considerably less attention.

To pick up the epidemics example once more, again governance for sustainability is frequently characterized narrowly in terms of stability. This is the case for many outbreak narratives, which, as we have seen, emphasize 'stamping out' short-term disease shocks to return to a previous status quo. Again, a variety of governance pressures is in play. Eradicating a disease or controlling an epidemic – or at least claiming to do so – is a powerful way of asserting political authority, whether this is the authority of an international health regime or of a national political one. Routine responses and institutionalized practices emphasize a preoccupation with stability. Such practices are, for instance, encoded in the standard, global surveillance, early warning and rapid response repertoires of the main agencies. In the case of many diseases, huge amounts of public cash have been invested in these, bringing financial and economic pressures to maintain certain styles of response and their associated funding streams (Calain, 2007). Added to these are professional, disciplinary and cognitive pressures. These include the dominance of disciplinary cultures – often centred around biomedicine and epidemiology – which value short-term disease-focused assessments over more complex analyses which might emphasize longer-term, less equilibrial dynamics. Understandings from ecology, history, social sciences and local knowledge are thus squeezed out (Dry and Leach 2010). Finally, the media often plays key roles in supporting and amplifying powerful outbreak narratives and associated public fears, in turn generating weight and appeal for powerful agencies' claims to control the threat. In sum, then, conventional policy responses to epidemics represent challenges of sustainability mainly in terms of stability. These are in essence 'equilibrium' responses – seeking new forms of stable state through a set of interventions, guided by a particular set of knowledge framings, generated by particular practices and institutions. This creates a particular pathway – or trajectory for socio-technical and governance intervention and change. Yet there is very little attention to the specific challenges presented by long-term, external changes which are not amenable to prediction and control (Leach et al, 2010).

In all these examples, the point is not that the property of stability is necessarily invalid. Rather, the issue is that there exist powerful pressures to exaggerate its salience or importance. This, in turn, means that the other properties of sustainability are left unaddressed or underplayed.

Governance in a world of dynamism and incomplete knowledge

Despite the complex dynamics and multiple areas of incomplete knowledge in the contemporary world, the narratives which come to drive and be embodied in powerful pathways of intervention and change often emphasize much narrower notions of stability and risk. Furthermore, such ideas of risk and equilibrium, and power relations, are themselves interlocked: ideas, institutions and practices reinforce each other, and certain ways of seeing and acting in the world, through a process akin to Foucault's governmentality. It is through this mutual reinforcement of narrative and action that certain pathways become 'motorways', unrolling powerfully across the landscape of understanding and intervention, narrowing other tracks to minor bush paths or obscuring their traces altogether.

Such narratives and pathways may sustain a myth of a manageable world. This is a world amenable to neat interventions by corporate or state actors, civil society or international institutions and partnerships, underpinned by scientific expertise, through uniform approaches to problem and risk assessment based on singular views of evidence. But, as we have argued in this and earlier chapters, the melee of real-life dynamics and interactions and of everyday practice suggests a far more turbulent, complex and messy world in which knowledge and notions of 'the system' and 'the problem', and of 'sustainability goals', are contested. Approaches based on static, narrow views of problems and solutions shore up those very institutions. In effect, the perspectives and the institutions evolve in tandem; they are co-produced. Much governance is, as we have argued above, built upon such myths, and indeed it needs them as a source of justification. Yet the resulting interventions can be highly problematic. They may put into play forms of power and governmentality that have negative effects on people's livelihoods and well-being. While they may expediently sustain a sense of order and control, at least in the short term, for some this is often a fragile, problematic and ultimately illusory order. It may deny and suppress the dynamism of human–nature–technology interactions and the multiple framings of these and, in this, marginalize further the perspectives of people already poor and marginalized.

Yet, as both action in the real world and theorists of governmentality remind us, there is always space for alternatives. Alternative forms of knowledge, practice and institutional arrangements may be suppressed, but are never fully wiped out. Modern governmentality and biopolitics often generate new kinds of counter-politics, as people come to resist, subvert or sidestep the terms of governmental practice (Scott, 1985, 1990). Thus the history of governance as the 'conduct of conduct' is interwoven with the history of dissenting 'counter-conducts (Burchell et al, 1991, p5).

Referring back to the review with which we started this chapter, the pressures and processes in play in such 'closing down' do not map neatly onto particular styles and practices of governance. Thus it is not that state-centric approaches or those resting on singular global institutions necessarily narrow down towards risk and stability. Nor is it that net-worked, participatory and messy politics-in-practice forms of governance necessarily provide the basis to resist, avoid or build alternatives.

Participatory approaches, for instance, can bring about such narrowing if power–knowledge relations are such that people express their own subjectivities in terms of narrow risk or equilibrium-based framings. In certain contexts and for certain issues, alternative politics may need to be built through more conventional antagonistic forms, emphasizing alternative organizations: of the state, civil society, or social movements. Thus the implications of particular political and institutional arrangements, and the politics of knowledge and practice, depend very much on the issue and the context.

Nevertheless, as we go on to explore in the rest of this chapter and in the two that follow, there are some candidate styles and practices – in politics, institutions, and knowledge-making – which are worthy of greater attention in attempts to understand and construct pathways to sustainability. With many health warnings about contexts and care in application, these offer prospects for countering or side-stepping the political, institutional and power–knowledge pressures that lead narratives to close down around narrow risk and stability framings, and so favour pathways dominated by goals and priorities of powerful groups. They thus offer, perhaps, greater prospects for 'opening up' to embrace more fully the challenges of a dynamic world. These include shifting governance discourses towards the bottom and right of Figure 4.1 – to embrace the implications of uncertainty, ambiguity and ignorance/surprise; and shifting to the bottom and right of Figure 4.2 – to take on board wider dynamic properties of sustainability, including durability, resilience and robustness. This 'opening up', we argue, also needs to involve taking seriously and pursuing the implications of alternative narratives that respond to the particular system-framings, goals and priorities of poorer and marginalized people.

In this, a number of the insights in the literatures considered earlier in this chapter are useful. The move from government to networked, multi-levelled governance is helpful in recognizing multiple interactions across scales between types of 'actor' whose status and boundaries are often fuzzy. This potentially opens up scope to recognize poorer people's agency in mobilization and networking, and to address the power relations that enable and constrain this. Insights from literatures on the politics of knowledge and governmentality enable important attention to the interplay of politics and institutions with processes of framing. This potentially opens up scope to recognize alternative framings and counter-politics. However, as we have already indicated, each of these contributory literatures also has certain limitations. Hitherto, they have also not been integrated very effectively with each other.

Integrating the adaptive and reflexive turn

There are, however, two sets of governance processes, styles and practices that aim explicitly to address these challenges. These potentially offer ways forward in addressing the multiple dynamic properties of sustainability and the multiple dimensions of incomplete knowledge. The first is adaptive governance, which aims explicitly to respond to dynamic systems and situations. The second is the cluster of approaches which can be grouped as deliberative and reflexive governance. As explored in the next two chapters, deliberation and reflexivity may come about and take the form of orchestrated designs (Chapter 5) or more antagonistic processes involving social movements and challenges to powerful institutions (Chapter 6).

In the rest of this chapter, we outline some of the key insights and emphases brought by these adaptive and reflexive perspectives as currently developed. We consider some of their insights and gaps, and their implications in relation to other processes of governance introduced earlier.

Adaptive governance of dynamic systems

Recent work on adaptive governance, emanating in large part from the work of the Resilience Alliance (see Olsson et al, 2006), helps address some of the key challenges of dealing with ecology in a dynamic way, addressing the intertwined nature of dynamic social–ecological–technological systems and taking account of the uncertainties and possibilities of surprise inherent in these.

It has largely been failures in conventional modes of governing social–ecological systems, such as the management of water basins, agro-ecosystems and other common pool resources, that have led to calls for 'adaptive governance' (Dietz et al, 2003; Folke et al, 2005). There has been less explicit focus on disease ecology or health-related issues – although arguably the dynamics in play in the health field are just as suited to an adaptive governance approach as are environmental and agricultural issues. As Per Olsson and colleagues put it: 'adaptive governance relies on polycentric institutions that are nested, quasi-autonomous units operating at multiple scales' (Olsson et al, 2006). Such forms of governance are deemed appropriate to situations of rapid change and high uncertainty. Thus:

> *We focus on transformations within the social domain of the SESs [socio-ecological systems] that increase our capacity to learn from, respond to and manage environmental feedback from dynamic ecosystems. Such transformations include shifts in social features such*

> *as perception and meaning, network configurations, social coordina-*
> *tion, and associated institutional arrangements and organizational*
> *structures. Transformations also include redirecting governance into*
> *restoring, sustaining and developing the capacity of ecosystems to*
> *generate essential services (Olsson et al, 2006, p2).*

Rather than seeking any grand theory of how to govern complex systems, adaptive governance is essentially experimental in nature, seeking to build capabilities based on past experiences and a commitment to social learning. Adaptive governance arrangements are conceptualized to consist of self-organizing and self-enforcing networks of individuals, organizations and agencies that have the capacity for flexible, collaborative and learning-based approaches to managing ecosystems. This means breaking away from routines that are no longer appropriate to the problem, and experimenting, adapting and reviewing new measures in a search for more resilient social–ecological relations (Folke et al, 2005). As such, adaptive governance aims to intervene in a complex socio–ecological system and guide it to some more favourable state or trajectory (Walker et al, 2006). Adaptive governance approaches accept that the outcomes of intervention will remain uncertain, and strategies for anticipating unintended consequences rest upon the emphasis on flexibility and learning. Conditions identified as important for adaptive governance include an ability to consider alternative system configurations and strategies for choosing between alternatives, creating knowledge and social networks committed to change; trust-building and sense-making processes and leadership in mobilizing support and managing conflicts. More problematically, however, profound disagreements and polarized interests are not addressed by adaptive governance strategies. Such cleavages hinder the kind of consensual knowledge production, voluntaristic strategic action and shared mission that those advocating adaptive governance see as essential for effective socio-ecological management. Politicization of issues or knowledge about them is considered problematic, as this undermines the independent authority of scientific knowledge and hinders the identification of common ground (Olsson et al, 2006). Rather, adaptive governance approaches assume that consensus-building on goals is possible, and that these goals will become evident to all through better scientific knowledge of the problem. Consensus is assisted by the experimental nature of adaptive governance: initial goals will be checked and monitored as events unfold, and opportunities for their revision are built into the process. In this respect, adaptive governance may be quite inadequate to deal with the clashes of framing that arise around many social, technological, environmental and health issues, whether or not these are made explicit. They invite the danger of simply upholding dominant 'expert' views and supporting those in power, marginalizing the perspectives and priorities of the poor.

Work on adaptive governance has also largely focused on local scales. While sometimes calling for coordination across multiple scales, primarily as a way of trying to safeguard local ecosystem management from higher-level socio-political, economic and ecological dynamics, work on and advocacy for adaptive governance remains weak in addressing these broader-scale processes.

A final difficulty is a lack of attention to the politics of knowledge. Adaptive governance is built upon recognition of the complex, uncertain dynamics of systems. Both lay and scientific knowledge about these dynamics is, as constructivist perspectives remind us, socially situated, partial, plural, contingent and often contested (Mehta et al, 1999, 2001). Adaptive governance claims to offer a way of dealing with this situation, treating 'knowledge uncertainties' as part of the realm of uncertainties to which governance must flexibly respond. But this ignores more fundamental questions and perhaps contestations over how 'the system' is framed in the first place, and what is to be sustained for whom and why. Implicit in some of the literature is a self-evident goal and an image of a natural system 'out there', knowable through science. Sometimes actors' different 'mental models' are acknowledged, but as partial constructs that can be verified empirically and which can contribute to more scientific and formal models of the system further down the line (Walker et al, 2006). In other words, each is seen as part of the same epistemological jigsaw, and not as a different world view in the way that our focus on framings and narratives would emphasize.

In sum, proponents of adaptive governance present it as a flexible, learning strategy that offers important advances in dealing with the complexities and uncertainties of socio–ecological–technological systems. However, there is limited consideration of questions of power, knowledge and framing. With respect to these dimensions, insights from recent literatures on deliberative and reflexive governance are helpful.

Deliberative and reflexive governance

In contrast with many contemporary mainstream approaches and with adaptive governance, deliberative and reflexive approaches consider the question of goals to be much more problematic and contested. In this, they build – both implicitly and explicitly – on many of the insights of constructivist approaches to knowledge and knowledge politics. Governance is seen to be as much about shared problem construction as it is about collective solutions. Indeed, the two are intimately and recursively linked. Since various groups of people conceive of the world in different ways (Hajer and Wagenaar, 2003, p11), different actors will frame the 'object' of governance and its boundaries differently. How these different framings are interactively and mutually negotiated has an important bearing in reflexive governance. As such, governance and the 'object' to be governed are inter-subjectively negotiated: governance arenas and social–technological–ecological systems are 'co-constructed' (Smith and Stirling, 2006).

Like adaptive governance, reflexive governance is aware of the inevitability of unintended consequences arising from earlier interventions. But it goes further to consider the effects that such reflection has upon the governing actors and how they come to terms with the impossibility of having full and complete knowledge of the governed object (Smith and Stirling, 2006; Voss et al, 2006). Thus adaptive governance involves addressing a wider and more dynamic range of issues, options, interactions, uncertainties and possibilities than are normally considered in more conventional, instrumental approaches to governance. But this quality of more comprehensive *reflectiveness* does not fully address the implications of *reflexivity* (Stirling, 2006). Reflexivity proper, by contrast, refers also to a capacity to engage with the ways in which framings of 'the system' are themselves plural, contingent and conditioned by divergent values, interests and institutional commitments. Thus reflexive governance is also open to, and seeks accommodations with, ambiguity over sustainability goals and differentials of power, control or influence over implementation strategies. Goals are rarely determined once and for all, since knowledge, values and interests in social–technological–ecological systems evolve and develop over time. Indeed, even at a given point in time, closure around sustainability solutions for some groups may simply reframe the sustainability problem for others.

Voss et al (2006) recommend a number of strategies to advance reflexive governance. These include integrated, transdisciplinary forms of knowledge production; adaptive strategies and institutions; anticipation and explorative evaluation of the possible long-term effects of different action strategies, the use of iterative, participatory processes in goal formation, and the interactive development of strategies to reach goals. Each of these broad strategies in itself involves many challenges. The strategies are not intended to reduce complexity, but to help learn better how to live with it.

Deliberative governance approaches aim to bring diverse actors and perspectives together, into forums for debate, dialogue and negotiation. Potentially, then, they offer a way to acknowledge and address ambiguities, as well as the diverse narratives that different actors may adhere to regarding system framings and sustainability goals. Indeed attention to narratives is often part of the approach: one strategy that researchers arguing for *deliberative* governance have identified is the development of simplifying

narratives about issues that facilitate dialogue, argumentation and engagement with problems (Fischer and Forester, 1993; Roe, 1994). Such
arguments are tested, re-constructed and developed through day-to-day
practice (Schön and Rein, 1994):

> *[Stories and arguments] are assessed in communities of people who
> are knowledgeable about the problem at hand, and who are all too
> conscious of the political, financial and practical constraints that
> define the situation for which they bear responsibility. These are peo-
> ple who realize that stories and arguments are always provisional,
> never the last word on the situation. They hold up until the situation
> changes, constraints are tightened or relaxed and/or a better story is
> told. Action, thus, structures and disciplines understanding (Hajer
> and Wagenaar, 2003, pp14–15).*

Rather than devise strategies for how governance practitioners *ought* to
behave with respect to complex problems, deliberative governance begins
by trying to understand how practitioners *actually* behave and cope with
these problems, focusing on their practical judgements, interpretations and
deliberations. In following this emphasis on practice-oriented sense-making
of complex policy problems, deliberative governance approaches thus pick
up on many important features of the more recent governance literatures
that we identified earlier – including new spaces and networks for governance, more dynamic and fluid processes, conditions of radical uncertainty,
interdependencies in action and the significance of actors' everyday practices (Hajer and Wagenaar, 2003).

This deliberative approach to governance embraces constructivist perspectives on knowledge. Difficulties in separating facts from values, and
analysis from the normative aspects of social life, come to the fore as part of
a post-positivist turn in social science (Fischer and Forester, 1993;
Flyvbjerg, 2001):

> *Such a social science is based on a turn from the dominant emphasis
> on rigorous empirical proof and verification to a discursive, contex-
> tual understanding of social knowledge and the interpretative
> methods basic to acquiring it... Rather than altogether rejecting the
> empirical methods of the social sciences, [the deliberative argument] is
> that the issue is how to situate them within the context of normative
> concerns that give the findings their meaning (Fischer, 2003, p211).*

Accordingly, deliberative governance has to be concerned, reflexively, with
the social processes that define and give meaning to accounts of both the

governed object and interventions aimed at improving or sustaining that object. Analysis is considered as stimulating debate and improving argumentation, rather than settling debate and arriving at definitive solutions.

A range of strategies is identified for 'doing' deliberative governance (Flyvbjerg, 2001; Fischer, 2003). These include facilitating interpretive interactions between different perspectives; reformulating and rendering participatory the relations between analyst, citizen and decision-maker and recasting the role of the expert as a facilitator of public learning. They include moving to consensus through a discursive synthesis of competing views and recognizing dissent as a legitimate discursive contribution. Deliberative governance advocates multi-methodological, contextually situated approaches to appraising and generating system and policy goals, and democratizing policy evaluation in ways that include analysis of normative goals. The validity of any one interpretation is tested against earlier interpretations and is accepted or rejected through dialogue between them.

Deliberative governance can, at times, seem to require conditions in which everyone is able to speak openly and rationally – what Jurgen Habermas termed 'communicative rationality' (Habermas, 1987). As Flyvbjerg (2001) emphasizes, however, there is a need to attend to power relations and discourse as part of the process, using research and reflection to understand why some interpretations and not others are taken forward and agreed or imposed as the basis for public decisions. Addressing the relations of power and framing within deliberative governance procedures – as well as in processes of participatory democracy and development more generally – is therefore critical. However, in some cases the positions and claims of marginalized people may fail to feature in any form of institutionalized deliberative practice. Rather than hope optimistically to 'bring them in', it is important also to acknowledge counter-politics in relation to the state or global agencies that operate outside such arenas, whether through subtle forms of subaltern resistance or more organized forms of mobilization and movement. A focus on such dissenting, antagonistic politics is an important complement to the focus on argumentation, deliberation and reasoning, and one that may be in tension with such consensus-driven processes (Mouffe, 2005, 2006).

We need to consider what conditions enable an opening up of more rigid governance arenas so as to permit deliberative governance; and, having identified power relations that hinder deliberation, define what scope and processes help bring about improved forms of deliberation that include the interests and perspectives of poorer people. We also need to recognize that, for certain issues and settings, deliberative approaches may be unrealistic and inappropriate. Counter-claims, conflict and contestation in relation to power and political economy may continue to demand alternative, radical democratic political strategies of mobilization and resistance that enable the poor to exert their agency in relation to modernist political institutions (Laclau and Mouffe, 2001).

The literatures concerning adaptive, deliberative and reflexive governance therefore display many parallels, convergences and overlaps. Yet there are also some quite distinct differences, with some important implications. Table 4.1 summarizes the key distinguishing features of these inter-related approaches to governance for sustainability. Key issues around the distinction between reflective 'broadening out' and reflexive opening up in appraisal are addressed in the next chapter.

Conclusion

Governance is central to how narratives – and associated pathways – are constructed and to where they lead: To which goals and dynamics of sustainability, defined in whose terms? Yet, as we have shown, there are many ways of conceptualizing the political and institutional processes that constitute governance. Approaches to understanding are often co-constructed with the practices of policymakers, state agents, managers and private organizations in 'doing governance'. With the analytical lenses afforded by recent debates, a variety of processes, styles and practices in contemporary governance is coming into view. Among these are the relevance of multi-scale, networked governance; of participatory processes; of politics-in-practice as a negotiated, messy affair in which the agency of local-level bureaucrats is key; of the politics of nature and the politics of knowledge; and of the importance of political culture, history and context.

A range of questions thus arise which are central to understanding how governance processes are shaping and being shaped by dynamic,

Table 4.1 *Comparing adaptive, deliberative and reflexive approaches to governance*

Approach to governance	Main focus	Key dimensions
Adaptive	Dynamic (not static) systems	Inter-/trans-disciplinarity
	Unintended effects	Reflective learning
	Uncertainty and complexity	Flexible adaptation
Deliberative	Exclusion by power	More inclusive participation
	Discursive process	Transparent discussion
	Narratives	Prioritizes social learning
Reflexive	Contingency	Humility over basis for action
	Social construction	Reflexivity in knowledge claims
	Framing by power	More plural interventions

social–technological–environmental systems – and, normatively, how they might do so in ways that produce better outcomes for poorer and marginalized people. How are multiple actors interacting across local and global scales, through what forms of network and blurred boundaries? How have particular governance arrangements emerged in particular political contexts, through what contingencies and path dependencies? How is governance responding to the interlinked dynamics of social–technological–ecological systems? What forms of power/knowledge and participation shape the interaction between framings and narratives? How are knowledge of system dynamics and governance arrangements co-constructed? These are not new questions, but as we have argued, to date they have been addressed in rather separate, poorly connected literatures.

We have argued that very often, and for many issues and settings, the answers to such questions end up in a closing down around narratives and pathways that prioritize interests that are already powerful – and thus militate against sustainabilities that are attuned to real-world dynamics and to the perspectives of people who are currently marginalized. That is, governance processes, styles and practices create powerful tendencies to treat issues in terms of narrow notions of risk (underplaying wider forms of uncertainty, ambiguity and ignorance) and to focus on stability and control (at the expense of other dynamic properties of sustainability – durability, resilience, robustness) in ways that inhibit capacities to deal with longer-term and less controllable dynamics. Power relations, governmentality and other sectional interests often work to promote dominant narratives, thus fostering particular pathways and obscuring alternatives that might better respond to the goals of poorer people.

There is thus a fundamental need to open up; to reveal and give voice to marginalized narratives and so enable pathways which do address poorer people's goals and take greater account of multiple dimensions of incomplete knowledge and of sustainability. Governance processes, again, are key to such opening up. While no particular process, style or practice provides a panacea, we have argued that some offer potential ways forward – and drawing these together can help fill gaps in each. The relevance, appropriateness and combination of these will of course depend very much on the issue and the context. Thus networked and participatory governance processes potentially offer ways forward in recognizing and building on people's own agency. Appreciation of power/knowledge and governmentality can help identify spaces and forms of counter-politics from which alternative narratives and pathways might grow. Approaches to adaptive governance offer insights in responding to highly dynamic systems so as to build resilience and robustness. And deliberative and reflexive governance approaches emphasize negotiation among multiple narratives and ongoing reflection on actors' positions and framings – so enabling ambiguity and contestation among sustainability goals to be addressed.

How might such opening up be pursued in practice? In the next two chapters we elaborate further on the forms this might take and on the deliberative, reflexive and counter-political processes, styles and practices which might assist it. We focus first, in Chapter 5, on the role of orchestrated methods and appraisal designs, and then, in Chapter 6, on broader forms of engagement in the politics of sustainability.

Chapter 5

Opening Up, Broadening Out: Empowering Designs for Sustainability

Introduction

In the previous chapter we saw how a variety of processes can close down ways of understanding and responding to dynamic, complex situations. This chapter explores one set of ways of opening up and broadening out analysis and action. This, we suggest, is important if narratives are to be recognized – and pathways pursued – which address all the different dynamics of sustainability as well as the goals of reducing poverty and promoting social justice.

The focus in this chapter is on what we term 'empowering designs'. This refers to diverse, deliberately configured processes for consciously engaging with the challenges of sustainability – involving a 'broadening out' of the inputs to appraisal and an opening up of the outputs to decision-making and policy. In particular, empowering designs for appraisal aim at eliciting and highlighting marginalized narratives and thus exposing and exploring hidden pathways. In this way, 'inclusion' goes beyond simply the bringing of frequently excluded groups to the table – but extends to detailed and symmetrical treatment of alternative pathways for social, technological and environmental change. Crucially, these empowering designs for appraisal also aim at facilitating processes of negotiation between protagonists of different narratives and thus promote explicit deliberation over the detailed implications of contending possible pathways. They thus aim to facilitate processes that are adaptive, deliberative and reflexive (Chapter 4). As discussed in this chapter, this is an intensely political process; politics and power influence both process and outcomes. This theme is picked up in the next two chapters where we address more explicitly the politics of designs and how they interplay with wider social and political processes.

This chapter focuses in on a potential array of methods and tools that can be used in the appraisal of sustainability issues. Which method is chosen, and how a particular tool is applied, can make a huge difference to which type of narrative and subsequent pathway is exposed – and which remain hidden. This does not imply some simple instrumental relationship between 'tools' and 'outcomes'. There is no method that cannot be employed in inappropriate ways. Context is always crucial and the devil is often in the proverbial detail. Appraisal tools may encourage a broadening out or opening up in relatively direct ways through explicit features and characteristics. Or they may have this effect through more subtle effects – perhaps acting like 'Trojan horses' to gain access to relatively closed organizational cultures and then, through unfolding practice, stimulate forms of reflection or reflexivity that need not be explicitly proclaimed in the methodology itself. Whichever the mechanisms in question, the influence of methodological choice on practices and contexts for appraisal is a vital consideration.

Following a discussion of what is meant by appraisal, we examine a range of approaches which offer good prospects for broadening out and opening up complexity, and addressing the diverse dimensions of incomplete knowledge and sustainability, in line with the framework presented in Chapter 3. Thereafter we return to the discussion of framing and look in particular at the interaction between different methodological approaches and framing effects. We then outline key ingredients of effective appraisal to help define pathways to sustainability.

Approaching appraisal

By appraisal, we mean the ensemble of processes through which knowledges are gathered and produced in order to inform decision-making and wider institutional commitments (Stirling, 2005, 2008). Appraisal for sustainability must engage with complex dynamic systems (Chapter 2) and the governance context in which they are embedded (Chapter 4) (Smith and Stirling, 2007). Yet this is no easy task. Conventional methods and approaches often fail to grasp complexity and dynamics, and the challenges of incomplete knowledge. It is all too easy to assume that, if an appraisal process produces 'evidence', governance and decision-making processes will respond in an appropriate manner. And, inevitably, appraisal processes are social activities, where both those conducting the appraisal and those contributing to it in other ways are situated in a wider social and political field, bringing their own interests and assumptions to bear.

A wide diversity of tools, methods, techniques, frameworks, approaches and processes exist under the label 'appraisal' (Pearce and Nash, 1981; Chambers, 1994; Levett, 1997; Stirling, 2005). In practice this takes multiple forms, from rapid assessments as inputs to development project planning, to longer-term processes of research, monitoring and wider learning. Those involved in the production of such socially situated knowledge may range from government agencies and commercial corporations to wider civil society; from certified experts and specialists to citizens and members of the public. How the different groups – and their respective forms of knowledge – interact during processes of appraisal is a crucial issue. These more deliberately designed, structured processes often co-exist with more spontaneous, contingent and self-organized ones and, as we argue in the next chapter, the ways these mutually interact, exclude or shape each other are of central interest. Table 5.1 lists some illustrative examples among the rapidly growing array of appraisal approaches.

Table 5.1 *Examples of appraisal approaches*

	Examples	Reference
Organized scientific and broader academic and consultancy research	Involving universities, corporations, agencies	Nowotny et al, 2001
Codifications of more experiential knowledges and learning processes	Representations by farmers, workers, local communities	Kolb, 1984
Structured or unstructured forms of social, ecological, environmental and public health surveillance and monitoring		Canadian Journal of Public Health, 1993
Systematic *ex ante* procedures for project planning, programme evaluation or logframe analysis		Julian, 1997
Formal *ex post* bureaucratic enquiries	Quasi-/judicial and political	Hogwood and Gunn, 1984
Public interest political interventions	NGO communication initiatives	Sale, 1993
Discursive processes embodied in cultural activities and narratives	Performance, art, popular media, literature	Allan et al, 2000
Aggregative quantitative assessment	Cost-benefit/decision/risk analysis	Byrd and Cothern, 2000
Applications of heuristic techniques	Multi-criteria methods (MCM), scenarios, sensitivity analysis	Stagl, 2007

Table 5.1 *Examples of appraisal approaches (contd)*

	Examples	Reference
Iterative procedures for adaptive learning, using various permutations of modelling and monitoring		Jones, 1992
More open-structured approaches to mental modelling, morphological or soft-systems analysis		Checkland, 1999
Use of interpretive social scientific and ethnographic methods	Participant observation, focus groups	Grove-White et al, 2000
Quantitative social scientific and social psychological elicitation techniques	Surveys, contingent values, repertory grid, Q-method	McKeown and Thomas, 1988
Structured forms of participatory deliberation or inclusive engagement	Participatory rural appraisal (PRA), rapid rural appraisal (RRA), village meetings, consensus conferences	Chambers, 1994
Stakeholder negotiation forums	Strategic commissions, roundtables	Renn et al, 1995
Codified contractual bargaining procedures	On intellectual property rights, regulatory standards	RCEP, 1998

How can such a suite of approaches be deployed in appraisal for sustainability? What criteria can be used in different contexts to identify one set of approaches as more appropriate than another?

Broadening out and opening up

As we saw in Chapter 4, ways of understanding and intervening in issues concerning sustainability often close down around particular narratives, highlighting certain pathways and excluding alternatives. Thus processes defined in terms of risk can obscure valuable recognitions of other forms of incomplete knowledge, including ambiguity and surprise. In the same way, conceptions of sustainability may end up focusing on stability to the exclusion of perspectives that might help enhance resilience and robustness. Through the exertion of different forms of power, there are many ways closing down can take place. These can include the choosing of particular styles of method or tools for the framing and understanding of the problems in question.

Despite increasing interest in addressing wider social issues and perspectives in sustainability assessment (Holmes and Scoones, 2000; Munton, 2003), the dominant influence on appraisal remains with conventional expert-analytic methods (Flyvbjerg, 1998). These include a range of quantitative and/or expert-based assessment techniques, notionally based on evidence generated in scientific experimentation, modelling and monitoring (von Winterfeldt and Edwards, 1986; Morgan et al, 1990). These are framed and interpreted through use of probabilistic and statistical procedures, often as part of wider forms of cost-benefit (Pearce and Turner, 1990; Hanley and Spash, 1993), risk (Suter, 1993), decision (DTLR, 2001) or log-frame (Julian, 1997) analysis.

Taken together, it is these kinds of frameworks, techniques and tools that are implicitly referred to wherever calls (or claims) are made for (or to) 'sound scientific' decision-making on issues such as water resource management, health planning or agricultural systems appraisal. In particular, such methods are held to provide 'decision rules' of a kind that are applicable, appropriate and complete (Peterson, 2006). The strong implication is that appraisal can thus achieve a high level of confidence and lack of bias. Yet, though they may appear as neutral technical details, many features of expert analytic methods can carry profound implications for the kinds of results that are obtained. The routine practice of time-preference discounting in cost-benefit analysis, for instance, involves an implicit assumption that flows of value occurring in the future are less important than those occurring at the time of appraisal (Portnes and Weyant, 1999). Thus longer-term dynamics, and the requirement for durable and robust responses, are underplayed (Howarth and Norgaard, 1997).

Returning to our case study examples, expert analytics, and especially cost-benefit analysis, have been widely used in appraisal of water issues – and especially to inform decision-making around the construction of large dams (Mehta et al, 2007).[9] Developed by the US Tennessee Valley Authority in the 1930s specifically to appraise large dam projects, cost-benefit analysis claims to address the diverse range of issues by focusing on identifying and measuring the contending associated costs and benefits emerging out of individual projects. Yet the application of cost-benefit analysis privileges particular dimensions of the problem, while downplaying or obscuring others. While direct financial costs or benefits are easy to calculate and so rendered visible, less tangible economic factors and social issues and the ambiguities related to these are often neglected – such as changes in socio-cultural identity and gender relations (Elson, 1997) or impacts on geographical space and the environment (Cornerhouse, 1998).

Classic applications of cost-benefit analysis focus narrowly on a single intervention – such as a large dam project – to the exclusion of alternatives associated with other technological or policy pathways. As traditionally practised, the risk-based characterization of incomplete knowledge conspicuously fails to account for uncertain dynamics (e.g. changes in river flow). Problems of water scarcity, underdevelopment and poverty are typically framed in highly specific ways, such as to reduce ambiguity and privilege the benefits of large dams. The political attributes of the issues in question are typically reduced to a simple linear balance between the rights of the majority (or nation as a whole), pitted against the rights of a small minority who are asked to sacrifice their interests in the face of this greater good (Roy, 1999). Such cost-benefit analyses also privilege prevailing values in existing markets, attributing greater value to powerful, incumbent interests. Thus irrigated land is valued more highly than common-property land or men's economic activities are valued above those of women. Beyond this, it is often impossible to put a discrete monetary cost or benefit on intangibles such as the loss of livelihoods that have never entered the market-place, making it especially difficult to calculate the gendered nature of costs and benefits.

It was not until the 1980s and 1990s that the social and environmental impacts of dams came to be properly documented (Goldsmith and Hildyard, 1992; Cernea, 1997; Scudder, 2005). In this context, critics of cost-benefit analysis have increasingly highlighted the importance of making the invisible more visible. They have been sceptical of reductive–aggregative approaches to the measuring of costs and benefits and their respective distributions. In particular, gender scholars have demonstrated how a balance-sheet approach serves to legitimize the unequal distribution of resources (Elson, 1997).

Thus the case of cost-benefit analysis and its application to large dams illustrates how methods can contribute to processes of closing down – the shifts documented in the last chapter towards considering issues narrowly in terms of risk and stability, underplaying broader dimensions of incomplete knowledge and the range of dynamic properties of sustainability. But this need not be the case. Appraisal methods and tools can also contribute to the reverse processes of broadening out. Thus appraisal methods can be evaluated in terms of the degree to which inputs are responsive to the dynamics and uncertainties of social, economic, technological and ecological systems. 'Breadth' refers to the depth, extent and scope with which appraisal succeeds in fostering effective reflection over the full character of dynamic systems and diverse knowledges of them. Appraisal methods can also be evaluated according to the degree to which the outputs offer an array of options for policies, institutions, commitments and decisions (Smith and Stirling, 2006). 'Openness' refers to the degree to which appraisal conveys the plural and conditional nature of appraisal outputs into wider processes of governance (Stirling, 2005, 2008).

Figure 5.1 provides a schematic representation of how a variety of different methods, widely employed in appraisal, might be grouped in relation to these two dimensions. The fact that cases of more expert-analytic and participatory-deliberative appraisal methods are fairly evenly scattered, with strongly overlapping distributions, shows that contrasts between broadening out/narrowing in and opening up/closing down are applicable equally to quantitative expert-analytic methods as to qualitative, participatory, deliberative processes.

The issue of breadth or narrowness of inputs to appraisal refers to the kinds of options, methods, issues, possibilities, conditions and (crucially) perspectives that are taken into account – issues that relate closely to the processes of framing discussed in the last two chapters. Before turning to the specific methodological implications summarized in Figure 5.1, however, we should consider further some of the detailed characteristics of what is meant by the horizontal axis in Figure 5.1 – the difference between opening up or closing down the outputs of appraisal.

If appraisal is about closing down, then the aim is instrumentally to assist incumbent policy actors (or perhaps other sectional interests) by providing a means to justify particular decisions or support for decision-making processes in general (Collingridge, 1980, 1982). Whether expert-analytic or participatory, the role of the appraisal process lies here in cutting through the messy diversity of interests and perspectives to develop a clear, authoritative, prescriptive recommendation to inform decisions. The output of this kind of closing down in appraisal takes the form of what might be called 'unitary and prescriptive' policy advice. This involves the highlighting of a single (or very small sub-set) of possible courses of action (or policy or technology choices), which appear to be preferable under the particular framing conditions that happen to have been privileged. These framing conditions and sensitivities will typically not be explored in any detail. The outputs will therefore have the instrumental merit of conveying practical implications for policy and a clear justification for decision-making (Stirling, 2005).

On the other hand, if appraisal is aimed at opening up, then the emphasis lies in revealing to wider policy discourses any inherent open-endedness and contingency. Instead of focusing on unitary, prescriptive recommendations, such appraisal poses alternative questions, focuses on neglected issues, includes marginalized perspectives, contrasts contending knowledges, tests sensitivities to different methods, considers ignored uncertainties, examines different possibilities and highlights new options. Under an opening up approach to appraisal – whether expert-analytic or participatory – the outputs are what might be termed 'plural and conditional' policy advice (Stirling, 2003).

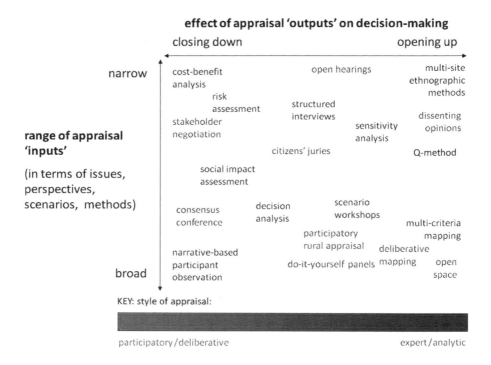

Figure 5.1 Characteristics of appraisal methods

With this dimension clarified, we can turn to the schematic ordering of methods offered in Figure 5.1. Starting in the top left corner, both (quantitative) cost-benefit analysis and (qualitative) stakeholder negotiation are conventionally conducted in ways that simultaneously narrow in inputs and close down outputs to appraisal. The inputs to appraisal are circumscribed by the methods used: for example, a limited array of quantifiable costs or benefits. These approaches can close down decision-making, because the outputs to wider governance debates often take the form of unitary, prescriptive findings – identifying single configurations for understandings and/or interventions that have the effect of uniquely prescribing policy and so closing down the scope for wider political discussion.

In a similar way, appraisal conducted through certain types of decision analysis or participant observation both represent very different forms of expert-analytic approach that have the effect of broadening out the inputs to appraisal. The first does this by engaging quantitatively with diverse actors, the second by eliciting disparate, local perspectives. Yet both can still have the effect of closing down appraisal: participant observation through privileging the analyst's own interpretive narrative and decision analysis through various aggregative procedures for combining the different quantitative inputs. Likewise, a consensus conference or citizens' jury may also display similar conjunctions of breadth but closure, through including diverse specialist and citizen values and knowledges during the process, but then arriving, in the end, at a particular 'consensus' or 'verdict' for policymaking.

Turning to the opening-up axis, there are many procedures for highlighting dissenting or minority views in conventional expert scientific committees. In a similar vein, an ethnographic appraisal of possible consequences of a particular policy may deliberately explore implications as seen from diverse settings or perspectives and thus yield a richer, less prescriptive and more multivalent output to policymaking. Yet both these approaches can remain relatively narrow if attention is restricted to a small subset of contexts or perspectives. A similar opening-up effect may be achieved even with otherwise quite narrow quantitative methods, for example risk assessment or cost-benefit analysis, simply by using techniques such as sensitivity or interval analysis to explore the many ways in which different values, in even a rather narrow range, can quickly yield highly divergent results.

Finally, there are a number of quantitative and qualitative, specialist and participatory approaches that display properties both of broadening out inputs and opening up of outputs. Participatory methods such as 'open space' incorporate many qualitative features designed to facilitate this, which can be applied with diverse specialists or in more inclusively participatory ways. Quantitative methods such as multi-criteria mapping can, properly used, also have the effect of simultaneously opening up and broadening out appraisal. This is because they explicitly require attention to be given to a range of different options, perspectives, criteria, scenarios and uncertainties. At the same time, the results obtained are not simple prescriptions of some 'optimal', 'most reasonable' or 'most legitimate' course of action. Instead, they focus on systematically exploring the ways in which different framing assumptions yield a different picture of the right course of action; although of course some possible interpretations are just plain wrong.

Different methods and tools for appraisal thus address contrasting aspects of opening up and closing down. Relatively few single approaches fully incorporate both qualities, irrespective of context. Likewise, it will often be apparently obscure features of detailed implementation (such as recruitment, facilitation, the boundaries of analysis or the expression of uncertainty) that determine the degree to which a particular appraisal exercise may be considered to broaden out or open up decision-making. In particular, the top right and bottom left corners of Figure 5.1 illustrate how it cannot be assumed that methods which broaden out inputs will also necessarily be those that open up outputs to decision-making.

As the pathways framework laid out in Chapter 3 describes, two key moves in particular are critical to the broadening out and opening up of appraisal for sustainability, in ways that resist the constraining effects of power documented in the last chapter. The first is a move away from narrow risk-based framings, which restrict attention to a circumscribed set of outcomes, each with an associated probability (Figure 3.4). The other is a shift away from preoccupations with stability-oriented interventions and towards strategies addressing less tractable dynamic properties of sustainability, such as resilience and robustness (Figure 3.7). The addressing of uncertainty, ambiguity and ignorance (Figure 3.4) requires the broadening out of attention to a wider range of options, perspectives, scenarios and possibilities, addressing incomplete knowledge head on. Yet this will not in itself have the effect of opening up wider debates about policy and governance, unless the key implications of different framings are explicitly distinguished – for instance by identifying and exploring alternative narratives and their implications for pathways. Likewise, the broadening out of attention to long-run stress, as well as short-term shocks, or to intractable, as well as readily controlled factors (Figure 3.7) does not of itself constitute an opening up of decision-making, again unless the implications for divergent pathways and policy interventions are clearly conveyed to wider governance debates.

In sum, there can be no simple methodological fixes for the challenges of opening up and broadening out. The wider political implications of this will be returned to in the next chapter. Nonetheless, with the 'devil in the detail' it follows that methods remain important. Figure 5.2 therefore provides a schematic illustration of some of the tools and methods that can be employed in order both to broaden out and open up appraisal designs, such as to better address the various aspects of incomplete knowledge that are routinely neglected in reductive-aggregative techniques such as risk assessment (moving from the top left corner to other quadrants). Taking these in turn, we can see uncertainty heuristics identified in the lower left corner. These take the form of rules of thumb – such as 'maximize the worst case outcome' (maximin) or 'minimize regrets' – that can be employed as a guide to the interpretation of uncertainty in the absence of aggregated probabilities. These have the effect of broadening out attention to scenarios that might otherwise be marginalized in appraisal. By also highlighting the intrinsically subjective and thus political values involved in choices between seeking to minimize worst-case outcomes or maximize best-case outcomes, these can also have the effect of opening up subsequent decision-making. Likewise, by making the contingencies more explicit, various forms of interval and sensitivity analysis (Saltelli, 2001) can (if properly conducted) also help to contribute to this dual role.

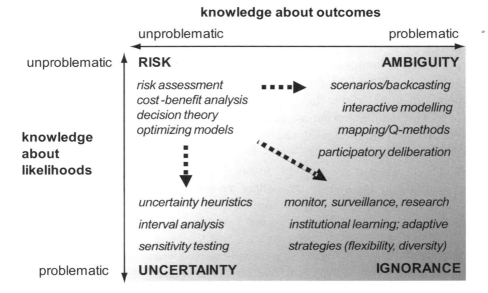

Figure 5.2 Appraisal methods for addressing contrasting aspects
of incomplete knowledge

Turning to the right-hand side of Figure 5.2, we can see a similar potential on the part of approaches to ambiguity as diverse as interactive
modelling, scenario analysis (Ogilvie, 2002; Werner, 2004) and participatory deliberation (Bohman, 1996). These can also have the effect of
broadening out attention to a range of perspectives – and thus associated
issues, options or conditions – of a kind that are typically side-lined in the
aggregative procedures routinely employed in risk assessment. Building on
this, techniques such as multi-criteria mapping explicitly focus on exploring
the detailed implications of different framing assumptions in appraisal, and
presenting this as a map of possible pathways and their respective advantages and disadvantages under contrasting viewpoints. However, though
offering to broaden out attention in many ways, these kinds of interactive
and participatory approaches will only open up debates if the divergent
findings that they reveal are clearly conveyed into the political decision-
making process. This is the reason, for instance, that multi-criteria (Stirling
and Mayer, 1999) and deliberative mapping (Davies et al, 2003)
approaches focus on mapping a set of alternative possible findings and their
respective assumptions and conditions, rather than prescribing a single,
ostensibly definitive result. Likewise, this is why Q-method (McKeown and
Thomas, 1988) focuses on the construction of a detailed picture of contrasting discourses, each of which yields a different implication for

'reasonable decisions'. Either way, the degree to which any given appraisal exercise is successful in opening up wider governance will often be a consequence of the detailed design and context and the style of communication.

Finally, although a state of ignorance is often treated as inherently indeterminate, we find in the lower right corner of Figure 5.2 a range of methodological approaches that can be useful in appraisal, even under these demanding conditions. Deliberate prioritization of monitoring, surveillance and targeted research, for instance, all offer ways to learn quickly from unfolding complexities and so reduce dangers of over-reliance on modelling. Measures to promote institutional learning help avoid the pitfalls of constraints on knowledge, where relevant implications may be well known to particular communities or disciplines but remain effectively unknown to those making decisions. Likewise, ignorance prompts greater attention in appraisal to strategies such as adaptation, agility, flexibility and diversity, whose benefits are all too easily missed when it is believed that the disciplines of risk assessment have effectively eliminated surprise. As our discussion of the avian influenza example in Chapter 3 showed, rethinking surveillance approaches in order to encompass the diverse forms of incomplete knowledge is essential.

Of course none of these methods offers a magic bullet; the specific contributions to broadening out or opening up will depend on details of context, design and implementation. In reality, conditions of uncertainty, ambiguity and ignorance are inextricably intertwined and indeed mutually co-constituting. Applications of specific approaches will therefore likewise often address aspects of all these conditions together. The point is that there exist no shortage of practical tools and methods for the design of more effective forms of appraisal. It is the fixation with risk-based approaches that tends to leave these, like Cinderella, uninvited to the party.

Just as it is critical to extend the range of methods and institutions in the appraisal of incomplete knowledge, so is it necessary to expand the repertoire of appraisal approaches and associated governance interventions to address all dynamic properties of sustainability. Here too, as discussed in the last chapter, we find a similar picture, in which attention is preoccupied with stability-based strategies, rather than the contrasting dynamic properties of durability, resilience and robustness. Here, existing literatures are less well developed than those reviewed earlier concerning alternative approaches to appraisal under conditions of incomplete knowledge. Nonetheless, it is possible to sketch some general implications. Appraisal approaches that illuminate the temporality of change become critical in distinguishing between shocks and stresses and their implications and their importance over different timescales. These range from quantitative environmental monitoring approaches through longitudinal analysis of landscapes, resource and technological systems, to *longue-durée* historical and archaeological analysis. There are roles here for participatory as much as expert-led analysis. Linking appraisal to action, the discipline of social ecology, making use of some of these appraisal approaches, has done much to highlight the importance of qualities such as flexibility and adaptability as attention moves away from a fixation with conventional control-based strategies (Adger et al, 2001; Berkes et al, 2006). In general, the distinctive characteristics of responsive action lie in the more qualified, conditional, iterative and reflexive style than is typically associated with interventions oriented towards control (Stirling, 2010).

Whether appraisal approaches actually succeed in broadening out and opening up depends not just on the methods themselves, however, but also on the ways in which they are applied. The next section therefore turns again to the question of framing, but this time within appraisal processes themselves.

Framing and appraisal

As discussed in Chapter 3, consideration of framing underlies all the more specific issues of context discussed so far. It refers to the particular contextual assumptions, methodological variables, procedural attributes or interpretive issues that different groups might bring to a problem – including those relating to understandings of risk, uncertainty, ambiguity and ignorance – and the prioritization of stability, durability, resilience and robustness in thinking about sustainability. Attention to framing addresses the ways in which problems are bounded and constituted, the way different aspects are related and their relative importance. Evidence for the importance of framing effects in the conduct of appraisal is widespread (Goffman, 1975; Wynne, 1987; Jasanoff, 1990; Schwartz and Thompson, 1990; EEA, 2001). Framing effects together condition the ways in which even the most finely specified method is implemented in practice and thus strongly influence the patterning of results. As we saw in Chapter 3, through the example of the appraisal of energy systems, because of different configurations of framing conditions, even expert-analytic approaches can yield radically divergent results. However, given their reliance on particular disciplinary criteria of rigour or consistency, many expert-analytic approaches fail to recognize this. The result is a false impression of precision, rigour and neutrality which masks real and sometimes important biases linked to framing.

Table 5.2 identifies a series of framing effects that commonly arise in appraisal processes. These lead to a variety of ways in which the answers can depend on the questions. As can be seen, these framing effects apply as much to qualitative approaches as to quantitative ones, albeit in different ways (Stirling, 2005, 2008). Thus, substituting one form of appraisal for another does not resolve the problems of the contingent effects of framing; nor does it remove the pressures exerted through power relations for particular framing conditions to be adopted; often those that justify decisions that work in the interests of powerful groups or institutions (Denzin and Lincoln, 2003; Kanbur, 2003). Therefore attention to framing effects should be part of any sound scientific, rigorous procedure and so central to any appraisal approach, whether quantitative, qualitative, participatory or not.

Towards empowering designs: Five principles

So far in this chapter we have identified three challenges for appraisal for sustainability. These are, first, the need to broaden out the inputs to appraisal, to be more inclusive of diverse perspectives and priorities, and attendant to the complex dynamics and diverse forms of incomplete knowledge that pervade social, ecological and technological systems. Second, the need to open up how the results of appraisal articulate with decision-making and policy processes so that, instead of a narrow set of options, a wider array of possibilities is acknowledged, along with explicit acknowledgement of their distributional and sustainability implications. Third, there is a need to

Table 5.2 *Framing effects in appraisal*

Equally relevant to quantitative and qualitative approaches	Setting agendas	Defining problems	Posing questions
	Prioritizing issues	Deciding context	Choosing methods
	Addressing power	Definition of options	Selecting alternatives
	Handling dissensus	Designing process	Drawing boundaries
More relevant to expert and quantitative approaches	Discounting time	Formulating criteria	Characterizing metrics
	Setting baselines	Deriving probabilities	Including disciplines
	Expressing uncertainties	Recruiting expertise	Commissioning research
	Constituting proof	Exploring sensitivities	Interpreting results
More relevant to participatory and discursive approaches	Identifying stakeholders	Phrasing questions	Bounding remits
	Recruiting participants	Providing information	Focusing attention
	Engaging personalities	Conducting discourse	Facilitating interactions
	Documenting findings	Persuading critics	Adopting norms

attend to the framing effects and power relations that pervade appraisal processes themselves, ensuring that these do not (deliberately or inadvertently) constrain the range of alternatives that are examined or prioritize attention to the pathways favoured by particular groups.

Moving beyond the specific focus on methods and their choice, in this section we outline five key principles of appraisal for sustainability. Our focus is on the ways in which methods are deployed and the practices, styles and ethos of appraisal. This echoes and draws on some of the reflections from, for example, literatures on precaution (O'Riordan and Cameron, 1994; Harding and Fisher, 1999; ESTO, 1999; Raffensberger and Tickner, 1999; O'Riordan and Jordan, 2001; EEA, 2001), as well as literatures on the conduct of participatory processes in settings pervaded by steep gradients of power (Chambers, 1997; Cornwall and Gaventa, 2000; IIED, 2006).

Include a diversity of knowledges through participatory engagement

Rather than privileging a particular body of elite or disciplinary knowledge (such as economics or risk assessment), appraisal should be deliberately configured to draw symmetrically on the full diversity of different methods and salient knowledges – emphasizing where necessary to correct for the neglect of weaker voices (EEA, 2001). In this, quantitative expert-analytic knowledges will often remain relevant (and sometimes essential) but need to be recast as necessary, rather than sufficient, inputs to the structuring of appraisal (ESTO, 1999). Depending on the context, other relevant bodies of knowledge might variously include those of marginalized scientific disciplines, local communities, farmers, women, workers, consumers, 'users', citizens, children or those living with particular health or livelihood conditions (Fischer, 1990). Although they may share many features, the knowledges associated with such varied social groups may also embody sometimes subtle but important differences arising from divergent experiences, conceptualizations, values and priorities (Wynne, 2001; Feenberg, 2002). They may also be associated with important differences concerning the ways that relevant knowledges are (or should be) constructed, accredited, interpreted or validated (Scoones and Thompson, 1994; Agrawal, 1995; Fairhead and Leach, 2003).

To achieve this more symmetrical approach to different knowledges, many argue that an overarching open process of participatory deliberation is needed, taking precedence over the application of different specific methods (Irwin, 1995; Sclove, 1995). This should be subject to principles of accessibility, fairness, transparency, mutual respect, free expression, public reasoning and good faith; principles that are widely established to characterize rational, equitable discourse (Joss and Durrant, 1995; Renn et al, 1995). Only once such broad criteria of high-quality deliberation are established for a particular appraisal process should attention turn to finer-grained conventions to be adopted over the choice and use of more specific methods (Rowe and Frewer, 2000; Petts, 2001). This includes attention to the framing of techniques such as risk or cost-benefit analysis (where these are applied) and deliberate iteration between disparate and complementary methods to compensate for any difficulties or 'blind spots' and stimulate challenges to further learning (EEA, 2001).

Establishing such open, equitable discourse, especially in power-laden settings, is of course extremely challenging (Dryzek, 1990; Bohman, 1996). At the very least, particular efforts must be made to bring the voices and perspectives of groups disempowered by prevailing social and institutional structures into this deliberation over framing (Gaventa and Valderrama, 1999; Holmes and Scoones, 2000; Wakeford, 2001). Making use of a mix of methods can help, each drawing on a range of different inter- and trans-disciplinary contributions. Qualitative, discursive and interpretive methods, for example, may assist in establishing and rendering more explicit and accountable the principal elements in the framing of analysis. Quantitative metrics, heuristics and analysis, on the other hand, can reinforce the transparency and clarity with which these principles are implemented and their implications communicated to third parties. By pursuing a range of disparate methods in parallel, appraisal can triangulate and validate findings in order to yield more robust policy recommendations and to identify more confidently areas where further attention is required.

Extend scope and enable choice

To be effective and rigorous, appraisal for sustainability needs to focus with comparable vigour on a range of different criteria – rather than being circumscribed or dominated by a particular focal consideration. Among other things, this means broadening the scope of appraisal to enable choice among different options (O'Brien, 2000). This is especially important where a policymaking initiative is driven by a specific problem (such as a threat to economic welfare) or beset with urgent priorities (such as a pressing risk issue). In practice, this means taking care that appraisal moves away from narrow assessments of the efficacy, efficiency, acceptability, safety or tolerability of a single possible course of action – often that favoured by powerful institutions or under prevailing market forces (ESTO, 1999). Instead, appraisal should address a range of contending possible options and future pathways favoured – or salient under – a diversity of different interests and perspectives (Collingridge, 1980). Pursuing a diversity of options may also help accommodate such plural perspectives, hedge ignorance and foster more robust and innovative future strategies (Stirling, 1997, 2007d). Only in this way can appraisal genuinely address the dynamics of alternative pathways for change and so enable real choices among a variety of different possible technology, policy or institutional trajectories.

This essentially comparative character to appraisal should also move beyond preoccupations with negative 'impacts' or 'risks', in order to allow a balanced consideration of the *pros* as well as the *cons* of different possible courses of action. This means paying attention to claims or expectations over the positive dimensions of each option, such as its driving needs or purposes, or associated benefits and justifications (Jackson and Taylor, 1992; MacGarvin, 1995). A final aspect of this extended scope concerns the need to consider indirect, cumulative and synergistic social, economic and environmental effects – as well as the direct impacts that are more tractable to conventional forms of assessment (EEA, 2001).

Take a dynamic perspective, accept incomplete knowledge

Appraisal processes need to move beyond static 'snapshot' approaches to the assessment of benefits and impacts, to adopt a dynamic perspective. This requires an approach that attends directly to the passage of time. This applies both retrospectively and prospectively – involving an empirical grounding in historical knowledges, as well as the use of a longitudinal framework to look forward to the future. It is only in this way that appraisal can give proper consideration to issues such as path-dependent events, and additive, cumulative, synergistic or life-cycle effects (ESTO, 1999). An historically grounded, longitudinal approach can also help reveal the complex and sometimes unexpected consequences of individual and organizational behaviour, as shaped by different contexts and governance arrangements (EEA, 2001).

A further crucial feature of such a dynamic perspective is that it prompts greater humility over the implications of uncertainty, ambiguity and ignorance discussed in Chapter 3, and a search for more appropriate methods. Collectively these approaches are increasingly well documented as elements of more 'precautionary' approaches to the appraisal of environmental and human health threats (Stirling, 2007c).

Appraisal therefore becomes part of an ongoing learning process, continually learning from and responding to a dynamically changing world. Instead of seeing the relationship between appraisal and decision-making as a monolithic, linear sequential procedure, it becomes instead a more multi-stranded and finely iterated process of interactions between deliberation and intervention – allowing continuous adaptation to shifting knowledges, values and priorities and the persistent inevitability of surprise. Appraisal is undertaken not as a means to produce and defend claims to definitively complete bodies of knowledge, but as a means to catalyze, facilitate and empower more effective social learning.

Attend to rights, equity and power

Although a broadening out of appraisal may open the door to the more effective prioritizing of the concerns and priorities of the poorest and least powerful groups, it is not sufficient. It does not provide any guarantee that these will actually be treated with the seriousness that they are due. Power operates in more persistent and concrete ways than simply through framing and needs to be challenged in a variety of ways. Nevertheless there are some direct measures in appraisal which can help. These include a shift away from three dominant tendencies.

First, rather than viewing different policy options purely in terms of utilitarian trade-offs, appraisal might also adopt alternative 'lexicographic' frameworks (Spash, 2001) – for instance highlighting consequences in terms of the fundamental rights and entitlements of the poorest groups in society (Sen, 2001). Second, rather than concentrating predominantly on aggregate notions of economic benefit, social utility, human welfare or 'the public good', appraisal should focus more on distributional issues and impacts on equity and equality with respect to all these (and other) parameters (Rawls, 1971, 1993).Third, against the tendency to concentrate on apparently transcendent qualities such as 'objectivity', 'authority', 'representativeness' and 'legitimacy', appraisal should deliberately reflect on the ways in which such qualities (even when ostensibly progressive) can become re-defined and manipulated through the exercise of power (Pellizzoni, 2001; Stirling, 2005). In other words, considerations of rights, entitlements, equity and power should be central to processes of appraisal and the way its outcomes are dealt with (Gaventa 2006, Pettit and Musyoki, 2004). Thus, among a plurality of outcomes suggesting alternative possible pathways, there are grounds for explicitly highlighting and elaborating on those that work in the favour of the perspectives and goals of poorer and marginalized groups and towards social justice. How such pathways actually become realized, sometimes in the face of entrenched power relations that push in opposing directions, is a major challenge which we consider further in the next chapter.

Be reflexive

Reflexivity in appraisal compels explicit acknowledgement of the rationales and approaches being prioritized. This applies both at the level of institutions and methods and at the level of individual practitioners and commentators. In both cases, the challenges are considerable. For institutions constrained by statutory frameworks or responsibilities to particular stakeholders, this can be difficult not only in terms of the required levels of humility, deliberation and communication, but also in terms of legal duties, administrative remits or political accountabilities. In the case of individuals, the required degree of self-reflexivity can be in stark tension with principles of professionalism – under which the distinguishing imperative is often seen to lie precisely in disengaging from (and by implication denying) one's own personal subjective context and commitments (Chambers, 1997; Eyben, 2006).

A further manifestation of reflexivity in appraisal is to focus attention on the relationship between an appraisal process and the wider governance structures which shape it and in which it is embedded (Fischer, 1990; Dryzek, 1990; Pellizzoni, 2001). The quality of reflexivity applies both to the inputs to appraisal and also to the outputs to wider governance (Stirling, 2006).

Appraisal in practice

So what might these five principles for more effective appraisal look like in practice? How can they contribute together to more empowering designs? Returning to our case studies, in this section we look at two examples of where attempts have been made in the directions we have discussed. The first focuses on the appraisal of options for agricultural futures and particularly the role of GM crops. The second looks at the design of HIV prevention programmes and in particular an NGO response to the HIV/AIDS epidemic in Africa. Both of these examples had limitations.

Case 1: Voice, vision and rural futures in Zimbabwe

A series of workshops leading to a citizens' jury were held in Zimbabwe in 2002 to explore rural futures and particularly the role of biotechnologies within them (Rusike, 2005). The methodologies chosen were firmly focused on those aiming to be both broad and open (see Figure 5.1) and that could address the ambiguities in the debate due to diverse and divergent perspectives. In particular a participatory scenarios approach was combined with a citizens' jury approach.

In recent years attempts to encourage greater inclusivity in deliberations on controversial policy issues have involved experimentation with citizens' juries. As one among a number of new approaches to fostering more deliberative explorations of ordinary peoples' views on issues of wider interest, citizens' juries emerged in the USA in the 1970s (Rowe and Frewer, 2000). Since then, a range of related approaches have been applied under a variety of names to a broad range of policy issues, including major challenges of radioactive waste management and genetically modified food production (see www.juryworld.com). Since 2000 a number of such processes have been conducted around the future of farming and especially the role of GM crops in the developing world, including in India, Brazil and Mali (IIED, 2006). The Prajateerpu citizens' jury in Andhra Pradesh, India, held in 2001 (Pimbert and Wakeford, 2001, 2002), proved the most controversial to date, generating substantial institutional and policy reaction and an extensive reflection on institutional and methodological implications.

A classic citizens' jury process involves a number of key steps: a question is defined; a selection of jurors is made; a panel of 'experts' is invited; a deliberation on the issues is convened, including a cross-examination of expert witnesses; and finally a judgement is made (Wakeford, 2001). The overall aim is to encourage a broadening out of debate, going beyond a narrow, closed, expert-driven appraisal process. Through a thorough deliberation of issues, involving a representative group of stakeholders, the end result, it is hoped, is a decision or recommendation which has been tested rigorously by diverse opinions and perspectives. And, with an inclusive approach, it hopefully allows for wider ownership and buy-in to the result. In sum: better, more robust policies and recommendations.

The *Izwi ne Tarisiro* ('Voice and Vision' in Shona) process was convened by a group of NGOs and parastatal organizations in Zimbabwe and established links with government, non-governmental and private sector actors from the start. It was broadly framed around the question: 'What do you desire to see happen in the smallholder agriculture sector in Zimbabwe by 2020?' Rather than being focused on particular technology options, the framing was broad. A national scoping workshop involving 43 farmers from 16 districts, selected to represent a range of backgrounds, identified key issues and future scenarios. A jury of ten men and six women was then selected from this group and after a careful induction, which demystified the jury and policy processes, interrogated 17 specialist witnesses over a week. The process led to agreement on some basic principles about the local control of food and farming, as well as the importance of indigenous knowledge, practical skills and local institutions, alongside a verdict which questioned the use of GM crops. In subsequent reflections, participants felt they had had an unprecedented opportunity to interact directly with senior officials, and gain insights and information about the workings of the policy process that they could feed back to their communities and act on in pressing for desired change (Rusike, 2005).

Overall, the central lesson that emerged was the importance of reflexivity – the ability, honestly and openly, to reflect on framings, assumptions, interests and subject positions – among all parties. Processes that ensure reflexivity add both to the opportunities of inclusion and opening up, but also to methodological rigour and robustness, and ultimately effectiveness.

Case 2: Appraisal for the design of HIV/AIDS prevention programmes

Approaches to prevention of HIV/AIDS at the community level in developing countries have often been dominated by the top-down provision of information, education and communication on the assumption that this will bring about changes in individuals' behaviour. However, accumulated experience has shown that such expert-driven approaches, focused on individual behaviour change, often have little impact on people's ability to protect themselves from HIV infection (Edstrom et al, 2000, 2002).

Realizing this, the International HIV/AIDS Alliance, and the linking organizations that it supports to work with local NGOs in community prevention programmes, began from 1996 to adopt alternative approaches. These were characterized by two linked features. First, they broadened the framing and hence range of possible inputs to appraisal by shifting the focus away from the behaviour of individuals towards HIV-related vulnerability within communities. The vulnerability framing opened up a far wider range of possible factors at play, ranging from access to risk-reducing technologies such as condoms, to people's power to make choices, to infection levels within the broader community and partners.

Second, the approaches turned to community members themselves to identify the specific complexes of factors at work in their own local settings. In this they drew on and adapted a range of tools and methods used in participatory rural appraisal, including social maps, discussion groups, Venn diagrams, ranking and scoring, body mapping, life-lines, causal analysis flow charts, and HIV 'wheels', where vulnerabilities are identified as segments in a pie chart. Such a 'toolbag' was applied with community members to identify issues of local concern and their links to sexual vulnerability and HIV/AIDS. Emphasis was on creating and maintaining open deliberation among people with different perspectives on and experiences of vulnerability, airing and comparing the diverse views of different groups rather than establishing a single 'community view'. The HIV/AIDS Alliance and its partners realized that such participatory appraisal processes required highly skilled facilitation and attention to intra-community power dynamics to work effectively. Nevertheless, in a number of instances, the approach has resulted in highly inclusive processes of project appraisal.

These have led to the identification and implementation of projects that move well beyond awareness-raising and individual behaviour change, highlighting a diverse range of practical approaches that respond to people's diverse vulnerabilities as framed and experienced themselves.

Reflecting on these two cases, how do they match up to the principles of effective appraisal for empowering designs we outlined earlier? Table 5.3 offers a schematic overview.

Overall, in both cases, the use of broad-based, multi-method, participatory approaches to appraisal enabled a greater degree of reflexivity over the ways in which the knowledges informing policy decisions are conditional on different framings. Instead of closing down around a particular representation of the issues and perspectives, they helped open up the outputs of appraisal to policymaking and wider political discourse. However, as we have already discussed, the processes are not straightforward. Attention to issues of representation proved a challenge in both instances, and the assumption that a 'local' or 'community-based' approach is sufficient is challenged. Power dynamics pervade all appraisal processes, and these examples were no exceptions. Inclusions and exclusions occur at all points and attention to how this occurs is essential. With a dominant discourse prevailing, dissenting or even mildly differing, opinions can easily be silenced, often inadvertently. Reflexivity on the part of the convenors of appraisals about both the process and the outcomes is therefore paramount, as otherwise the rush to define a project solution or an advocacy message may close down the process.

Conclusion

This chapter has argued for the importance of taking seriously the imperatives to broaden out and open up appraisal. This serves to make associated decisions more rigorously accountable. Nowhere is such accountability more important than in relation to the interests of those who are already most disadvantaged and marginalized. Bringing together these discussions of broadening out and opening up appraisal, we can envisage four possible permutations of appraisal approach – depending on the degree to which inputs to appraisal and outputs to governance and decision-making are broad or narrow. Figure 5.3 illustrates each of these ideal types diagrammatically, together with a stylized example for each.

What are the implications of this framework for thinking about the design of appraisal approaches for the specific challenges of sustainability? Much of the preceding discussion has, in different ways, highlighted the strong value but relative neglect of broad and open appraisal designs.

Table 5.3 *Empowering designs: Five principles, two cases and some questions*

	Agricultural futures and GM crops	**HIV/AIDS prevention**
Include a diversity of knowledges	Local knowledge seen as critical. A deliberate sampling of representatives for the jury, including attention to gender representation. But how were these choices made? What is the basis for representation?	Beyond a top-down, expert model to a community-based, participatory approach. But who is represented in 'the community'?
Extend scope, enable choice	Broad framing of the question – rural futures, not a specific technology. Choice among different scenarios encouraged. But how constrained were scenario options? What room for dissent and debate was there?	A focus on vulnerability, with a broad definition, opening up debate about prevention options. Choice of projects which go beyond awareness raising and education. But how constrained were choices in the end?
Take a dynamic perspective, accept incomplete knowledge	A focus on longer-term futures, but without a specific focus on the multiple dimensions of sustainability. Scenario approaches addressed uncertainty to some degree. But what about ignorance and surprise?	Deliberation around diverse views of vulnerability, accepting ambiguities, Less attention to longer-term dynamics of change.
Attend to rights, equity, power	A specific focus on involving those who do not usually have access to decision-making, including women. But how were power dynamics – including dispute and dissent – dealt with as part of the process?	A rights-based focus, with the perspectives of the poor, marginalized and stigmatized prioritized. But who was left out from the group-based, community-level approach?
Be reflexive	Reflexive learning by participants, many who had not been engaged in such processes before. But a singular 'verdict' underplays the wider deliberation and debate involved.	Reflexive learning by the HIV/AIDS alliance and partners, extending the scope of their programming. But how did the process of reflection and learning continue into the project phases?

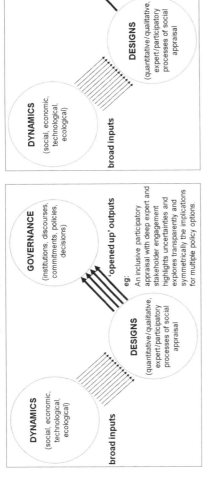

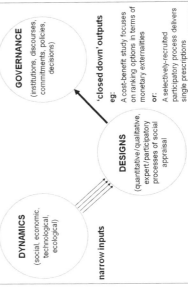

Figure 5.3 Permutations of breadth and openness in appraisal

Appraisal designs for sustainability need to attend to various synergies, tensions and sequences in the articulation of different expert-analytic and participatory-deliberative methods, as linked into wider appraisal and governance processes. By analysing significant tensions and contrasts, and by suggesting new complementarities or synergies, we emphasize two aspects. First, an enhanced understanding of the key features in appraisal designs, in relation to the dynamics of the social, technological and ecological systems with which we are concerned. Second, the importance of a more rigorous and grounded picture of how new articulations of different methods might help resolve the problems of current relatively narrow, closed approaches and so help address the concerns of marginalized people.

The chapter has underlined that incomplete knowledge of social, technological and ecological systems extends well beyond the conventional problem of 'risk' – as addressed in established 'science-based' techniques such as risk assessment, cost-benefit, decision and log-frame analysis. Rather, we face many situations of true uncertainty – in which there is no firm basis to assign probabilities, so these techniques are formally inapplicable. In addition, we face problems of ambiguity, where the possible outcomes are also indeterminate or contested, and we must deal with the challenge of ignorance, acknowledging persistent exposure to unknowns and the inevitable prospect of surprises.

Appraisal is deeply conditioned by a multitude of framing effects. This applies as much to qualitative as to quantitative methods and to participatory as well as expert processes. Some of these framing effects reflect the particular contexts in which the methods are applied, others relate to inherent features of appraisal procedures and structures themselves. An overarching challenge lies in the tendency for poorer people to be systematically marginalized and excluded by the power relations and governance institutions within which appraisal is conducted.

This chapter has therefore identified a number of key features of potentially more empowering designs for appraisal, giving rise to a series of practical responses. These include drawing on a diversity of knowledges, especially the knowledges of those who stand to be most affected. They include extending the scope of appraisal to consider a range of different options for action; considering a wider array of complex and indirect possible effects; and triangulating by using a variety of different disciplines and methods. Together, these 'empowering designs' offer better ways to help move towards more progressive outcomes for the poorest groups and to ensure their stability, durability, resilience and robustness. At the same time, however, appraisal should be designed to focus constantly on issues of equity, the rights of those who stand to be most affected and the ways in which power can operate to thwart these ends, both in appraisal and in wider governance.

Chapter 6

An Alternative Politics
for Sustainability

Introduction

The last chapter argued for broadening out the inputs to, and opening up the outputs of, appraisal – to offer a broader array of options, defining multiple potential pathways to sustainability. In particular, this means attention to those pathways that are sometimes hidden and especially to those that support the needs and aspirations of people struggling to escape poverty and marginalization. This chapter asks what would it take for governance processes themselves to broaden out and open up – to receive this richer and more plural knowledge and act on it, incorporating it into pathways to sustainability?

This takes more than methods. Appropriate choice of appraisal methods, if applied with all the qualifications and suggested practices outlined in the last chapter, can certainly help broaden out and open up governance processes. This can encourage reflexivity, challenge power relations and show policy actors alternative narratives. But what is actually taken up and acted upon will clearly still be influenced by power structures, politics and interests acting well beyond the domains accessible by any appraisal method. Good ideas and evidence do not necessarily result in change. As we saw in Chapter 4, there is a huge array of cognitive, institutional and political pressures, interacting through processes of governmentality, which often close down options towards narrow risk-based and stability-oriented perspectives, reinforcing the interests of the powerful. There is a need therefore to bring governance and politics back to centre stage. Attention to context and the particularities of institutions, politics and policy processes in different settings and to the networked, multi-level character of governance arrangements today must be part of this.

Governing for sustainability is not straightforward. As discussed at the beginning of the book, there appears to be an emerging contradiction: just as things are getting more complex, powerful narratives, supported by powerful institutions are on the rise with the consequence that options are being closed down and alternative pathways obscured or obliterated.

Yet alternatives are possible. As we argued in Chapter 4, governmentality always generates possibilities for counter-politics. In this chapter, we pursue further the argument that there are chinks and spaces in existing governance arrangements. If opened up, these might allow alternative narratives to be acknowledged and appreciated, towards enabling new pathways. Likewise, we have seen glimpses of how governance might be further opened up to accommodate the kinds of more adaptive and reflexive approaches that are needed to cope with the deeper indeterminacies of knowledge and intractabilities of action.

In this chapter we focus in on two arenas and forms of engagement which offer prospects for opening up governance processes. First we look at understanding and influencing policy processes. Second, we move to an exploration of the ways in which citizen action and social movements can affect change. Both policy and citizen engagement take place in a far wider landscape of knowledge and knowledge-making, however, and in this light the last part of the chapter considers roles for researchers, public intellectuals and the media in seeking out and supporting pathways to sustainability.

Influencing policy processes[10]

Understanding what policies are and how policies change is an important first step for influencing them. For a term so commonly taken for granted, 'policy' is a remarkably slippery one – it has been suggested that 'policy is rather like an elephant: you know it when you see it, but you cannot easily define it' (Cunningham, 1963, in Keeley and Scoones, 2003). But if putting one's finger on what constitutes policy is difficult, then assessing why particular policies take the shape they do – and working out what can be done to change them – is often an even more daunting challenge. Some have gone as far as to say that 'the whole life of policy is a chaos of purposes and accidents. It is not at all a matter of the rational implementation of so-called decisions through selected strategies' (Clay and Schaffer, 1984, p192).

Being a policymaker does not necessarily make the task of understanding policy any easier. Indeed, one policymaker working in a rural development setting in Africa commented on the often confused and complex nature of policy:[11] 'I thought all I had to do was explain the science and all would change – I was wrong.' As another put it: 'Policy says something, and implementation on the ground is something else. How do you reconcile these?' And another argued: 'There are so many interests around policy. It's like moving a big wheel. It's a long struggle.'

In exploring policy processes with a view to enabling pathways to sustainability, a series of questions arise: Why is it that particular narratives about the nature and causes of problems stick with such tenacity in policy debates? How do particular perspectives and the interests they represent find their way into policy? How might policy processes be changed to encourage a greater inclusion of otherwise excluded voices?

There is a need for a sceptical step away from the assumption that research is a neutral and objective exercise in gathering 'correct' evidence that will make a positive difference – in other words, what ought to be done and how to do it. Instead, as we have argued earlier in this book, the process of gathering knowledge to inform – and evidence for – policy (which we call appraisal) is less the result of a pure and rational quest for what is technically correct (where the task is to develop more refined tools to provide 'better' information, which leads to better policy). Instead, it is more about the establishment of 'facts' within particular networks, and in relation to particular framings of the problem and sustainability goals. It is thus the reach and influence of such networks, and their stability or capacity to shape what goes on in mainstream institutions, nationally and internationally, that is key.

Understanding policy – the conventional view

The traditional and highly stylized model of policymaking views it as a linear process in which rational decisions are taken by those with authority and responsibility for a particular policy area (Simon, 1957). This model assumes that policymakers approach the issues rationally, going through each logical stage of the process and carefully considering all relevant information. If policies do not achieve what they are intended to achieve, blame is often not laid on the policy itself but on political or managerial failure in implementing it (Juma and Clarke, 1995) – through a lack of political will, poor management or shortage of resources, for example.

It is also assumed that there is a clear separation between fact (identified through a rational approach based on evidence, science and objective knowledge) and value (seen as a separate issue, dealt with in the political process). Policymaking is thus seen as a purely bureaucratic or administrative exercise (Jenkins, 1978; Hogwood and Gunn, 1984; Weber, 1991). If politics enter the fray, it is around decision-making (in the realm of value); implementation is an entirely technical procedure (in the realm of facts). The role of experts is seen as critical to the process of making rational decisions, and scientific expertise is presumed to be independent and objective. The familiar refrain is that of 'evidence-based policy', or policy rooted in sound science.

While many would disregard this as a caricature – which it undoubtedly is – the underlying assumptions are remarkably pervasive, and this linear model remains a prevalent mindset – particularly in development practice. However, research on policy processes shows it to be an inadequate reflection of reality (Keeley and Scoones, 2003).

What are policy processes?

To understand and influence policy processes towards pathways to sustainability we need to cast aside this linear, rational policy model. Instead, policy needs to be understood as a more complex and messy process involving a multiplicity of actors, with several key characteristics. These features of the policy process echo arguments we have made in earlier chapters when discussing governance, politics, institutions and decision-making more broadly (Chapters 3 and 4).

First, policymaking must be understood as a political process as much as an analytical or problem-solving one. The policymaking process is by no means the purely technical, rational activity that it is often held up to be. Second, policymaking is incremental, complex and messy, a process of 'disjointed incrementalism or muddling through' (Lindblom, 1959; see also Etzioni, 1967; Smith and May, 1980). This suggests a more 'bottom-up' view of policy (Hjern and Porter, 1981), whereby the agency of different actors across multiple 'interfaces' is emphasized (Long and Long, 1992). An understanding of practitioners and their day-to-day dealings with policy issues is therefore key (see Schön, 1983; Mosse, 2005). Third, implementation involves discretion and negotiation by front-line workers (giving staff more scope for innovation than they are often credited with). Thus Lipsky (1980) makes clear that so-called street-level bureaucrats – or field-level ones, such as health workers or agricultural extension agents – may exercise considerable agency in the policy process. They prioritize, interpret instructions, deal with overlapping and contradictory directives, and sometimes even take the initiative in high-profile policy change (see Joshi, 1997).

Third, there are always overlapping and competing agendas; there may not be complete agreement among people over what the really important policy problem is. Different actors will always bring different framings and narratives to bear (Chapter 3), so policy processes always involve a degree of argumentation, even if this remains implicit (Fischer and Forester, 1993; Hajer, 1995). Fourth, decisions are not discrete and technical: facts and values are intertwined. Value judgements play a major role (Fischer, 1990). Fifth, technical experts and policymakers 'mutually construct' policy (Shackley and Wynne, 1995). This means that scientists contribute to the framing of policy issues by defining what evidence can be produced and its policy significance. And those working in policy also frame scientific enquiry by defining areas of relevance and pertinent areas for investigation – jointly negotiating what questions need to be answered and what knowledge can be provided to answer them. And finally, the co-production of science and policy (Barnes and Edge, 1982; Jasanoff and Wynne, 1997; Jasanoff, 2004) often acts to play down scientific uncertainties and ignorance, as scientists attempt to satisfy the demand for answers from policymakers (Wynne, 1992). Thus, as we discussed in Chapter 4, plural and partial debates often become recast as singular, closed and certain.

The study of policy processes therefore involves understanding the mechanics of decision-making and implementation. Just as important, as we discussed in Chapter 3, it requires an understanding of more complex underlying practices of system framing – the way boundaries are drawn around problems, how policy problems are defined and what is included and excluded.

There is of course an extensive literature on the policy process. Summarized in the briefest possible terms, this reveals three broad approaches to understanding policymaking. One emphasizes political economy and the interactions of state and civil society, and different interest groups (Grindle and Thomas, 1991; Hill, 1997). Another examines the histories and practices linked to shifting discourses and how these shape and guide policy problems and courses of action (Hajer, 1995; Apthorpe and Gasper, 1996; Grillo, 1997; Shore and Wright, 1997). The third gives primacy to the roles and agency (or capacity to make a difference) of individual actors (Giddens, 1984; Haas, 1992; Hempel, 1996; Long, 2001). These different ways of understanding the policy process echo and overlap with different traditions and literatures for understanding governance (Chapter 4).

Bringing these different perspectives together, three lenses on the policy process are suggested (Figure 6.1). These prompt a series of questions:

- Knowledge and discourse: What is the 'policy narrative'?
- Actors and networks: Who is involved and how they are connected?
- Politics and interests: What are the underlying power dynamics?

Understanding policy processes, as Keeley and Scoones (2003) suggest, requires looking through all three lenses together – at the intersection of the three overlapping perspectives. Thus, to understand why policies take particular shapes, it is necessary to understand not only the framing of issues – the narratives that tell the policy stories – but also the way policy positions become embedded in networks (of actors, funding, professional and other relationships, and particular institutions and organizations), and the enabling or constraining power dynamics.

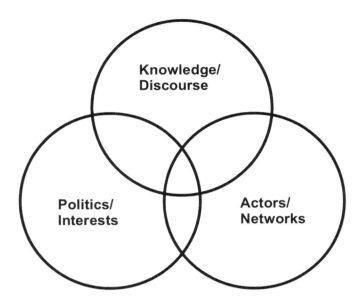

Source: After Keeley and Scoones, 2003

Figure 6.1 Three lenses on the policy process

Stories about policy change almost all have a beginning, a middle and an end. They describe events, or define the world in certain ways, and so shape policy decisions. As we saw in Chapter 3 and have explored through the cases of water in dryland India, seeds in Africa, epidemics and climate and energy systems, such 'policy narratives' provide both a diagnosis and a set of measures and interventions. They define a problem, explain how it comes about and show what needs to be done to avert disaster or bring about a happy ending: in other words, what is wrong and how it must be put right (see Roe, 1991, 1994). Policy narratives often gain validity despite (or even because of) the fact that they frequently simplify complex issues and processes. This simplification is seductive in that it sidesteps fuzziness and suggests a programme of action. This is what makes simple narratives appealing to politicians or managers – sweeping people along. Some narratives gain more authority, persisting at the expense of others, and hence have more bearing on policy decisions. Yet these will often be contested by alternative policy narratives that frame problems and solutions in different ways.

Policy narratives can stick with great tenacity, despite contrary perspectives and practices. This is true of the mainstream narratives we have explored in our case studies, as well as in other arenas – for instance around environment and development issues in Africa (Roe, 1994; Leach and Mearns, 1996). Why is this? Most obviously, they suit certain political interests. Simple, singular narratives are easily communicated, make for good sound-bite political marketing, and fit well with large-scale bureaucratic organizations' demands for clarity and measurable manageability. They also fit well with the practices of mass-media and education, which, as we discuss later in this chapter, perpetuate particular narratives and embed them in wider society and popular culture. The storylines and metaphors are so taken for granted that they limit thinking about particular areas – this becomes the way things are thought about over time. Single, dominant narratives – associated with particular pathways – reduce the 'room for manoeuvre' or 'policy space' of policymakers (Cobb and Elder, 1972; Kingdon, 1995) – that is, their ability to think about alternatives or different approaches. These become embedded in particular institutional structures, bureaucracies or actor networks. They become normalized – part of people's everyday practices, and so perpetuated and reinforced through them – from bureaucratic routines to institutional patterns.

Networks, coalitions and alliances of actors (both individuals and institutions) with a shared vision – similar belief systems, codes of conduct and established patterns of behaviour – are important in spreading and maintaining narratives through chains of persuasion and influence such as journals, conferences, education or informal introductions. Through these networks 'norms of good and bad practice are reinforced, research agendas are set, and orthodoxies or conventional wisdoms are reiterated and, very often, dissenting opinions or unconventional views are suppressed' (Keeley and Scoones, 1999, p20).

In any given policy domain, and given the complexity of the contemporary networked governance arrangements we described in Chapter 4, actor networks are not exclusively confined to state institutions. Rather, they link up parts of the bureaucracy and government with the private sector, donors and actors in civil society – such as journalists, researchers and NGOs. Thus the existence of actor networks can make for highly pluralist styles of policymaking involving a range of different stakeholders or actors, often across local and global scales. Processes of negotiating and bargaining between competing interest groups are central to policymaking. Policies rise and fall in prominence as a result of the changing effectiveness of different networks of actors in the debate. Networks can gradually change narratives as well as reinforce them – as they bring people together who exchange ideas and strategize.

Perhaps it seems obvious that policy is inherently political and contested. But the conventional view of policy, in which fact and value are separated, denies this. Indeed, summing up from the discussion above and looking back to Chapter 4, it should be clear that politics shape policy processes in several important ways. First, the political context is moulded by the interests of particular regime authorities to remain in power. Competition also exists between groups in society, based on their differing interests with regard to allocation of resources, for example, or social concerns. Second, the policy process is influenced by a range of interest groups that exert power and authority over policymaking. These influences affect each stage of the process, from agenda-setting, to the identification of alternatives, weighing up the options, choosing the most favourable and implementing it. The vested interests of various actors in policy – government agents, officials of donor organizations and independent 'experts' – might be served by the perpetuation of certain narratives. Third, policy is often set out as objective, neutral and value-free, and is often phrased in legal or scientific language. In this way, the political nature of the policy is hidden by the use of technical language, which emphasizes rationality and objectivity. But the technical is always in some way political. Finally, bureaucrats are not simply neutral executors of policy; they have their own personal and political agendas to negotiate. Bureaucratic politics, such as battles within ministries for control over policy arenas, are therefore relevant.

Effecting policy change

Policies often have a certain inertia: particular ideas and practices stick, despite concerted challenges to their basic concepts and implied ways of working. If actor networks are tightly formed and impenetrable, and contexts and circumstances are not conducive to change, no amount of rational argument will shift a dominant policy narrative. However, things do change once distinct and well-guarded policy positions begin to fall apart, chinks and spaces open up and other arguments become incorporated, softening the stance and, through this process, enlarging the associated actor network. But by what strategies can this be catalyzed? How would one set about creating opportunities for challenging existing policy and opening debate in order to define alternative pathways to sustainability? Here we outline five practical means which might be used to assist this.

Telling persuasive stories

Clearly there is often a need to challenge entrenched policy stories and their underlying assumptions. But it is not enough simply to critique the status quo and the conventional wisdoms of the mainstream. In order to effect change, opening up new pathways to sustainability, alternative storylines must be offered – developing pragmatic, clear and simple policy stories that challenge dominant policy positions, suggesting, in turn, alternative policies and institutional structures (Wolmer and Scoones, 2005).

It may appear to go against the grain to challenge one simple storyline with another. After all, one could argue, the simplifications of policy narratives are part of the problem, when what we need is better ways to understand and respond to the complexity and diversity of the real world. Yet 'strategic simplifications' are warranted and justified when one is clear about the contexts and goals of their use. Moreover, alternative storylines can be developed which combine clarity and persuasion with recognition of diversity. In the case of water in India, for example, a mainstream narrative that 'water scarcity needs to be addressed through a large dam' might be challenged through alternative, simple storylines of a number of kinds, depending on the particular goal and context. 'Irrigation water will benefit only large farmers; smallholders need alternative water harvesting technologies'; or 'women's concerns are with the scarcity of drinking water, requiring investment in domestic water supplies' are examples of simple storylines supporting the goals of particular groups. Or these might be combined with an appreciation of complex dynamics and diversity, in a storyline such as: 'Scarcities are multiple, and adapting to uncertainties must be central – we need diverse practices and technologies suited to local settings.'

Building networks and encouraging champions of change

It is one thing to come up with an effective story, but convincing others that this is the idea to back – especially if it means abandoning other ideas, supported by powerful players – is a more challenging task. This means understanding where the power lies – knowing which actors and institutions are important, both governmental and non-governmental, public and private – understanding the jostling of positions and interests at the global, national and local levels, and tracing the connections between them. With this knowledge it is much easier to target the right people in the right places at the right time.

Building and linking networks is a key part of policy change – particularly linking very local networks to broader coalitions operating at national, continental and international levels. New ideas gain purchase when there is strong backing or where obstacles (in the shape of existing networks) are circumvented. Without support and advocacy, even brilliant new ideas or approaches may sink without trace. For instance, in relation to introducing adaptive governance approaches, Olsson et al (2006) identify the importance of informal, 'shadow networks', whose coordinated efforts to develop alternatives, build the case for adaptive governance and identify and exploit political opportunities are seen as essential.

Encouraging reflexivity

As an African policymaker working in rural development put it: 'We've seen government policy change, but it is slow. Seeing things on the ground helps change policy.'[12] 'Seeing is believing' is a powerful route to changing policy. Field days, demonstrations and exposure visits are time-honoured means of enrolling actors into networks and opening up the perspectives of senior officials to alternative realities.

Reflections emerge most effectively when people are exposed to others' views and lived experience, across hierarchies, between institutions and away from the capital city office to the urban neighbourhoods, villages and fields where poorer people create their livelihoods. A senior official who took part in the World Bank's Grass Roots Immersion Programme (GRIP) in India explained how:

> *Witnessing the life of a family that has no assurance that it can survive until the next harvest, going to bed at 8pm because there is no light and nothing else to do and talking with parents and children who have no expectations that the government will improve their lives had a remarkable effect on me (IDS, 2004).*

Such experiences can help to shift the worldview of senior policymakers and, at their best, help fold poor people's perspectives into policy and practice at the highest level.

Critical reflection can also focus on the policy process itself. This is a luxury few policymakers have the time to enjoy. Policymakers find tidy, closed stories and certainties easier to deal with than messy, plural and partial scenarios with multiple and contested perspectives. Yet despite, or perhaps because of this, an understanding of the nuances of policy processes can potentially provide valuable insights – an opportunity for reflexive learning. This was certainly the case for a group of African agricultural policymakers who, given the space in a workshop setting to reflect on the networks, discourses and political interests that they encountered, appreciated the opportunity to think about their own work and strategies in new ways (Scoones and Wolmer, 2005).

Opportunism, flexibility and adaptive governance

While the best-laid plans often go wrong, sometimes new, wholly unexpected opportunities arise and spontaneous, seemingly unconnected actions or groups come together. Opportunism and serendipity are thus key aspects of any strategy. They are difficult to fit into fixed, formal plans or log-frames, administrators often are fearful of such apparent randomness and donors are often reluctant to play along. Yet alongside long-planned and well-prepared events and processes, effective leveraging of policy change demands an aptitude for seizing particular policy moments or windows of opportunity as they arise, to get policy messages on the agenda and to open up the argument for policy reform. Such opportunities may be triggered by acknowledged 'crises' in the management of a particular issue. In the health arena, for example, this was the case when the Global Polio Eradication Initiative was derailed by resistance from northern Nigerian states in 2003, forcing donors and government agencies to rethink their approach radically (Yahya, 2006; Leach and Fairhead, 2007). Opportunities may also be triggered by wider political transitions and changes; for instance an election which brings in a change of government.

Such moments can also be important for introducing new governance approaches, such as those better attuned to the dynamics of complex systems. For instance, Olsson et al (2006) identify three basic phases for moves towards adaptive governance. The first phase is preparatory and involves the perception among key constituencies that the system is 'in trouble' and needs some form of change in approach to its 'management'. These stress or crisis situations open up windows of opportunity for the second phase, which is the 'transition to a new social context for ecosystem management', namely adaptive governance (Olsson et al, 2006, p3). It helps if advocates of new, adaptive governance measures have a portfolio of projects primed and ready to take advantage of opportunities when these occur. This is a highly unpredictable dynamic, but when some purchase for adaptive governance is realized, then the third phase institutionalizes the new approach.

Ideas about how adaptive governance might arise are inspired by work on 'policy entrepreneurs' and 'political windows' (Kingdon, 1995). This emphasizes the importance of timing and wider conditions to enable the initiation of adaptive governance (as an alternative to established approaches and routines), as well as the role of building supportive 'social capital' to take it forward.

Building new skills and professionals

Faced with complex, dynamic policy challenges, many professionals in policy positions are not necessarily equipped with the skills and insights necessary. They may have been trained in different, less relevant areas or narrow technical or administrative disciplines and are expected to learn how to 'do policy' on the job. Yet what is needed is investment in a new generation of sustainability professionals who are committed to and rewarded for cutting across a number of key boundaries.

A first important boundary is between the natural and social sciences, where skills are needed which facilitate an understanding of complex socio-ecological and technical systems in ways that do justice to the underlying dynamics and issues of uncertainty and surprise. This might come about through formal training – a variety of degree and diploma programmes now offer professionals and practitioners the opportunity to cross disciplinary boundaries – or through learning networks of other kinds. The Institutional Learning and Change initiative of the international agricultural research centres exemplifies one attempt to enable scientists to reflect on and challenge their own professional and disciplinary biases and to learn from interdisciplinary practice (Watts et al, 2003). Notably, this initiative has continually faced threat and marginalization – underlining the difficulties, yet also the importance, of bringing challenges to conventional disciplinary and professional hierarchies and reward systems.

A second boundary that needs to be crossed is between the assumed linear and rational policy process and the more messy and complex realities through which narratives, actor networks and political interests interact. Seeking ways that diverse perspectives, particularly those of poorer and marginalized people, can be articulated in policy processes is a key challenge, for which new skills in understanding policy processes and facilitating policy change are needed.

A third boundary exists between local-level reactive micro operations, drawing on specific events and single cases and on experiential and tacit knowledge – including the knowledge and experiences of field-level bureaucrats and front-line workers – and macro design, drawing on aggregative understandings and formal, deductive principles. To be able to respond to uncertainty and surprise and ensure 'high reliability' amidst complex dynamics requires a tacking between these. Carving out a middle ground, new professional skills need to link localized scenario development, based on particular cases and events, with wider pattern recognition – leading to the ability to anticipate and respond appropriately (Schulman and Roe, 2008).

In building such new sustainability professionals, there are roles both for formal processes – training, workshops, learning initiatives – and less formal ones, involving learning-by-doing in flexible institutional contexts where boundary-crossing is encouraged. Recognizing and validating new skills in turn requires broader notions of what constitutes 'capacity' and 'excellence' (Chataway et al, 2007; Waldman and Leach, 2009) and appreciation of these in incentives, rewards and institutional arrangements.

Thus these five routes to opening up policy debates about diverse pathways to sustainability offer some practical starting points for building sustainable futures. Each of these approaches to effecting policy change may take place across a diversity of policy spaces, a subject to which we now turn.

Creating and using policy spaces

The concept of 'policy space' (Cobb and Elder, 1972; Kingdon, 1995) relates to the extent to which those involved in the policy process are restricted by forces such as the opinions of a dominant actor network or narrative. For instance, if there are strong pressures to adopt a particular strategy, a decision-maker may not have much room to consider a wider set of options. On the other hand, there may be times when an individual has a substantial amount of leverage over the process and is able to assert his or her own preferences and significantly mould the way policy choices are considered.

Understanding policy processes through an examination of knowledge/discourses, actors/networks and politics/interests (Figure 6.1) can help with identifying policy spaces. For example, the articulation of alternative narratives is possible where there is a weakness in the articulation of the dominant narrative. This in turn requires the identification of spaces within networks (spaces to join the network or key actors who can be enrolled into an alternative network). A clearer assessment of strategies for changing and influencing policy can then be achieved by looking at such policy spaces, where they lie and what they consist of. Depending on the policy issue, there may be important interactions between such spaces – from the very local to the regional, national and global, while a number of different types of policy space are evident. Table 6.1 illustrates a range of types of policy space, together with suggested strategies for opening them up – as identified by African agricultural policymakers during a workshop in Kenya.[13]

While certainly nonlinear, policy processes are clearly not simply chaotic and governed by chance and accident. An analysis of the policy process highlights the complex interplay of narratives underpinning the policy, the actor networks promoting or resisting it and the political interests driving the process and opening up potential strategies and tactics. An understanding of the politics, bureaucracy, power and interests behind policies gives clues as to how their formulation and implementation are open to interpretation and manoeuvre; of where the openings might lie and of how these might be enlarged.

Opening alternative pathways to sustainability need not just involve formal policy processes and spaces. As Table 6.1 has already identified, there are roles for citizen mobilization in creating 'popular spaces' where alternatives are imagined and created, and through which pressure may be exerted on wider politics and institutions. In the following section, we turn to consider these processes in greater detail.

Table 6.1 *Policy spaces – and strategies for opening them up*

Policy space	Strategies for opening up
Conceptual spaces (where new ideas are introduced into the debate and circulated through various media)	Publish papers on proposed policy in scientific journals Quote other important, influential people Influence consultants 'after hours' Learn the 'official language' and use it
Bureaucratic spaces (formal policymaking spaces within the government bureaucracy/ legal system, led by government civil servants with selected input from external experts)	Lobby peers and key players Select an internal champion Get the boss to relay new ideas and to get praise for it
Invited spaces (consultations on policy led by government agencies, involving selective participation of stakeholders)	Gatecrash other people's meetings and hijack agenda Influence/write opening speech Show videos in workshop to introduce stakeholders' opinions Get official blessing – write the speech
Popular spaces protests (demonstrations led by social movements, putting pressure on formal policymaking)	Join change agent/direct action movements and actively get involved Petition Participate in membership organizations, e.g. farmers' or patients' groups Use the media: radio, TV, posters
Practical spaces (providing opportunities for 'witnessing' by policymakers)	Pilot project Case studies Study tours

Mobilizing citizens[14]

A second route towards the opening up of governance processes concerns citizen action and mobilization. Social movements and citizens' groups can help to prize open the cracks in policy processes and in standardized ways of doing things. They can push for particular perspectives and interests, redefining ideas about and pathways to sustainability.

Let us look at a couple of examples from our case studies. One well-known example from the health arena and concerning the AIDS pandemic is the successful mobilization by the Treatment Action Campaign (TAC) in South Africa. This grassroots organization successfully fought through linked local and global networks to gain access to antiretroviral drugs for working class and poor people, taking on the global pharmaceutical industry and international patenting laws (Robins, 2005a,b). In 2001, the country was in the midst of an HIV/AIDS epidemic but also a raging controversy within South Africa's scientific and political establishments over whether HIV was the cause of AIDS (Nattrass, 2007). TAC cut through this debate with a campaign centred on the perspectives and immediate concerns of poor and unemployed black women and men, many of whom were HIV positive and desperate for drugs for themselves and their children. Drawing on activist styles, symbols and songs from the earlier struggle against apartheid, TAC's mobilization spread through schools, factories, community centres, churches, shabeens (drinking dens) and door-to-door visits in the townships. TAC also engaged with scientists, the media, the legal system, NGOs and government, using sophisticated networking channels that crossed race, class, occupational and educational lines, and extended internationally in what has been dubbed 'grass-roots globalization'. By focusing on moral imperatives, TAC successfully forced drug companies to bring their prices down and it persuaded the Ministry of Health to make anti-retroviral drugs more widely available. TAC's mobilization was a struggle for poor people to gain access to life-saving drugs – opening up a particular treatment pathway – but it was also a campaign to assert the rights of citizens to scientific knowledge, treatment information and the latest research findings.

The case of water in India has also generated many examples of activism and mobilization. Large dams and river-linking systems, undertaken by government with international backing as large-scale technological 'solutions' to assumed problems of water scarcity, have long been a focus of mobilization and protest. One of the longest-running anti-dam movements is the Sardar Sarovar (Narmada) movement, which has opposed the government/World Bank project to dam the Narmada river (Fisher, 1995; Pate, 2002; Mehta, 2005). With the leadership of NGOs and spokespeople, and through local meetings, demonstrations and campaigns on the global stage, the Narmada movement has given voice to citizens' concerns. These include the loss of forest-based livelihoods and cultural values centred on the river implied by flooding upstream of the dam; whether the dam will really help downstream issues of water uncertainty as lived and experienced by local farmers and pastoralists; and concerns about the elite, industrial and political interests that are perceived to drive large dam approaches. Linking up with similar movements across the world, the Narmada mobilization has helped to broaden out debate and open up governance, provoking a wave of questioning around the appropriateness of large-scale engineering technologies versus alternative approaches to addressing water issues that are better attuned to local ecological and social perspectives. In more recent years, however, while the life and death struggle for villagers faced with submergence by the Narmada dam continues, the anti-dam struggle has lost much of its high profile. Mobilization and protest around water in India, as elsewhere, has come to focus more on the spectre of large-scale privatization of water management regimes; another blanket, singular solution to so-called problems of scarcity which threatens to ride roughshod over the rights and concerns of marginalized people in dryland areas.

As we saw in Chapter 5, much debate has focused on institutionally orchestrated forms of participation in appraisal. As discussed, there has been an explosion of efforts to involve citizens in policy and decision-making, ranging from classic consultations to more innovative forms such as citizens' juries and participatory appraisal. However, as these examples highlight, many instances of citizen engagement take place outside such institutionally orchestrated spaces, through more spontaneous forms of mobilization. These have been the subject of extensive scholarship on social movements, whether around classic struggles for material resources and political power (so-called old social movements; e.g. Olsen, 1965; Oberschall, 1973; Tilly, 1978) or around emergent issue or identity-focused struggles (so-called new social movements; e.g. Melucci, 1985, 1989; Offe, 1985; Touraine, 1985). The importance and roles of social movements and citizen engagement in environmental, health and energy politics is now well recognized and the subject of a large literature (Fischer, 2000; Jamison, 2001; Peet and Watts, 2004).

As discussed in Chapter 4, citizen mobilization can be seen as part of the complex, multi-levelled networked processes that characterize so much governance and politics today. Yet citizen mobilization, we argue, also has particular roles to play in challenging and opening up other parts of these networked interactions, towards achieving greater recognition and support for alternative narratives and pathways to sustainability and for otherwise marginalized perspectives and goals.

Key questions thus arise both in understanding such mobilization and assessing its potential and means to open up governance processes around particular issues and settings. Who mobilizes and who does not, and why? What are the patterns of experience, profiles and identities of activists? How are activist networks constituted and what diverse forms do they take? What forms of identity, representation and processes of inclusion and exclusion are involved? What forms of knowledge – including values, perceptions and experiences – frame these public engagements and movements? Within what spaces do debates take place and what resources are drawn upon? How do citizens and 'experts' of various kinds interact in processes of mobilization?

Understanding the politics of mobilization for sustainability, we suggest, requires a combination of perspectives drawn from the wide and highly diverse literatures on social movements. These include perspectives which emphasize the resources available to movements and the mobilization of these within political processes (Tilly, 1978; Tarrow, 1998). They include a focus on how mobilization takes shape around and actively involves the construction of particular ideas, meanings and cognitive and moral constructions of a 'problem' (Benford and Snow, 2000). They include perspectives on movement identity, focusing on the processes and sources through which common identities and subjectivities are formed, and perhaps dissolved and reformed, through movement processes and the 'politics of presence' (Young, 1990; Phillips, 1995). And they include appreciation of the spatial location and contexts of movements as critical to why they unfold as they do (Miller, 2000). Movements may link participants in diverse local sites across global spaces, constituting what has been called 'globalization from below' (Appadurai, 2002).

All this points towards an understanding of 'mobilizing citizens' as knowledgeable actors engaged in a dynamic, networked politics. This involves shifting and temporary forms of social solidarity and identification, through processes that are sometimes local or national but sometimes involve networks that span local sites across the world (Leach and Scoones, 2007). In a world increasingly influenced by the dispersing and fragmented effects of globalization, and in the context of multi-levelled, networked politics (Chapter 4), there is a need to go beyond either state-centred or pluralist accounts of citizenship. People clearly have multiple memberships of different groupings, both in institutional and cultural terms. Such a multiplication of identities, affiliations and forms of solidarity, Ellison (1997) argues, requires the dissolving of more conventional boundaries between the public and private, the political and social, thus situating citizen mobilization in relation to – and as part of – governance in new ways.

Such an approach to citizen engagement in turn challenges mainstream ideas of 'the citizen'. Dominant narratives about problems concerning agriculture, water, health or energy often include and promote particular views of people which either deny their agency and citizenship, or construct this in particular ways. Thus narratives underpinned by the politics of liberal modernization, see citizens as passive beneficiaries of plans developed with formal scientific expertise and implemented through public sector institutions and global funds. In another version of the liberal view, gaining growing currency, citizens are seen as consumers of science and technology and its products, driven by market-led growth. Citizens are assumed to follow the market, while the liberal state provides a regulatory function which protects their safety. In contrast to both these views, we suggest that a more active version of citizenship is needed, in which citizens are understood as knowledgeable actors, engaging through various forms of social solidarity and identification in networked politics around issues of concern (Leach and Scoones, 2007).

These forms of engagement, involving new processes of social and political mobilization, are, as Ellison emphasizes, 'increasingly messy and unstable' (1997, p712). Despite this, several key themes emerge. These draw attention to different dimensions of the opening up of governance processes to citizen claims and perspectives.

Mobilizing knowledge

Contests over knowledge are central to the dynamics of mobilization. Epstein (1996) argues that:

> *Increasingly, science is the resource called on to promote consensus, and experts are brought in to 'settle' political and social controversies. Yet this 'scientisation of politics' simultaneously brings about a 'politicisation of science' ... political disputes tend to become technical disputes' (Epstein, 1996, p6).*

Our case examples illustrate this tendency for social and political disputes to become technical disputes – but also possible ways in which they might be opened up. For example in the case of seed systems in Africa, disputes about the desirability or otherwise of GM seed technologies have often been couched in terms of technical advantages and risks (Scoones, 2005; Glover, 2009). Thus, while GM advocates point to potential productivity increases, these are pitted against the dangers of genetic drift, ecological and health impacts – claims which have been at the forefront of anti-GM activism. Enwrapped with such technical claims and counter-claims, however, have often been deeper social and political claims and anxieties – for instance about corporate control over agriculture, loss of local autonomy to manage food systems, or growing inequalities between farmers more or less capable of benefiting from GM technologies. In the case of the South African HIV/AIDS controversy, the dispute over whether HIV was the cause of AIDS was often fought out in technical terms and around discussions of the relative efficacy of biomedical or 'traditional' treatments. Yet enwrapped with the stance of President Mbeki and his supporters were broader nationalistic and anti-colonial perspectives, while TAC and the many others who opposed his AIDS denialism drew on broader commitments to social justice and rights for people living with HIV (Robins, 2005c; Nattrass, 2007). Thus, in both these examples, mobilizations were about broader social and political issues and claims, yet became framed in technical terms.

Epstein (1996) proposes four possible ways in which social movements might engage with science. All of these can be seen as part of routes to opening up governance (and its interlocked scientific claims). Thus movements might engage by: disputing scientific claims; by seeking to acquire a cachet of scientific authority for a political claim by finding a scientific expert to validate their political stance; by rejecting the scientific way of knowing and advancing their claims to expertise from some wholly different epistemological standpoint; or by attempting to 'stake out some ground on the scientists' own terrain' by questioning 'not just the uses of science, not just the control over science, but sometimes even the very contents of science and the processes by which it is produced' (Epstein, 1996, pp12–13). Our cases offer examples of each of these. In the case of mobilization around GM crops, activists in South Africa (Scoones, 2005) used all these forms of engagement, deploying them strategically depending on the setting. Whereas in the courts they disputed scientific claims about GM safety, in the media they rejected scientific arguments about risk altogether in favour of a wider debate about corporate control, globalization and livelihood futures. TAC's mobilization around HIV/AIDS in South Africa was in part a response to attempts by Mbeki and the 'AIDS dissidents' to acquire a cachet of scientific authority for their political claim that there was no viral cause of AIDS. TAC drew on mainstream understandings of virology and disease causation to argue for investment in anti-retroviral treatments (see Robins, 2005c), exemplifying Epstein's fourth category of engagement.

A classic case of this opening up of knowledges by social movements is the history of nuclear power, especially in Northern settings (Smith et al, 2005). Over recent decades, the anti-nuclear movement (in the USA, Europe and Japan in particular) has exerted profound and multiple influences on the direction taken by knowledge production and innovation in and around the energy sector (Smith, 2007). Pressures began with the raising of explicitly normative concerns over associations with nuclear weapons and of ethical questions over issues such as the dumping of radioactive wastes in the global commons and contrasting exposures on the part of differently distributed communities (Flam, 1994). As the movement grew in scale and influence, attention turned increasingly to a more scientific idiom, deconstructing the many sources of uncertainty, ambiguity and ignorance in ostensibly precise expert assessments of nuclear risk and energy demands (Patterson, 1976). In the process, regulatory processes became destabilized, leading to an accumulation of additional safety requirements. This in turn exerted effects on the economic performance of nuclear power, with interlinked processes of liberalization and privatization further highlighting financial challenges. At the same time, other branches of the anti-nuclear movement were engaged in knowledge production concerning 'alternative energy' pathways – both in terms of experimental engineering (Harper, 1976; Dickson, 1977) and high-level policy analysis (Leach, 1979; Lovins, 1979). In countries such as Denmark that lacked strong nuclear interests in suppressing these incipient bodies of expertise, social movements played a formative role in fostering entirely new design traditions and management capacities for emerging renewable energy sources such as wind power (Garud and Karnøe, 2001). With long-run rises in energy prices and associated expectations, influenced by the changing critical expert discourse, this combination of pressures on the incumbent system and the substantiation of alternative pathways is now beginning to bear fruit. Despite continued contention between nuclear power and renewable energy – and persistently high stakes – the energy debate in states with nuclear power has been effectively transformed over the space of just two decades. Throughout the many strands of this process, a crucial role has been played by the emergence of significant new bodies of knowledge and forms of expertise fostered by social movements.

In such examples we see diverse forms of expertise at work. In some cases, mobilization draws on lay knowledge and forms of experiential expertise that people have acquired in everyday life. For instance, cultural understandings of bodily and disease processes shaped movements around HIV/AIDS in South Africa, while experiences of complex local agroecologies shaped opposition to GM crops. In some cases, such experiential expertise has become recast as 'citizen science' (Irwin, 1995; Fischer, 2000), in which people actively worked to produce new knowledge according with their own experiences. Thus in India, NGOs have provided communities mobilizing against dams with water-testing kits to challenge the Pollution Control Board's own monitoring data. Activists have also facilitated community surveys of malaria incidence and related this to the extent of stagnant water arising from industrial operations in the area. Such community-derived evidence has been compiled as part of 'People's Development Plans', which are presented to local assemblies and government officials.[15]

In many cases, citizens have enrolled accredited scientific experts sympathetic to their perspectives, forming alliances that give their claims greater strength and legitimacy (see Nelkin, 1987; Hoffman, 1989). Through these alliances, certain citizens may themselves learn new forms of scientific expertise: what Epstein terms the 'expertification of lay activists'. At the same time, accredited experts confront their institutionalized and professional knowledge, reclaiming their role as citizens. Through these processes, boundaries between citizen and expert become much more fluid and hybrids emerge. In some cases, activists themselves embody hybrid identities.

Clashes over knowledge are therefore central to mobilization dynamics. As we have seen earlier in the book, they are equally central to how different actors frame systems – and in turn define pathways to sustainability. However, cases show how the oppositions involved rarely conform to simple views of 'science versus people' or 'experts versus indigenous/lay knowledge'. Instead, differently constructed discourses and discourse coalitions (Hajer, 1995) emerge. Thus, in mobilization around large dams, the key opposition has been more between their proponents (embracing particular types of engineer, large-scale commercial agricultural interests and urban consumers) and the proponents of alternative, small-scale water interventions (including other hydrologists and engineers, small farmers and dam oustees). Fundamentally, in such cases different forms of knowledge alliance are linked to different social and political interests, and interact with each other in highly politicized and power-laden processes.

In some instances, citizens may successfully press knowledge claims and framings from which flow alternative pathways to sustainability. In other cases, such mobilization around knowledge may help create a more general process of opening up, leading to transformations in the ways issues are understood and debated in policy and public arenas, and thus creating space to consider a wider range of options. As Jamison suggests:

> *Out of the alternative public spaces that have been created by social and political movements has emerged a new kind of scientific pluralism, in terms of organization, worldview assumptions and technical application (2001, p136).*

In the practices of science-related mobilization, both movement actors and their opponents create, consolidate and extend their claims by enrolling other actors and institutions into knowledge/power networks. Particular events and forums shape the co-production of scientific and social, political or policy positions (Jasanoff and Wynne, 1997). Thus new narratives around pathways to sustainability are created through the coming together of different actors in networks – formed as discourse coalitions or advocacy groupings. In this, citizen engagement goes well beyond just the involvement of lay publics or people at the 'grassroots'; scientists, administrators and policymakers are citizens too and may become enlisted or actively involved in processes of mobilization. This suggests a process of reflexivity, in which scientists, citizens and policy actors are explicit about their goals and commitments and their positions in knowledge politics.

Strategies, tactics and spaces of mobilization: opening up, broadening out

There are a wide range of styles and practices of citizen mobilization and activism. These can be seen to represent particular strategies and tactics for opening up governance. Different styles and practices may be relevant for different issues and contexts. In some cases, contemporary mobilizations draw on longer histories and experiences, as in the example of the South African TAC activists who utilized knowledge and experiences from the anti-apartheid movement. Yet novel repertoires may also be created to provide new idioms for motivating activism or holding together collective identity. Thus in the South African case the notion of almost ritualized transformation of a person from 'near death to new life' which comes about through anti-retroviral therapies has come to unite and motivate activists in arguing for expanded treatment availability (Robins, 2005a).

Not all movement participants, however, necessarily have this common, intense shared experience. Sometimes movements involve a diverse group, with different social backgrounds, educational profiles and personal life histories. The pattern of diversity and its key axes in movement participants clearly shape different interests in pursuing a particular cause. These may create tensions, but mean that the performative and ritualized moments of commonality – in protests, demonstrations, fasts, court cases – are all the more significant. Thus at its height in the 1990s, the anti-dam movement in India drew people from all walks of life to its high-profile events and protests, including well-known individuals on the international activist circuit. Where movements are made up of socially diverse participants, the roles and charisma of individual leaders in holding them together, or at least presenting a public face of a united movement, also become more significant.

At the extreme, direct actions have been a tactic of some mobilizations. Thus protesters against GM crops have often resorted to uprooting or burning trial plots, while anti-dam protesters have lain in front of approaching bulldozers or destroyed dam foundations. In addition to the creation of new expertise discussed above, the conduct of direct action by the anti-nuclear movement has had a formative influence on international energy strategies – most notably in helping to condition an end to ocean dumping of radioactive wastes and to the domination of reprocessing strategies in nuclear infrastructures.

Yet alongside overt, extravagant performances through protest, direct actions and engagements with the courts or media, movements may engage in more everyday resistances. Perhaps especially where the resources or political opportunities for organized movements are lacking, people who feel their livelihoods or well-being threatened by technologies express their concerns in less visible ways – perhaps through irony, satire or jokes, or through the many forms of subtle resistance, foot-dragging and sabotage that James Scott termed 'weapons of the weak' (Scott, 1985, 1990). In the developing world, countless technology projects have met with opposition from local communities. Water pumps have mysteriously not been maintained or agricultural projects have found their supposed beneficiaries failing to turn up and comply with expected production schedules. Such forms of mobilization and cultural avenues of protest need to be taken more seriously as expressions of public concern. These other forms suggest alternative and complementary routes to citizen engagement that could enable fuller inclusion of the range of poor people's views.

In attempts to open up debate, there is frequently a dynamic, sometimes fraught connection between a multiplicity of spaces. Spaces for mobilization range from the formal to the informal, from the invited to the spontaneously claimed or even raided, from the popular to the top-down and from the permanent to the transient (Cornwall and Schattan P. Coelho, 2006). Thus contemporary mobilizations often link more conventional forms of protest in spaces established through face-to-face encounters, sit-ins, court cases, marches and demonstrations, with more diffuse communication processes over multiple locales, including the use of both conventional mass-media and new information and communication technologies.

It is often the connection between spaces – and the ways in which they are combined and sequenced – that proves key in processes of mobilization. Thus GM activism has combined, at different times and by different groups, direct action against field trials, supermarket-trolley dumping, protests outside facilities and research institutes, constitutional and public-interest litigation cases, media campaigns on TV, newspapers and radio, Internet-linked networks and resource materials, and e-mail protests (Scoones, 2005). Activism against large dams has linked marches and demonstrations with astute media interventions, multiple court cases and engagements in international deliberations on dams, complemented by e-mail networking and website publicity and connections. TAC activists in South Africa began in the locales of black townships, making use of local political forums, but then extended their movement into global spaces through forging connections around anti-patent law struggles in the spaces of international conferences, media and Internet debate (Robins, 2005c).

Legal spaces can be seen to present particular opportunities for opening up governance processes. In these, courts and related legal processes act as mediators. Legal arenas are sometimes seen by activists as spaces where their concerns can be heard and deliberated in a neutral, objective manner, in contrast to what are perceived to be more politicized arenas elsewhere. Yet processes of framing also operate in legal spaces, with legal processes shaping which kinds of knowledge are either accepted as 'evidence' or labelled as 'biased'. Thus 'science' and 'knowledge' come to be constructed (and legitimized and de-legitimized) in particular ways when put to work as legal evidence (Jasanoff, 1997).

Nor are legal spaces singular. Different routes of legal redress are available and activists may be able to exploit them strategically in a process of 'forum shopping' (von Benda-Beckman, 1981), highlighting the pluralistic nature of the legal system (Merry, 1998, 1992). In making use of different legal spaces, activists may frame movement concerns in different ways – and this can in turn lead to debate within movements themselves. In the case of the campaign for anti-retroviral treatment in South Africa, for instance, activists operated across multiple legal jurisdictions, engaging both at the international level around patent provisions and at the national level. Different types of court at a national level also offer different types of opportunity for legal argument. For example, in the case of GM seeds, constitutional courts have offered some opportunity to elaborate oppositions in terms of rights, justice and broader livelihoods, while other courts and the public interest litigation route have been more specifically focused on legally specified procedures and regulations, thus constraining the scope of claims that can be made.

Putting forward a court case is no minor task. Small activist organizations often have to link up with others to do so, while links between more diverse individualized claims may be strengthened through putting together a class action. The forms of coordinated action involved in turn shape the collective nature of movement identity in particular ways. Thus for example in the case of TAC in South Africa, engagement in court cases around patents drew the South Africa-based treatment movement into a wider collective identity associated with the anti-globalization movement (Robins, 2005a). Legal action also requires high levels of resource mobilization, not just of funds but of expertise, including legal advisors and representatives, and scientific 'expert witnesses'. Thus seeking legal redress requires movements to extend their networks, enlisting specialist expertise in mobilizations, often with attendant tensions.

Citizen mobilization can and does also make effective use of the rapidly growing variety of media spaces. As many media studies commentators have pointed out, the genre and style of media coverage tends to construct a particular kind of storyline: David versus Goliath, goodies versus baddies and so on (Lowe and Morrison, 1984; Hargreaves et al, 2002). Many social movement stories are easily presented in this mould, making them appealing subjects for media coverage. Activists can often gain access to such coverage despite their small size and limited budgets by the desire of the media to present 'two sides of the story' or 'a balanced picture' – for instance to counter dominant state or corporate interests – even though, in the process of turning mobilizations into media storylines, subtleties of their framings are often lost (Leach, 2005).

As the history of the anti-nuclear movement shows, in some – perhaps rare – instances a necessary determinant of successful radical change is that the right media message is articulated in the right manner – and at the right place and time. In the case of ocean dumping of radioactive wastes in the early 1980s, for example, the weakest point in the industrial infrastructure was identified and targeted by a multi-faceted but tightly interlinked strategy – of which prominent media interventions were the most visible aspect. Efforts by organizations such as Greenpeace aimed simultaneously to: destabilize established science (concerning uncertainties in marine dispersion models); build counter-expertise (concerning environmental behaviour of radionuclides and alternative management strategies); form strategic alliances (with fishing and marine labour constituencies); and exploit international tensions (between nuclear and non-nuclear states). These were then focused specifically on developments in a particular intergovernmental forum, the London Dumping Convention. When it works, this kind of media mobilization can achieve massive shifts in the momentum of a well-established global technological regime (Parmentier, 1999).

The multiple forms of contemporary media offer different spaces with different implications for movement access and framing. Even in countries with a notionally free press, this comes in many shapes and forms. Thus in some outlets, advertising revenues might be jeopardized by anti-corporate perspectives, making certain activist approaches unattractive. Some media outlets have long-established affinities with particular political interests or parties, shaping their receptivity to particular mobilizations. Some newspapers have had sympathetic journalists who take up a particular activist cause and may publicize it over several years, through a combination of headlines and detailed features. In such cases, journalists become, in effect, enrolled as movement activists. There are also important distinctions between the spaces offered by national media outlets, and local ones such as local and vernacular-language newspapers, and community radio stations. In the latter, movement storylines and framings may need to be constructed differently to appeal to locally relevant concerns. The use of different media spaces by activists is, in some respects, akin to forum shopping in plural legal spaces. This also enables appeal to different audiences who might lend popular support to a movement.

Increasingly, media networks are based on Internet connections through websites, e-mail lists, blogs and so on. The degree to which mobilizations are able to make use of such cyberspaces is varied, depending not least on degrees of Internet access and connectivity. Yet even in rural Africa and India, activist leaders have used Internet networks to forge links with movements elsewhere. These cyber spaces provide many resources for mobilization, enabling movement participants to have rapid access to information and connection with each other without the need for face-to-face encounters. This has implications for movement identity, which may become broader, more diverse and inclusive – but less cohesive (Bauman, 1998).

The politics of knowledge also become mediated in different ways through cyberspace. For instance movement participants can now gain direct access to scientific research papers posted on movement websites or sent out to e-mail lists. However, such access is not unmediated: just as Monsanto and its regionally based outposts have their own websites with links to news articles and scientific papers on the benefits of GM crops, so do global anti-GM campaigners, linking to different articles that stress the risks. Perhaps the most novel dimensions of the spaces opened up through the Internet are the ways in which they connect local and global sites and forms of knowledge, giving localized movements access to global debates and information sources, and global campaigns sources of local experience and forms of legitimacy. Cyberspace also enables localized mobilizations to connect with each other, sometimes resulting in a sharing of styles and practices of activism, as well as a sharing of framings. Such globalization from below (Falk, 1993; Appadurai, 2002) can contribute to the strength and claims of local movements, although it can also reduce the specificity of localized citizens' concerns in favour of appeals to global concerns and visions.

To be most effective in opening up governance, citizen mobilization often involves moving strategically between these different spaces. Styles and tactics, as well as representations and uses of different kinds of knowledge, may be adjusted accordingly. In a world of multi-levelled governance in which context and political culture matters, the ability to shift and adapt between levels, settings and appropriate cultural styles has become a vital part of engaging effectively in the politics of sustainability.

Conclusions: Knowledge-making and communication

This chapter has discussed a variety of contests around policy processes or struggles associated with citizen mobilization. Referring back to Figure 3.1 in Chapter 3, these contests are represented there by the ways that different system framings and associated narratives are constituted by different actors, and the politics through which these narratives and their associated pathways interplay. However, what gets opened up and what gets closed down, and how this happens, clearly does not just depend on particular policy processes and forms of citizen mobilization. It also depends on the ways that knowledge is constituted as part of society and politics. This is a much broader terrain, which – in the terms of Figure 3.1 – would constitute the enveloping background and context to the entire figure. This of course potentially includes vast areas of history, society and politics – extending well beyond the scope of this or any other single book. Nevertheless, the ways in which processes of opening up unfold in relation to the politics of policy processes and mobilization are deeply affected by several particular themes which it is important to acknowledge here, if briefly.

Policy processes and patterns of citizen mobilization are inextricably intertwined with rapidly expanding, accelerating flows of knowledge and information. Science, policy processes and mobilization – the forms they take, and the dynamics of opening up and closing down – are part of a wider informational realm including media, education and aspects of popular culture. The significance of this extends well beyond the use of particular media spaces by social movements or policy actors, as discussed above. More broadly, this informational realm helps to shape the ways in which people construct images and imaginations of the lives and practices of others.[16] Such images can become interlocked with scientific and policy institutions in various ways, serving to stabilize particular narratives, embedding them in wider society. Yet media and educational practices can also provide vehicles for opening up; for exposing alternative narratives, and fractures and disagreements within more dominant views.

Several factors complicate the picture. These include more rapid information flows in all directions via the Internet, including web-postings, listserves, twitters, blogs and social networking sites. These suggest contradictory tendencies. On the one hand, there is an opening up of opportunity for people to express diverse opinions and debates. Yet on the other, we see a tendency to limit analysis and reproduce 'sound-bite' styles of narrative. On the one hand, an emergent political economy and set of institutional practices around media production is multiplying outlets around the world. But on the other, political economy limits detail and original investigation, favours a recycling of stories and interpretations and is routinely engaged in corruption and propaganda (Davies, 2008).

Media and educational materials can be powerful in establishing particular images of sustainability issues, (re)producing moral images in which certain types of person are vilified as destructive and others lauded. Aspects of genre and style, such as photogenic, picturesque or crisis stories, the use of simplified narratives and of iconic characters – heroes and villains – amplify these images (Lowe and Morrison, 1984; Chapman et al, 1997). This plays into the use of simplified narratives and story lines, and into the wider field of public debate in which people reflect on and evaluate these. Thus in many settings one finds a remarkably closed, mutually referential field of interlocked institutions and available information, which contributes further to a closing down of public debate about sustainability issues.

Yet there are also many routes through which media and education can contribute to an informational environment which encourages and enables critique and the forwarding of alternative views. Indeed a huge variety of approaches which aim explicitly to broaden out and open up – in this sense, constituting what we term 'empowering designs' in this book (Chapter 5) – have been developed and advocated in diverse settings around the world. These range from approaches to participatory education and pedagogy (Freire, 1970), the transformation of educational systems and schooling (Neill, 1960; Illich, 1971, 1973), and approaches to research and learning that are embedded in action (Fals-Borda, 1986; 1987; Tandon, 2000; Reason and Bradbury, 2007) to participatory approaches to theatre (Boal, 1979; Abah, 1997; Okwori, 2005), video and other media.

All such media and educational practices must be seen in a wider context of the politics of knowledge-making in society. Research, evidence and knowledge more broadly are, as we have seen, central to the ways that policy processes and citizen mobilization play out. In asking how research might act to broaden out and open up, we need to ask – what kinds of knowledge are being generated by whom, and who is it for? Michael Burawoy (2005) suggests that there are four distinct types of knowledge-making which would answer these questions in very different ways (Figure 6.2).

One type of knowledge is for instrumental purposes, whether to inform and solve puzzles for academic audiences (professionalized knowledge-making) or to solve problems for policymakers, practitioners or groups of activists (policy knowledge-making). In recent years there has been much discussion about how to engage research more effectively with this policy

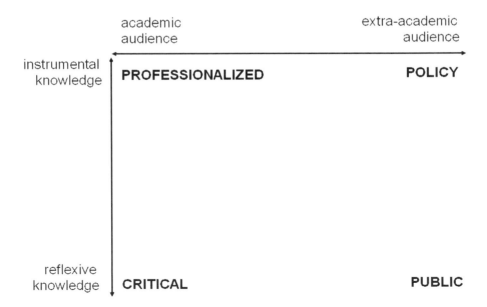

Figure 6.2 Types of knowledge-making

dimension, transferring instrumental knowledge from professional academic settings to those in which it might have influence and generate impact. These include considerable investments in information services (ID21, GDNet and others), as well as approaches for 'getting research into use' (Court et al, 2005; Stone and Maxwell, 2005).

Such approaches often fail to problematize questions of framing and wider challenges of subjectivity and reflexivity in knowledge-making and translation. They often slip into the trap of assuming a linear relationship between research and intervention whereby 'evidence' is all that is needed to inform and change policy or indeed guide activist movements. Yet as the discussion throughout this book has suggested, reflexivity and dialogue about goals and values needs to be central to all processes of knowledge-making. This points to the importance of reflexive knowledge-making which engages critically with the foundations and directions of academic research (critical knowledge-making) and articulates with the wider public sphere (public knowledge-making). The latter can include policy actors, but treats them as part of and in relation to wider society. It implies constant attention to the framings, narratives, values, implications and shortfalls, both of mainstream approaches and understandings of pathways and of alternatives.

Seen in this way, knowledge-making and communication becomes integral to wider conceptions of society and democracy. This appreciation of broader knowledge-politics needs to go hand-in-hand with the more specific processes of opening up discussed in this chapter, around policy processes and citizen mobilization.

As Sheila Jasanoff argues:

> *Contemporary societies are constituted as* knowledge *societies...* *important aspects of political behaviour and action cluster around the* *ways in which knowledge is generated, disputed, and used to under-* *write collective decisions. It is no longer possible to deal with such* *staple concepts of democratic theory as citizenship or deliberation or* *accountability without delving into their interaction with the dynam-* *ics of knowledge creation and use (2005, p6).*

In these terms, an alternative politics for sustainability is necessarily a politics of knowledge. In the next chapter, we explore what this might mean in practice for the four case studies that have run through this book.

Chapter 7

Towards Pathways
to Sustainability

Introduction

This concluding chapter summarizes the book's argument and revisits the major contradiction with which it started – the growing gulf between complex dynamics and approaches premised on a stable, manageable world. We return to our four case examples – of water in dryland India, seeds in Africa, epidemics and health systems, and energy and climate – and to specific questions being asked by policymakers. Systematically, we consider how these questions might be addressed differently through a pathways approach. Finally, we draw together the potential ways forward outlined in earlier chapters in relation to these cases, and consider how these add up to a new agenda for thinking and action towards pathways to sustainability and social justice.

In this chapter, we explore how the pathways approach laid out in this book might provide a helpful guide to thinking and action, given the challenges being faced by policymakers now. We return to the key themes explored in different chapters. We started by defining the narratives, the actors and the system framings and the priority goals for system change. We then reflected on how incomplete knowledge and dimensions of dynamics and sustainability are addressed to the governance, appraisal and wider power/knowledge processes. Finally, we showed how these processes are involved both in closing down around dominant narratives and offering possibilities for opening up to alternatives.

Confronted with a bewildering array of competing positions, disagreements, complex dynamics and often deep uncertainties, how might a policymaker address the challenge of sustainability? Too often, as we have seen, the response is to search for a blueprint solution to a defined and clear problem. This is, however, an illusory goal. As this book has repeatedly shown, negotiating sustainability is a process, one replete with politics and power. Instead, what is offered in this book, and explored in relation to the four case studies we have pursued throughout, is a route map for thinking about the issues at stake and practical ways of approaching them.

Above all this means asking the right questions and moving beyond the standard, dominant narratives – and associated pathways – that are usually invoked.

For each of our case study areas therefore, we offer a simple checklist which brings these themes together and relates them to contrasting dominant and alternative narratives. By presenting these contrasts, the aim is to illustrate the potentials of the analytical approach – not to suggest that these are the only dominant or alternative frames. As we have repeatedly argued, context matters, and in different settings and among different people a different range of alternatives might come into view. The aim is to offer a guide for thinking and action, highlighting questions around which more in-depth, context-specific analysis might turn.

While the dominant narratives are relatively well defined and have been discussed at various points during the book, the alternatives – almost by definition – remain more tentative and are often less powerfully articulated. They are often present only implicitly in tacit knowledge and experience – and are therefore in need of uncovering. Furthermore, as we have already discussed, alternatives are necessarily plural, offering a diversity of narratives and associated pathways which are able to respond to diverse settings and contexts. This does not mean that anything goes, however. The point is that among this plurality will be some narratives and pathways that support the goals and ambitions of particular groups of poorer and marginalized people, around which some more specific, simplified narratives and interventions can be constructed. Our concern here is, first, around opening up to create the space so that alternative narratives can be recognized and the potentials for building associated pathways to sustainability can flourish and be made real. Second, by revealing plurality and diversity – encompassing both the dominant and alternative narratives – the political choices that necessarily underlie constructing pathways to sustainability are highlighted.

In Chapter 3, the book laid out a pathways approach to exploring sustainability challenges. As part of the approach a series of building blocks were identified. These can be rephrased as a series of questions. For any particular case or issue, we can identify a range of dominant and alternative narratives. Of each we can ask in turn eight linked questions. We start by asking who are the actors and how are they connected. We then move to examining how the system is framed, and what goals and values are prioritized for system change. Then we look at how incomplete knowledge is addressed – whether in terms of risk, uncertainty, ambiguity or ignorance. We then look at which dynamic properties of sustainability are prioritized, whether stability, durability, resilience or robustness. Then, turning to the discussions of Chapter 5, we ask what appraisal approaches closed down (in the case of dominant narratives) or might help broaden out and open up (in the case of revealing alternatives). Turning to the discussions of Chapter 6, we then ask about the roles of policy and mobilization processes in such closing down or opening up. Finally, we ask what the narratives and their associated pathways imply for social justice and the priorities of poorer and marginalized people.

Water resources in dryland India

In Chapter 1, when introducing each of the cases, we posed a core question of current policy concern. In relation to the case of water resources in dryland India, we asked: 'Given the unfolding dynamics of climate change in dryland areas across the world, how might diverse and responsive pathways be built that respond to cross-scale water dynamics in ways that meet the needs and values of currently marginalized groups? Table 7.1 offers some tentative responses to the checklist of questions which reflect the different elements of the pathways approach laid out in this book. The table again draws closely on Mehta's (2005) research in Western India which has informed this case study throughout earlier chapters.

Clearly in Western India, just as elsewhere, there is no single dominant narrative, and there is of course a diversity of alternatives. The important point though is that, through a variety of framing processes that close down the debate, development pathways are constructed around the dominant approach. By exposing the array of alternatives a more symmetrical debate can ensue. This requires different disciplinary expertise, new stakeholders and different appraisal methods, alongside different governance approaches. Of course in the settings of dryland India, the world is not organized into neat, separate narratives, and many of the processes identified in Table 7.1 co-exist and inter-play. The default is often to ignore this or see it as impossibly difficult and complex – a mire of disagreement and conflict which deters effective policy action. But, through outlining the conflicts, untangling the stakes, highlighting the different ways of thinking, identifying the actors and their positions, a more realistic and effective approach to policy deliberation is made possible.

What might such a deliberation offer? Clearly, the top-down, large-scale engineering solutions have limits. But they also have benefits, providing secure water supplies in the face of highly variable and changing rainfall. As the World Commission on Dams discussed at great length (World Commission on Dams, 2000) dams need not be built in a way that always excludes the marginalized and disenfranchises the poor. Instead complementary designs that allow diverse usage are possible, but require a design process that is inclusive and not simply responding to the demands of elites. A set of pathways could be envisaged that includes the development of dam

Table 7.1 *Water resources in dryland India: Dominant and alternative narratives*

	Dominant narratives	Alternative narratives
Narratives	'Water scarcity must be dealt with using large scale technical solutions – big dams as a universal solution'	'Scarcities are multiple, and adapting to uncertainties must be central – diverse practices and technologies suited to local settings'
Who are the actors and networks articulating the narratives?	Engineers and planners, large-scale irrigation farmers, some politicians	Dryland farmers and pastoralists, certain researchers and NGOs
What is the specific framing of 'the system' and its dynamics – including the treatment of different notions of bounding and spatial and temporal scale, and the goals and values prioritized for system change?	Goals: broader economic development and water security System bounding: national or regional System framing: scarcity, low rainfall, drought, gaps between supply and demand	Goals: livelihoods, identity, sustained flows for diverse, gendered everyday needs Bounding: local Framing: living with uncertainty
How is incomplete knowledge dealt with – to what extent does the narrative address the issue in terms of risk, uncertainty, ambiguity or ignorance?	Risk focused – technological interventions (e.g. dams) to reduce variability of supply	Uncertainty and ambiguity focused: acknowledgement of different uses, needs, socio-cultural meanings of water
Which dynamic properties of sustainability are prioritized – in particular, to what extent is the narrative focused on shocks or stresses, control or response?	Stability focused – controlling supply against shocks (drought events)	Resilience and robustness focused – adaptively responding to uncertain rainfall and long-term shifts in hydrology and climate
What appraisal approaches close down or might help broaden out and open up towards alternative narratives – and pathways?	Cost-benefit analysis; aggregative supply demand surveys	Livelihoods analysis, including histories and biographies, leading to participatory mapping and needs assessments
What governance, policy and mobilization processes close down around the dominant narrative or provide opportunities for opening up around alternatives?	Certain styles of dam and irrigation engineering reinforced by education, training and professional norms; dominant cultural and media visions of resource 'limits' and 'security'; electoral politics, patronage and favours; practices and procedures of	Citizen mobilization and protest through anti-dam movements; alternative actor-networks, linking farmers, activists, journalists, public intellectuals and sympathetic judges and policymakers; local political and electoral processes; reflexive and critical research

	Dominant narratives	Alternative narratives
	water resource management and planning bureaucracies	into lived experiences of water dynamics; practised demonstration and communication of water harvesting technologies
What are the implications for social justice and perspectives and priorities of poorer and marginalized groups?	Unequal distribution of benefits	Targeted efforts, focused on women, poorer communities

infrastructure and other engineering solutions, but tailored in ways that minimize costs and assure rights to water. This requires a rethinking of engineering approaches, and new innovations that build resilience and robustness to fluctuating, uncertain climatic regimes and social and economic demands. But such approaches are insufficient and must be complemented with other pathways, requiring different types of innovation and mixes of social and technical strategies. Thus, for example, investment in an array of locally based water-harvesting approaches may be a critical addition to any redesigned dam-building programme, responding to people's own priorities and ways of life. These different elements of a more plural and integrated approach to water resources must take on the contrasts of framings, potential conflicts over goals and power relations among different groups, in ways that conventional approaches to 'integrated water resources management' have often so far failed to do (Mehta et al, 2007).

Seeds in Africa

Chapter 1 introduced the following question: 'Given the unfolding dynamics of environmental change, markets and politics that constitute the global food crisis, what pathways of innovation and mixes of technology make sense for poorer farmers as they live and work in diverse African settings?' As we have seen, this is a key debate around the nature of a new African Green Revolution. There are multiple, competing and highly contested narratives about the nature of the problem and possible solutions. Seeds, which were the focus of our earlier discussions, are central to these narratives, but in diverse ways. Table 7.2 offers two illustrative narratives, characterized as 'dominant' and 'alternative'.

Table 7.2 *Seeds in Africa: Dominand and alternative narratives*

	Dominant narratives	Alternative narratives
Narratives	'The technology is in the seed, and modern plant breeding and genetic engineering can deliver solutions to hunger which need to be rolled out at scale'	'No one size fits all. Socio-technological solutions must be diverse and adapted to ecological, market, social and institutional contexts. Farmer knowledge and local innovations have a central role to play'
Who are the actors and networks articulating the narrative?	Seed companies, international and national agricultural research institutes, plant breeders and biotechnologists, some funding organizations	Farmers, NGOs, other international and national agricultural researchers, agroecologists and social scientists, some funding organizations
What is the specific framing of 'the system' and its dynamics – including the treatment of different notions of bounding and spatial and temporal scale, and the goals and values prioritized for system change?	Goals: crop productivity increases Bounding: field and crop, extrapolated to national food security balances Framing: modern technological applications can solve the food supply problem	Goals: agriculture for livelihoods Bounding: the farm, community, the agro-ecological region Framing: Diverse solutions for context-specific livelihood challenges
How is incomplete knowledge dealt with – to what extent does the narrative address the issue in terms of risk, uncertainty, ambiguity or ignorance?	Not considered – the solution is in hand, or could be with the right scientific applications and technological advances	Ambiguity focused: hunger problems and livelihood challenges subject of intense debate and multiple understandings
Which dynamic properties of sustainability are prioritized – in particular, to what extent is the narrative focused on shocks or stresses, control or response?	Technological responses to a known range of variability: control focused (stability and durability)	Response focused: resilience and robustness generated through diverse approaches, including technological, market, institutional and social approaches
What appraisal approaches close down or might help broaden out and open up towards alternative narratives and pathways?	Narrowly framed and limited bounding of surveys, cost-benefit and impact analyses	Explorations of framings through multi-criteria approaches; deliberations around alternative food, agricultural and livelihood options (e.g. citizens' juries); surveys and participatory appraisal approaches looking

	Dominant narratives	Alternative narratives
		at social and technical aspects and wider livelihood implications
What governance, policy and mobilization processes close down around the dominant narrative or provide opportunities for opening up around alternatives?	Research funding, corporate control, intellectual property rights, disciplinary hierarchies, organizational priorities, media generated focus on the search for a magic bullet	Social movements, research and media debate, deliberative fora and policy assessment approaches
What are the implications for social justice and perspectives and priorities of poorer and marginalized groups?	Effects unclear and variable, despite the pro-poor claims	More explicitly focused on such groups

Clearly the narratives as laid out above are only illustrative of complex, ongoing debates. However, they do highlight some of the major contrasts and tensions around approaches to agricultural and rural development in Africa and the role of technology – and in particular seeds – in this. A well-rehearsed version of the dominant narrative focuses on the GM solution and the potential of a 'magic bullet' technological solution based on transgenic biotechnologies (see Paarlberg, 2008). This has been widely critiqued, but often in a way that suggests a similarly singular non-GM alternative. The debate has been stuck in a rather black-and-white argument about whether GM crops are the solution for agricultural development and poverty reduction. By unpacking the dimensions of the dominant narrative, a set of further, more nuanced questions are revealed about the conditions under which such technologies will result in the claimed benefits. Complex agroecological dynamics, deep uncertainties and variations in social, labour, market and production conditions all shape whether and how seeds work, for whom and in what ways. Alternative narratives draw attention to such diversity and suggest different pathways of innovation and mixes of technologies, linked to different social and institutional arrangements. Rather than defining a particular solution, the aim is to open up debate about the array of socio-technical trajectories.

Such debates about different options and pathways need to occur at different scales – among farmers in a particular locale, to district and national debates about agricultural futures, to regional and international deliberations about technology development and funding. Over several years from 2003, the International Assessment of Knowledge, Agriculture, Science and Technology for Development (IAASTD), involving over 400 contributors from across the world, discussed such issues, again highlighting the need for diverse approaches to the complex problems of agricultural development (IAASTD, 2008). For future, similar efforts, the type of questions posed by the pathways approach introduced in this book may help hone the discussion and focus the debate around key themes.

Epidemics and health systems

As various examples explored in other chapters have shown, the challenges posed by epidemic diseases are at the centre of current discussions about health policy. The question posed in Chapter 1 was: 'Given the major epidemic health challenges facing the world, and given the particular disease challenges of poorer people, what pathways of response would ensure good health in an equitable, socially just and sustainable way?'. This is clearly a huge question, one we have explored here in relation to debates around avian influenza, haemorrhagic fevers and HIV/AIDS, among others. The appropriate response – whether to focus on technological solutions, surveillance systems or wider, integrated disease-management approaches – is highly contested. Table 7.3 illustrates some of the major contrasts in this debate.

The dominant narrative, focusing on an 'outbreak' framing and its global implications, is clearly important in some situations. Alternative narratives thus do not reject the importance of such a framing, and the pathways of disease response that it informs and justifies, but they do draw attention to vital complementary and additional understandings. These are important, particularly in situations where outbreaks are a manifestation of underlying, longer-term social, disease and ecological dynamics, and where outbreaks occur in settings where diseases are endemic. Alternative narratives also highlight issues, understandings and forms of knowledge which are vital to ensure that outbreak responses are attuned to local ecological and social circumstances and so actually work.

Thus a pathways approach highlights the array of different options and their potential complementarities. It offers a broad route to thinking about disease dynamics which can guide understanding and action around particular health challenges in particular settings (see Dry and Leach, 2010; Scoones, 2010). The policy challenge is therefore: first to open up this array and make the more hidden alternatives explicit, elaborating their implications and trade-offs; second, to think hard about the context-specific requirements of any disease response, attuning the choice and selection of (often) multiple pathways to such settings; third, explicit attention needs to be given to issues of social justice and how the livelihood concerns of poorer and marginalized

Table 7.3 *Epidemics and health systems: Dominant and alternative narratives*

	Dominant narratives	**Alternative narratives**
Narratives	'Outbreaks are threatening humanity. They need to be controlled through effective surveillance and large-scale roll out of singular technological solutions'	'Underlying causes need to be tackled, requiring a rethink of surveillance and diverse social, cultural ecological and technological responses'
Who are the actors and networks articulating the narrative?	Mainstream public health professionals and organizations; pharmaceutical companies; philanthropic organizations	Diffuse networks of more field-based professionals, including epidemiologists, ecologists, social scientists; people living with and responding to disease environments
What is the specific framing of 'the system' and its dynamics – including the treatment of different notions of bounding and spatial and temporal scale, and the goals and values prioritized for system change?	Goals: global public health security Bounding: global Framing: outbreak control and preparedness to ensure security (especially the health of northern populations, and business continuity)	Goals: health systems that can respond to epidemic and endemic diseases, serving diverse needs Bounding: cross-scale (from local to ecosystem to globe). Framing: uncertain disease dynamics across scales
How is incomplete knowledge dealt with – to what extent does the narrative address the issue in terms of risk, uncertainty, ambiguity or ignorance?	Risk focused – controlling outbreaks at source, stamping out, eradication and mortality reduction	Ignorance and ambiguity focused – establishing surveillance and response systems for dealing with surprise and deliberation on diverse causes and effects
Which dynamic properties of sustainability are prioritized – in particular, to what extent is the narrative focused on shocks or stresses, control or response?	Stability focused – returning to the pre-epidemic situation as rapidly as possible. Health security linked to stability of economic activity and political regimes	Robustness in relation to long-term social and environmental dynamics; and resilient responses to disease shocks across multiple scales
What appraisal approaches close down or might help broaden out and open up towards alternative narratives – and pathways?	Standard epidemiological survey techniques (without social and ecological dimensions); knowledge, attitudes and belief surveys framed by existing assumptions	Ethnographic and ecological studies of disease dynamics and 'cultural logics'; multi-criteria mapping; participatory health systems needs appraisal
What governance, policy and mobilization processes	Narrow disciplinary foci, emphasizing epidemiology	Emerging alliances between different disciplines and close

Table 7.3 *Epidemics and health systems: Dominant and alternative narratives (contd)*

	Dominant narratives	Alternative narratives
down around the dominant narrative or provide opportunities for opening up around alternatives?	and medical perspectives; institutional remits of major organizations; planning procedures; funding flows; media and popular cultural imagery of pandemic threats	professions (e.g. links between epidemiology, ecology and anthropology), around new policy platforms (e.g. One World, One Health); learning processes linking local and macro scales, including systemic surveillance; recognition and communication of diverse and innovative health system arrangements in particular settings; citizen mobilization around perspectives and rights and claims of people living with disease
What are the implications for social justice and perspectives and priorities of poorer and marginalized groups?	Responses based on outbreak narratives often ignore local livelihood interests and those living with disease in local settings, in favour of broad 'global public good' and 'security' framings – and so other interest groups.	Approaches rooted in local contexts, cultures and ecologies respond to livelihood needs, goals and priorities of diverse populations, with more equitable, socially distributed outcomes.

people are responded to. This will require careful balancing and thorough deliberation of alternatives, involving a wider participation of people in health and disease planning, including those directly affected. The final challenge is to allocate resources and deliver the type of capacity – in terms of expertise and institutional arrangements – that allow this to happen. This may not be easy. As we have explored, the existing professional and institutional configurations of global and national health systems are often not geared up to encompass alternative pathways, and substantial institutional reform and capacity development will be required.

The One World, One Health platform, launched in 2008 in Egypt, offers a way forward in integrated human, animal and ecosystem health across spatial scales (FAO et al, 2008). The pathways approach introduced here may assist in elaborating the practical and governance implications of this, and the particular challenges of addressing complex dynamics, incomplete knowledge and socio-ecological diversity.

Energy and climate

In the context of global climate change, debates about energy supply systems have, as we have shown in earlier chapters, emphasized the imperative of a transition to a low-carbon economy. Given the dynamism of energy supply contexts, Chapter 1 posed a pressing question for current policy debates: 'how might technological and energy system pathways emerge which respond both to the diversity of both national and local demands?'. Table 7.4 summarizes some of the key contrasts between dominant and alternative narratives in this debate, as focused on the particular question of securing sustainable electricity supplies.

Table 7.4 *Energy and climate: Dominant and alternative narratives*

	Dominant narratives	Alternative narratives
Narratives	'The only way to achieve rapid, radical reductions in carbon emissions is to base strategies on incremental technological innovation in established centralized thermal generating systems (like carbon capture and new nuclear build)'	'Rapid, radical reductions are achievable by novel, small-scale, distributed, networked (interlinked technical and institutional) innovations for smart grids, efficient use, energy services, and autonomous micro-generation'
Who are the actors and networks articulating the narrative?	Electricity utilities; energy regulators; captive government departments; intensive electricity users; incumbent equipment suppliers; associated professional communities	Renewable energy producers; novel equipment supply chain; innovative appliance manufacturers; government environment bodies; suppliers of key IT and other services; environmental movements
What is the specific framing of 'the system' and its dynamics – including the treatment of different notions of bounding and spatial and temporal scale, and the goals and values prioritized for system change?	Goals: centralized energy production from concentrated sources to dispersed passive consumers Bounding: national/regional Framing: large-scale capital-intensive thermal generating units aiming at high 'load factors' at central points in one-way AC transmission systems controlled by oligopolistic supply based utilities trading with passive consumers under closely tied central regulation	Goals: distributed energy networks using ambient sources linking producers with active consumers Bounding: local/inter-regional Framing: a diversity of dispersed multi-scale technologies including household energy production (often at low load factors), with multiple small energy service companies linking users in smart two-way DC grids to manage intermittent supply and demand

Table 7.4 *Energy and climate: Dominant and alternative narratives (contd)*

	Dominant narratives	Alternative narratives
How is incomplete knowledge dealt with – to what extent does the narrative address the issue in terms of risk, uncertainty, ambiguity or ignorance?	Challenge framed as 'risk management' using long-term oligopolistic contracts and coercive intervention in rigid hierarchical planning frameworks; initiatives to control social dissent	Challenge framed as more one of more open uncertainty, responded to by distributed intelligence of multiple actors in 'flat' coordination systems, sensitive to mediation of ambiguity and ignorance by social pressures
Which dimensions of stability are prioritized – in particular, to what extent is the narrative focused on shocks or stresses, control or response?	Attention focuses on stability e.g.: controlling load factors and disruptive trends to optimize existing hierarchical centralized aggregate power production	Attention focuses on robustness – response strategies for foresight and adaptation to novel and inherently uncontrollable environmental and market conditions
What appraisal approaches close down or might help broaden out and open up towards alternative narratives and pathways?	Narrow expert-based quantitative methods, highly discounted financial assessment, cost-benefit analysis, probabilistic risk assessment, portfolio theory	Broad-based integrative assessment methods, including supply and demand options and environmental issues, subject to stakeholder deliberation
What governance, policy and mobilization processes close down around the dominant narrative or provide opportunities for opening up around alternatives?	Large scale traditional capital finance markets; grid regulation; centralized planning law; government industrial energy policy; large corporate technology strategies	Venture and low-carbon capital; new-entrants pressuring for grid competition; devolved planning; environmental energy policy; new commercial energy strategies
What are the implications for social justice and perspectives and priorities of poorer and marginalized groups?	Responses focus on aggregate economic priorities and associated commercial and state interests, with a focus on filling supply gaps through particular technological choices and energy policy pathways. Distributional questions – of both risk and reward – are not high priorities.	Taking diverse goals and priorities of different groups, as well as the social distribution of potential technological risk, allows diverse pathways to emerge, responding to different needs, including those of the energy-poor and less well-off.

There is, of course, much diversity and dynamism in current international policy discussions around transitions towards sustainability in electricity systems. These are, as we have seen, largely driven by imperatives to respond to global climate change, as represented most prominently in the 2009–10 international process around the Copenhagen revision of the Kyoto Treaty. But these debates are also heavily influenced by other environmental pressures, energy security considerations (including concerns over fossil fuel depletion) and radical processes of technology change (Mitchell, 2007). Despite the vitality of the wider debates, dominant narratives remain 'locked-in' to the presumed centrality of hierarchical one-way systems linking concentrated supply with distributed demand. Utility companies operate the same basic practices devised by Edison in the 19th century (Hughes, 1983). The favoured technologies (coal and nuclear) continue to be based on the same thermodynamic steam cycle that initiated the industrial revolution (Patterson, 1999). Emphasis is thus placed on relatively incremental innovations favouring the interests of powerful players in existing electricity systems – such as carbon capture and sequestration and new design features for nuclear fission reactors. More radical innovations tend to remain more peripheral – as ways to 'diversify' at the margins, systems that remain optimized in the same ways as they have for the past century (Stirling, 2009a). However, a variety of different pathways, justified by alternative narratives, are also emerging for transformation in energy systems towards more sustainable electricity. Innovations that are coming together to offer this kind of transformative change include the advent of energy service companies, information technology-intensive energy exchange markets operating in smart two-way grids, building-integrated photo-voltaics and cogeneration, offshore renewable energy and distributed storage embodied in shifts to electricity-based transport (Patterson, 2007).

It is still unclear how far these alternative narratives will drive actual pathways of change in particular national and local settings, and whether the pathways pursued will take the more conservative form emphasized by the industry itself or one of many contrasting configurations for more radical change. Although different constituencies, institutions, countries and regions will initially favour different strategies, powerful pressures from technical standardization, globalized finance, integrated regulation and cultural expectations are all likely to consolidate momentum in only a subset of the possible directions (Unruh, 2000). There is therefore particular value in ensuring that political and industrial choices are sensitive to socio-cultural and bio-regional contexts and are as robust as possible to long-term stresses. To this end, there is a vital need to broaden out and open up appraisal and decision-making processes within this currently rather closed sector

(Stirling, 2008). This means giving more attention to a wider range of stakeholder interests – including small consumers and civil society organizations, but also encompassing renewable and energy-efficient equipment suppliers, IT and domestic appliance producers, electric vehicle manufacturers and construction firms, environmental regulators and planning authorities (Scrase and MacKerron, 2009). In deliberating over the results of these broader-based assessments of options for change, the core issues are often fundamentally political rather than technical, and a diversity of responses will typically present the most robust and resilient solutions (Stirling, 2007). Governments need to take measures deliberately to foster experimentation and allow this diversity to flourish (Rotmans et al, 2001), resisting pressures towards inappropriate standardization and premature lock-in (Unruh, 2006). Governance also needs to involve new collaborations and networks between state institutions, private industry and civil society, to generate more effective learning about the many complexities of achieving transitions to sustainability in global electricity systems (Scrase et al, 2009).

Pathways to sustainability

By looking at the case studies and posing the questions suggested by the pathways approach, a wide range of different dominant and alternative narratives and associated pathways – some realized and some only potential – have been revealed. It is important to reiterate that by presenting the contrasts between 'dominant' and 'alternative' we are not suggesting a simple move from one to the other. A pathways approach aims to uncover diversity, broaden out the debate and open up possibilities for ways forward.

Such multiple pathways, as the tables indicate, mix high-tech and low-tech solutions. They are variously pitched at both local and global scales, and they focus on both issues of broad-based economic growth and questions of equity and social justice. Different pathways are nevertheless particular, associated with different goals, system bounding and framing assumptions, and so mix options in different, sometimes quite eclectic, but always context-focused ways. A pathways approach thus offers a way to overcome the kinds of simplifications that have limited options and stultified debate about sustainable development.

However, not everything goes. By emphasizing diversity and pluralism and an openness to alternatives, there are trade-offs to be assessed and choices to be made. Here the normative dimension of the pathways approach becomes central. We have argued that making explicit the actors, institutions and goals associated with different narratives is crucial. We have argued further for giving particular weight to those narratives and particular pathways that recognize and support the goals of people who are struggling to move out of poverty and marginalization, wherever they may be and whatever the particular problems they face. Pathways to sustainability, as we have defined them throughout this book, need to be identified, prioritized and shaped according to these normative considerations.

Thus in any policy arena – and in all of the cases we have discussed in the previous sections – different pathways will be highly contested. Politics and interests, and the power/knowledge relations that are part of what we have termed governmentality define which narratives become pathways and which pathways get the backing and come to prevail. Negotiating pathways to sustainability is not just about opening up a plurality of options, it is about the political process of building pathways which are currently hidden, obscured or suppressed, as well as countering the dominance of others. This may involve both new kinds of deliberative fora and intervention in the policy process and more antagonistic politics – through processes of protest, mobilization, citizen engagement and alliance building. These, in turn, involve the active opening up of and claiming of political and policy spaces and engagement with media, legal and wider knowledge-making processes.

Strategies for sustainability

A key feature of our argument has been to distinguish four properties of sustainability – stability, durability, resilience and robustness. In Chapter 5 we explored the implications of this disaggregation for appraisal approaches and the way debates about sustainability can be broadened out. In Chapter 4 we discussed the governance implications of taking resilience and robustness in particular seriously, and highlighted the opportunities and challenges of adaptive and reflexive governance approaches.

Returning to the diagram which we introduced in Chapter 3 (Figure 3.7) to map the different properties of sustainability in relation to both the temporality of change (contrasting shocks and stresses) and styles of action (how tractable changes are, contrasting control and response styles), we can now begin to explore the types of intervention that will be required to address all four properties of sustainability. Figure 7.1 offers some clues as to the different innovation, institutional and infrastructural requirements for realizing pathways to sustainability.

As Figure 7.1 distinguishes, different dynamic properties of sustainability require contrasting styles of intervention. These contrasts are of great practical relevance for building pathways to sustainability, which is why we have been at pains to differentiate the dynamics of sustainability throughout this book. Thus to be effective against shocks (stability or resilience), vigilant interventions are needed – ones based on rapid identification of the

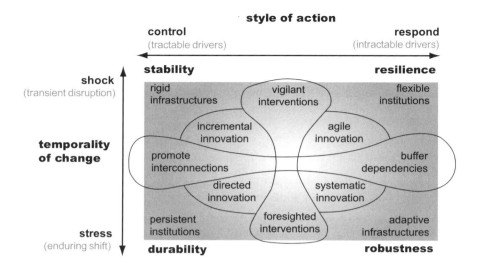

Figure 7.1 Realizing pathways to sustainability

nature of the shock and how to respond. On the other hand to be effective against stress (durability or robustness), interventions need to be based on foresight which picks up on and reacts to longer-term signals.

Strategies geared to these different dynamic properties of sustainability also require different kinds of institutional arrangement and different kinds of innovation. Thus strategies intended to foster stability can be based on rigid infrastructures, capable of controlling shocks while retaining their structural form. Likewise, technology policies for stability will prioritize incremental over more rapid forms of innovation, geared to preserving and building on existing institutional and technical structures. The property of durability, by contrast, will require institutions that are tailored for persistence in the face of long-term pressures, rather than rigidity in the face of short-term disruption. Innovation will need to be more specifically directed to address the orientation of the stress in question. Strategies for resilience differ from both of these in placing a premium on flexible institutions that can absorb uncontrollable shocks and bounce back afterwards. Innovation strategies here need to be agile, responding quickly to rapid change. Finally, the property of robustness requires a different quality again on the part of infrastructures and institutions, which need to be adaptive in the face of uncontrollable, long-run shifts in conditions. In this case, innovation strategies need to prioritize shifts in broader systems, to enable the kind of transition needed to cope with uncontrollably changing circumstances.

These practical distinctions are of crucial relevance to how government, policymakers, practitioners, private sector and civil society actors work and interact. They will have a major bearing on whether and how strategies deal effectively with the complex dynamics of social, technological and environmental systems that we have described in this book. Yet these important contrasts are missed in the many debates and practices around sustainability which fail to disaggregate its dynamic properties, or which emphasize one aspect – such as stability or resilience – alone.

Dynamic sustainabilities

By laying out and illustrating a pathways approach, this book has therefore argued for a rethinking of ideas and practices around sustainability more appropriate to the rapidly changing, diverse contexts of today's world. Embracing dynamic sustainabilities, we have shown, is a crucial challenge which requires shifts of several kinds. A basic shift is to make normative questions central: to specify clearly, for particular issues and settings, what is to be sustained for whom, and who will gain or lose in the process. Given the morally unacceptable and devastating impacts of poverty and inequality across the world, our pathways approach has thus given explicit priority to people living in poverty and marginalization, seeking out sustainabilities that meet their goals for better lives and livelihoods and greater social justice – diverse as these are. Following from this, we have underlined the need for some fundamental conceptual shifts. Our focus on framing and narratives has provided a systematic way to recognize that understandings of sustainability issues and goals are always multiple, as are views of dynamic social–technological–ecological systems and of why these dynamics matter. By exploring how different actors – whether governments, policymakers, scientists, private sector agencies, citizens or the diverse networks which connect them – construct and promote different narratives, we have cast light on the politics of sustainability. Recognizing multiple views also requires researchers, policymakers and others – indeed all of us – to be more humble and reflexive; to acknowledge how our own positions and assumptions shape our perspectives and the ways in which we participate in these politics.

Further conceptual shifts, we have shown, are important to unpack particular narratives and understand their implications for building pathways to sustainability. Thus we have argued for a move away from assumptions of an equilibrial world amenable to managerial solutions – so often part of dominant narratives, as views of stability and strategies to restore it suit those in power. Instead, to embrace the full implications of dynamics across different spatial and temporal scales requires narratives that recognize a wider range of dynamic properties of sustainability and which support appropriate strategies – such as those emphasizing adaptation, flexibility and agility. Amidst such dynamics, we have also argued for a move beyond treating situations only in terms of calculable risk, to embrace narratives and potential pathways which can address other forms of incomplete knowledge: uncertainty, ambiguity and ignorance.

These conceptual shifts in turn carry major practical implications. Recognizing and embracing the multiple dynamic properties of sustainability, and multiple forms of incomplete knowledge, requires different approaches to appraisal and different kinds of institutional and governance arrangement. We have explored many examples of these in relation to our cases and shown how they might make a difference. At the same time, embracing dynamic sustainabilities also requires a broadening out and opening up of appraisal and governance processes, to appreciate multiple narratives and the potential pathways they support. Again, we have exemplified a range of practical approaches to do this, ranging from forms of appraisal and deliberation through to styles, tactics and spaces for engaging in policy processes and citizen mobilization. These, we suggest, can contribute – albeit in different ways, attuned to different contexts and settings – to the core task advocated by this book: fostering an active process of revealing alternative narratives and elaborating and building pathways to sustainability.

Supporting and engaging in such a process, in turn, requires a series of professional shifts and forms of alliance-making: across disciplinary and sectoral boundaries, between researchers and practitioners and among policy actors and citizens. While recognizing the importance of diversity of pathways in any setting, there will never be any neat consensus on what mix is appropriate – and indeed this will continuously change over time. The challenge for policymakers and those who engage with them therefore is to ask repeatedly the questions highlighted by the pathways approach – as summarized in the checklist in the tables above. There is a need also to convene processes of deliberation that balance the needs and aspirations of different people, managing and negotiating conflicts, dissent and dispute along the way. This suggests a different way of conceiving of policymaking and the policymaker's role – whether this is someone operating within an international agency or a local NGO. The challenge is not to define a blueprint or even a portfolio of alternatives, but to engage in the process of both illuminating these and facilitating the negotiation of choices among them. This in turn is only one part of a wider politics of sustainability, where formal policymaking processes sit alongside processes of citizen engagement and mobilization, and public reflection on values and priorities within a broader knowledge landscape.

This book began with a glaring contradiction: that we are living in an era both of more rapid, complex, diverse and dynamic change in many spheres and across many scales and of pressure for quick-fix, blueprint solutions to generalizable problems. We have elaborated on and illustrated this contradiction, exploring how patterns of power, knowledge and politics often lead to a closing down around approaches geared to a relatively knowable and manageable world. The governance pressures which push powerful institutions, whether donor or government agencies, private sector actors, NGOs or networks to think and act in these terms are real and understandable. Yet the problems associated with water in dryland India, seeds in Africa, epidemics and health systems and energy and climate are, as the book has shown, not amenable to this kind of approach. Too often they leave the diverse perspectives and goals of poorer and marginalized people unaddressed, key aspects of dynamic change overlooked and crucial uncertainties and surprises unanticipated. Solutions, if achieved at all, may be temporary and fragile.

Dominant narratives and pathways are therefore not enough. A key task for the present and the future is therefore to make space for more dynamic sustainabilities. This means seeking out and articulating the alternative narratives around which a more effective and justice-oriented set of pathways may emerge. And it means concerted engagement in the process of building such pathways in contexts of deeply entrenched power and interests. These are difficult challenges, and this book has attempted to provide ways to think about and approach them. They are also vital challenges for our time if the pressing problems associated with climate change, energy, pandemic disease, water scarcity, hunger, poverty and inequality are genuinely to be addressed.

Notes

1   United Nations Environmental Programme.

2   This case study draws closely on a particular body of work on western India by Lyla Mehta (Mehta, 2005), as well as insights from David Mosse's work in southern India (2003).

3   This case study, as elaborated in the book, draws on a variety of sources. 'Farmer First' approaches (Chambers et al, 1989; Scoones and Thompson, 1994, 2009) and work on local social networks for seed selection and use (e.g. Richards, 1985, 2009) are particularly emphasized as elements of alternative narratives and pathways.

4   The following sections draw on a STEPS Working Paper on dynamics (Scoones et al, 2007).

5   This section draws on Scoones (1999).

6   This section draws substantially on Scoones (2007).

7   See also the debate between Wilfred Beckerman and Herman Daly and others on economic measures of sustainability (Beckerman, 1992, 1995; Daly, 1995; Common, 1996).

8   See reviews of these and other approaches by Hanley and Atkinson (2003); O'Connor and Spash (1999); and Hanley and Spash (1993).

9   This cost-benefit analysis example draws closely on Mehta et al, 2007.

10   This section draws on KNOTS (2006) and the longer term work on environmental policy processes (Fairhead and Leach, 2003; Keeley and Scoones, 2003).

11   Training workshop on Policy Processes for Veterinary Services in Africa, Mombasa, September 2004 (see Scoones and Wolmer, 2005).

12   Training workshop on Policy Processes for Veterinary Services in Africa, Mombasa, September 2004 (see Scoones and Wolmer, 2005).

13   Training workshop on Policy Processes for Veterinary Services in Africa, Mombasa, September 2004 (see Scoones and Wolmer, 2005).

14   This section draws on work on science and citizens conducted under the auspices of the IDS-based Citizenship Development Research Centre (DRC), particularly the set of cases and perspectives reviewed by Leach and Scoones (2007).

15   There are many similar examples of citizen science in action, ranging from Epstein's (1996) account of AIDS activism in the USA, to cases of popular epidemiology and patient/victim mobilization around issues of environmental and health risk (e.g. Brown, 1992; Di Chiro, 1992; Petryna, 2002), to parental science and mobilization around anxieties about children's vaccines (Leach and Fairhead, 2007).

16   This discussion on media and its relationship with science and policy processes draws on Fairhead and Leach (2003).

References

Abah, O. S. (1997) *Performing Life: Case Studies in the Practice of Theatre for Development*, Zaria, Shekut, Nigeria

Abraham, T. (2005) *Twenty-First Century Plague: The Story of SARS*, Johns Hopkins University Press, Baltimore

Adger, W. N., Kelly, P. M. and Ninh, N. H. (eds) (2001) *Living with Environmental Change: Social Resilience, Adaptation and Vulnerability in Vietnam*, London, Routledge

Agrawal, A. (1995) 'Dismantling the divide between indigenous and scientific knowledge', *Development and Change*, vol 26, pp413–439

Agrawal, A. (2005) *Environmentality: Technologies of Government and the Making of Subjects*, Duke University Press, Durham

Ahmed, E. and Hashish, A. H. (2006) 'On modelling the immune system as a complex system', *Theory in Biosciences*, vol 124, no 3–4, pp413–418

Aldy, J. E. and Stavins, R. N. (eds) (2007) *Architectures for Agreement: Addressing Global Climate Change in the Post-Kyoto World*, Cambridge University Press, Cambridge

Allan, S., Adam, B. and Carter, C. (2000) *Environmental Risks and the Media*, Routledge, London

Allen, P. (1997) *Cities and Regions as Self-Organizing Systems: Models of Complexity*, Gordon and Breach, Amsterdam

Allen, T. and Starr, T. (1982) *Hierarchy: Perspectives for Ecological Complexity*, University of Chicago Press, Chicago

Amendola, A., Contini, S. and Ziomas, I. (1992) 'Uncertainties in Chemical Risk Assessment: results of a European benchmark exercise', *Journal of Hazardous Materials*, vol. 29: pp347–363.

Anderson, P. W. (1997) *Basic Notions of Condensed Matter Physics*, Perseus Publishing, Cambridge, MA

Anderson, R. M. (1994) 'Populations, infectious disease and immunity: A very nonlinear world', The Croonian Lecture, 1994, *Philosophical Transactions of the Royal Society B: Biological Sciences*, vol 346, pp457–505

Appadurai, A. (2000) 'Grassroots globalisation and the research imagination', *Public Culture*, vol 12, pp1–19

Appadurai, A. (2002) 'Deep democracy: Urban governmentality and the horizon of politics', *Public Culture*, vol 14, pp21–47

Apthorpe, R. and Gasper, D. (eds) (1996) *Arguing Development Policy: Frames and Discourses*, Frank Cass, London

Argyris, C. and Schön, D. (1978) *Organizational Learning*, Addison-Wesley, Reading, MA

Arrow, K. (1963) *Social Choice and Individual Values*, Yale University Press, New Haven, CT

Arthur, W. B. (1989) 'Competing technologies, increasing returns and lock-in by historic events', *Economics Journal*, vol 99, pp116–131

Axelrod, R. (1997) *The Complexity of Cooperation: Agent-Based Models of Competition and Collaboration*, Princeton University Press, Princeton, NJ

Bache, I. and Flinders, M. (eds) (2004) *Multi-level Governance*, Oxford University Press, Oxford

Bak, P. (1996) *How Nature Works: The Science of Self-Organized Criticality*, Copernicus, New York

Ball, P. (2005) *Critical Mass: How One Thing Leads To Another*, Arrow Books, London

Barbier, E. B., Pearce, D. W. and Markandya, A. (1990) *Sustainable Development: Economics and Environment in the Third World*, Edward Elgar, Aldershot

Barnes, B. and Edge, D. (eds) (1982) *Science in Context*, MIT Press, Cambridge, MA

Barnsley, M. (1993) *Fractals Everywhere*, 2nd edn, Morgan Kaufmann, San Francisco

Bateson, G. (1972) *Steps to an Ecology of Mind: Collected Essays in Anthropology, Psychiatry, Evolution, and Epistemology*, University of Chicago Press, Chicago

Bauman, Z. (1998) *Globalization: The Human Consequences,* Polity Press, Cambridge, UK

Bawden, R. J. (1995) 'On the systems dimension of FSR', *Journal Farming Systems Research and Extension*, vol 5, no 2, pp1–18

Beckerman, W. (1992) 'Economic growth and the environment: Whose growth? Whose environment?' *World Development*, vol 20, pp481–496

Beckerman, W. (1995) 'How would you like your sustainability, sir? Weak or strong? A reply to my critics', *Environmental Values*, vol 4, no 1, pp169–179

Beddington, J. (2009) 'Professor Sir John Beddington's speech at SDUK 09', www.gov-net.co.uk/news/govnet/professor-sir-john-beddingtons-speech-at-sduk-09, accessed 12 August 2009

Behnke, R., Scoones, I. and Kerven, C. (eds) (1993) *Range Ecology at Disequilibrium. New Models of Natural Variability and Pastoral Adaptation in African Savannas*, Overseas Development Institute, London

Bell, S. and Morse, S. (1999) *Sustainability Indicators: Measuring the Immeasurable*, Earthscan, London

Bellwood, D. R., Hughes, T. P., Folke, C. and Nystrom, M. (2004) 'Confronting the coral reef crisis', *Nature*, vol 428, pp827–833

Benda-Beckman, K. von, (1981) 'Forum shopping and shopping forums: Dispute settlement in a Minankabau village, West Sumatra', *Journal of Legal Pluralism*, vol 19, pp117

Benford, R. D. and Snow, D. A. (2000) 'Framing processes and social movements: An overview and assessment', *Annual Review of Sociology*, vol 26, pp611–639

Berkes, F., Colding, J. F. and Folke, C. (eds) (2003) *Navigating Nature's Dynamics: Building Resilience for Complexity and Change*, Cambridge University Press, New York

Berkhout, F. (2002) 'Technological regimes, path dependency and the environment', *Global Environmental Change*, vol 12, no 1, pp1–4

Berkhout, F., Leach, M. and Scoones, I. (eds) (2003) *Negotiating Environmental Change: New Perspectives from Social Science*, Edgar Elgar, London

Berkhout, F., Smith, A. and Stirling, A. (2004) 'Socio-technological regimes and transition contexts', in Elzen, B., Geels, F. W. and Green, K. (eds) *System Innovation and the Transition to Sustainability*, Edward Elgar Publishing Limited, Cheltenham, UK

Bertalanffy, L. (1968) *General System Theory: Foundations Development Applications*, Allen Lane, London

Bijker, W. E. (1997) *Of Bicycles, Bakelites, and Bulbs: Toward a Theory of Sociotechnical Change*, MIT Press, Cambridge, MA

Blaikie, P. and Brookfield, H. (1987) *Land Degradation and Society*, Routledge, London

Bloom, G., Edström, J., Leach, M., Lucas, H., MacGregor, H., Standing, H. and Waldman, L. (2007) *Health in a Dynamic World*, STEPS Working Paper 5, STEPS Centre, Brighton, UK

Boal, A. (1979) *Theatre of the Oppressed*, Pluto Press, London

Bohman, J. (1996) *Public Deliberation: Pluralism, Complexity and Democracy*, MIT Press, Cambridge, MA

Bonner, J. (1986) *Politics, Economics and Welfare: An Elementary Introduction to Social Choice*, Harvester Press, Brighton, UK

Bossel, H. (1999) *Indicators for Sustainable Development: Theory, Method Applications*, IISD, Winnipeg, Canada

Botkin, D. B. (1990) *Discordant Harmonies: A New Ecology for the Twenty-First Century*, Oxford University Press, New York

Brookfield, J. F. (2005) 'The ecology of the genome – mobile DNA elements and their hosts' *Nature Reviews Genetics*, vol 6, no 2, pp128–136

Brooks, H. (1986) 'The typology of surprises in technology, institutions and development', in Clark, W. C. and Munn, R. E. (eds) *Sustainable Development of the Biosphere*, Cambridge University Press, Cambridge

Brown, N. and Michael, M. (2003) 'A sociology of expectations: Retrospecting prospects and prospecting retrospects, *Technology Analysis and Strategic Management*, vol 15, no 1, pp3–18

Brown, P. (1992) 'Popular epidemiology and toxic waste contamination: Lay and professional ways of knowing', *Journal of Health and Social Behavior*, vol 33, pp267–281

Brundtland, G. H. (1987) *Our Common Future: Report of the World Commission on Environment and Development*, Oxford University Press, Oxford

Burawoy, M. (2005) 'Presidential address: For public sociology', *The British Journal of Sociology*, vol 56, no 2

Burchell, P., Gordon, C. and Miller, P. (eds) (1991) *The Foucault Effect: Studies in Governmentality*, University of Chicago Press, Chicago/Harvester Wheatsheaf, Hemel Hempstead, UK

Byrd, D. and Cothern, C. (2000) *Introduction to Risk Analysis: A Systematic Approach to Science-Based Decision Making*, Government Institutes, Rockville

Calain, P. (2007) 'From the field side of the binoculars: A different view on global public health surveillance', *Health Policy and Planning*, vol 22, no 1, pp13–20

Callon, M., Law, J. and Rip, A. (eds) (1986). *Mapping the Dynamics of Science and Technology: Sociology of Science in the Real World*, Macmillan Press, London

Canadian Journal of Public Health (1993) Special issue of *Canadian Journal of Public Health*, 002 September–October

Carpenter, S. R., Brock, W. A. and Hanson, P. (1999) 'Ecological and social dynamics in simple models of ecosystem management', *Conservation Ecology*, vol 3, no 2, pp4

Castells, M. (1996) *The Rise of the Network Society*, Blackwell, Oxford

Casti, L. (1995) *Complexification: Explaining a Paradoxical World through the Science of Surprise*, Harper Collins, New York

Catley, A. (2006) 'Use of participatory epidemiology to compare the clinical veterinary knowledge of pastoralists and veterinarians in East Africa', *Tropical Animal Health and Production*, vol 38, no 3, pp171–184

Cernea, M. (1997) 'The risks and reconstruction model for resettling displaced populations', *World Development*, vol 25, no 10, pp1569–1587

Chambers, R. (1981) 'Rapid rural appraisal: Rationale and repertoire', *Public Administration and Development*, vol 1, no 1, pp95–106

Chambers, R. (1982) *Rural Development: Putting the Last First*, Longmans, London

Chambers, R. (1994) 'Participatory rural appraisal (PRA): Challenges, potentials and paradigm', *World Development*, vol 22, pp1437–1454

Chambers, R. (1997) *Whose Reality Counts? Putting the First Last*, Intermediate Technology Publications, London

Chambers, R., Pacey, A. and Thrupp, L. (1989) *Farmer First: Farmer Innovation and Agricultural Research*, Intermediate Technology Publications, London

Chapman, G., Kumar, K., Fraser, C. and Gaber, I. (1997) *Environmentalism and the Mass Media: The North–South divide*, Routledge, London

Chapman, J. (2002) *System Failure: Why Governments Must Learn to Think Differently*, Demos, London

Chataway, J., Smith, J., and Wield, D. (2007) 'Shaping scientific excellence in agricultural research', *International Journal of Biotechnology*, vol. 9, no. 2, pp172–187

Checkland, P. B. (1981) *Systems Thinking, Systems Practice*, John Wiley, Chichester

Checkland, P. B. (1999) *Soft Systems Methodology in Action*, John Wiley, Chichester

Chen, S. and Ravallion, M. (2008) 'The developing world is poorer than we thought, but no less successful in the fight against poverty', Policy Research Working Paper Series 4703, The World Bank, http://ideas.repec.org/p/wbk/wbrwps/4703.html (accessed 12 August 2009)

Chesson, P. and Case, T. (1986) 'Overview: Non-equilibrium theories: Chance, variability, history and coexistence', in Diamond, J. and Case, T. (eds) *Community Ecology*, Harper and Row, New York

Chomsky, N. (1998) *Profit Over People: Neoliberalism and Global Order*, Seven Stories Press, New York

Clark, J. (2003) *Globalizing Civic Engagement: Civil Society and Transnational Action*, Earthscan, London

Clark, W. C and Dickson, N. M. (2003) 'Sustainability science: The emerging research programme', *Proceedings of the National Academy of Sciences*, vol 100, no 14, pp8059–8061

Clay, E. and Schaffer B. (eds) (1984) *Room for Manoeuvre: An Exploration of Public Policy in Agriculture and Rural Development*, Heinemann, London

Cobb, R. and Elder, C. (1972) *Participation in American Politics: The Dynamics of Agenda-Building*, Johns Hopkins University Press, Baltimore, MD

Cohen, J, and Stewart, I. (1994) *The Collapse of Chaos: Discovering Simplicity in a Complex World*, Penguin, London

Collingridge, D. (1980) *The Social Control of Technology*, Open University Press, Milton Keynes

Collingridge, D. (1982) *Critical Decision Making: A New Theory of Social Choice*, Pinter, London

Collingridge, D. and Reeve, C. (1986) *Science Speaks to Power: The Role of Experts in Policymaking*, St Martins, New York

Collins, H. and Evans, R. (2007) *Rethinking Expertise*, The University of Chicago Press, Chicago

Commission of the European Communities (2004), *New Elements for the Assessment of External Costs from Energy Technologies*, Brussels, 2004

Common, M. (1996) 'Beckerman and his critics on strong and weak sustainability: Confusing concepts and conditions', *Environmental Values*, vol 5, no 1, pp83–88

Common, M. and Perrings, C. (1992) 'Towards an ecological economics of sustainability', *Ecological Economics*, vol 6, pp7–34

Common, M. and Stagl, S. (2005) *Ecological Economics – An Introduction*, Cambridge University Press, Cambridge

Connell, J. and Sousa, W. (1983) 'On the evidence needed to judge ecological stability or persistence', *American Naturalist*, vol 121, pp789–824

Conway, G. R. (1985) 'Agroecosystem analysis', *Agricultural Administration*, vol 20, pp31–55

Conway, G. R. (1987) 'The properties of agroecosystems', *Agricultural Systems*, vol 24, pp 95–117

Cooke, B. and Kothari, U. (2001) *Participation: The New Tyranny?* Zed Books, London

Cornerhouse (1998) 'Dams on the rocks: The flawed economics of large hydroelectric dams', Briefing (9 May 2007), www.thecornerhouse.org.uk/item.shtml?x=51963, accessed 11 August 2009

Cornwall, A. and Gaventa, J. (2000) 'From users and choosers to makers and shapers: Repositioning participation in social policy', *IDS Working Paper*, no 127, IDS, Brighton, UK

Cornwall, A. and Schattan P. Coelho, V. (eds) (2006) *Spaces for Change? The Politics of Citizen Participation in New Democratic Arenas*, Zed Books, London

Court, J, Hovland, I and Young, J. (2005) *Bridging Research and Policy: Evidence and the Change Process*, ITDG Publishing, London

Cowan, R. (1990) 'Nuclear power reactors: A study in technological lock-in', *Journal of Economic History*, vol 50, pp514–567

Cowan, R. (1991) 'Tortoises and hares: Choice among technologies of unknown merit', *Economic Journal*, vol 101 pp. 801–814

Cowen, M. P. and Shenton, R. W. (1996) *Doctrines of Development*, Routledge, New York

Crawford, D. (2007) *Deadly Companions: How Microbes Shaped our History*, Oxford University Press, Oxford

Crush, J. (1995) *The Power of Development*, Routledge, London

Cumming, G. S., Cumming, D. H. M. and Redman. C. L. (2006) 'Scale mismatches in social-ecological systems: Causes, consequences, and solutions', *Ecology and Society*, vol 11, no 1, pp14, www.ecologyandsociety.org/vol11/iss1/art14/, accessed 11 August 2009

Dalal-Clayton, B., Bass, S., Sadler, B., Thomson, K., Sandbrook, R., Robins, N. and Hugues, R. (1994) *National Sustainable Development Strategies; Experience and Dilemmas*, Environmental Planning Issues No. 6, IIED, London

Daly, H. E. (1991) 'Towards an environmental macroeconomics', *Land Economics*, vol 67, pp255–259

Daly, H. E. (1995) 'On Wilfred Beckerman's critique of sustainable development', *Environmental Values*, vol 4, pp49–50

Daly, H. E. (1996) *Beyond Growth: The Economics of Sustainable Development*, Beacon Press, Oxford

David, P. (1985) 'Clio and the Economics of QWERTY', *American Economic Review*, vol 75, pp332–337

Davies, G., Burgess, J., Eames, M., Mayer, S., Staley, K., Stirling, A. and Williamson, S. (2003) *Deliberative Mapping: Appraising Options for Addressing 'the Kidney Gap'*, final report to The Wellcome Trust, June

Davies, N. (2008) *Flat Earth News*, Random House, New York

De Alcantara, C. (ed) (1993) *Real Markets: Social and Political Issues of Food Policy Reform*, Frank Cass, London

DeAngelis, D. L. (1992) *Dynamics of Nutrient Cycling and Food Webs*, Chapman and Hall, New York

DeAngelis, D. L. and Waterhouse, J. (1987) 'Equilibrium and non-equilibrium concepts in ecological models', *Ecological Monographs*, vol 57, pp1–21

Deb, D. (2008) *Beyond Developmentality: Constructing Inclusive Freedom and Sustainability*, Earthscan, London

De Finetti, N. (1974) *Theory of Probability*, Wiley, New York

Denys, C., Lecompte, E., Calvet, E., Camara, M. D., Dore, A., Koulemou, K. Kourouma, F., Soropogui, B., Sylla, O., Allai-Kouadio, B., Kouassi-Kan, S., Akoua-Koffi, C., Meulen, J. ter and L. Koivogui (2005) 'Community analysis of Muridae (Mammalia, Rodentia) diversity in Guinea: A special emphasis on *Mastomys* species and Lassa fever distributions', in Huber, B. A., Sinclair, B. J. and Lampe, K-H. (eds) *African Biodiversity: Molecules, Organisms, Ecosystems*, Springer, The Netherlands

Denzin, N. K. and Lincoln, Y. S. (2003) *Strategies of Qualitative Enquiry*, Sage, London

Descola, P. and Palsson, G. (eds) (1996) *Nature and Society: Anthropological Perspectives*, Routledge, London

Diamond, J. (2005) *Collapse: How Societies Choose to Fail or Succeed*, Viking, London

Diamond, L. (ed) (1993) *Political Culture and Democracy in Developing Countries*, Lynne Reinner Publishers, Boulder, CO

Di Chiro, G. (1992) 'Defining environmental justice: Women's voices and grassroots politics', *Socialist Review*, October–December, pp93–130

Dickson, D. (1977) *The Politics of Alternative Technology*, Universe Books, London

Dietz, T., Ostrom, E. and Stern, P. (2003) 'The struggle to govern the commons', *Science*, vol 302, pp1907–1912

Dobson, A. P. (1999) *Justice and the Environment: Conceptions of Environmental Sustainability and Dimensions of Social Justice*, Oxford University Press, New York

Dosi, G. and Labini, M. (2007) *Technological Paradigms and Trajectories*, Edward Elgar, Cheltenham

Dosi, G., Freeman, C., Nelson, R., Silverberg, G. and Soete, L. (1988) *Technical Change and Economic Theory*, Pinter, London

Dry, S. (2008) *Epidemics for All? Governing Health in a Global Age*, STEPS Working Paper 9, STEPS Centre, Brighton, UK

Dry, S. and Leach, M. (2010) *Epidemics: Science, Governance and Social Justice*, Earthscan, London

Dryzek, J. (1990) *Discursive Democracy: Politics, Policy, and Political Science*, Cambridge University Press, Cambridge

Dodgson, J., Spackman, M. and Pearman A. (2001) *Multi-criteria Analysis: A Manual*, Department of Transport, Local Government and the Regions, HMSO, London

Easton, D. (1965) *A Systems Analysis of Political Life*, John Wiley & Sons, New York

Edström, J., Cristobal, A., Soyza, C. de and Sellers, T. (2000) '"Ain't misbehavin"': Beyond individual behaviour change', *PLA Notes*, February, pp22–27

Edström, J., Cristobal, A., de Soyza, C. and Sellers, T. (2002) '"Ain't misbehavin"': Beyond awareness and individual behaviour change', in Cornwall, A. and Welbourn, A. (eds) *Realizing Rights: Transforming Approaches to Sexual & Reproductive Well-Being*, Zed Books, London

Edwards, M. and Gaventa, J. (2001) *Global Citizen Action*, Earthscan, London

Elkington, J. (1997) *Cannibals with Forks: The Triple Bottom Line of 21st Century Business*, Capstone, Oxford

Ellis, J. and Swift, D. (1988) 'Stability of African pastoral ecosystems: Alternative paradigms and implications for development', *Journal of Range Management*, vol 41, pp450–459

Ellison, N., 1997, 'Towards a new social politics: Citizenship and reflexivity in late modernity', *Sociology*, vol 31, no 4, pp697–717

Elson, D. (1997) 'Micro, meso, macro: Gender and economic analysis in the context of policy reform', in Bakker, I. (ed) *The Strategic Silence: Gender and Economic Policy*, Zed Books, London

Elton, C. (1930) *Animal Ecology and Evolution*, Oxford University Press, Oxford

Elzen, B., Geels, F. and Green, K. (eds) (2005) *System Innovation and the Transition to Sustainability: Theory, Evidence and Policy*, Edward Elgar, Camberley

Epstein, S. (1996) *Impure Science: Aids, Activism and the Politics of Knowledge*, University of California Press, Berkeley, CA

Ericksen, P. J. (2008) 'Conceptualizing food systems for global environmental change research', *Global Environmental Change*, vol 18, pp234–245

Esteva, G. (1992) 'Development', in Sachs, W. (ed) *The Development Dictionary: A Guide to Knowledge and Power*, Zed Books, London

Etzioni, A., (1967) 'Mixed-scanning: A "third" approach to decision-making', *Public Administration Review*, vol 27, pp385–392

European Environment Agency (2001) *Late Lessons from Early Warnings: The Precautionary Principle 1898–2000*, EEA, Copenhagen

European Science and Technology Observatory (1999) *'On "Science" and "Precaution" in the Management of Technological Risk'*, report to the EU Forward Studies Unit, IPTS, Seville, EUR19056 EN, ftp://ftp.jrc.es/pub/EURdoc/eur19056en.pdf, accessed 11 August 2009

Eyben, R. (ed) (2006) *Relationships for Aid*, Earthscan, London

Fagerberg, J., Mowery, D. and Nelson, R. (2005) *The Oxford Handbook of Innovation*, Oxford University Press, Oxford

Fairhead, J. and Leach, M. (1996) *Misreading the African Landscape: Society and Ecology in a Forest-Savanna Mosaic*, Cambridge University Press, Cambridge

Fairhead, J. and Leach, M. (1998) *Reframing Deforestation: Global Analyses and Local Realities with Studies in West Africa*, Routledge, London

Fairhead, J. and Leach, M. (2003) *Science, Society and Power: Environmental Knowledge and Policy in West Africa and the Caribbean*, Cambridge University Press, Cambridge

Falk, R. (1993) 'The making of global citizenship', in Childs, J. B., Brecher, J. and Cutler, J. (eds) *Global Visions: Beyond the New World Order*, South End, Boston, MA

Fals-Borda, O. (ed) (1986) *The Challenge of Social Change*, International Sociology Series, Sage, London

Fals-Borda, O. (1987) 'The application of participatory action-research in Latin America', *International Sociology*, vol. 2, no. 4, pp329–347

FAO, OIE, WHO, UNSIC and World Bank (2008) *Contributing to One World, One Health: A Strategic Framework for Reducing Risks of Infectious Diseases at the Animal–Human–Ecosystems Interface*, 14 October 2008, Consultation Document Sharm-el-Skeikh, Egypt, http://www.fao.org/docrep/011/aj137e/aj137e00.htm accessed 23 February 2010

Farman, J. (2001) 'Halocarbons, the ozone layer and the precautionary principle', in Gee, D., Harremöes, P., Keys, J., MacGarvin, M., Stirling, A., Vaz, S. and Wynne, B. (eds) *Late Lessons from Early Warnings: The Precautionary Principle 1896–2000*, European Environment Agency, Copenhagen

Farmer, P. (2003) *Infections and Inequalities: The Modern Plagues*, University of California Press, California

Feenberg, A. (2002) *Transforming Technology: A Critical Theory Revisited*, Oxford University Press, Oxford

Feigenbaum, M. J. (1979) 'Universal metric properties of nonlinear transformations', *Journal of Statistical Physics*, vol 21, pp669–706

Ferguson, N. M., Cummings, D. A., Cauchemez, S., Fraser, C., Riley, S., Meeyai, A., Iamsirithaworn, S. and Burke, D. S. (2005) 'Strategies for containing an emerging influenza pandemic in Southeast Asia', *Nature*, vol 437, no 7056, pp209

Fidler, D. (1998) 'Microbialpolitik: Infectious diseases and international relations', *American University International Literature Review*, vol 14, pp1–53

Fischer, F. (1990) *Technocracy and the Politics of Expertise*, Sage, Newbury Park, CA

Fischer, F. (2000) *Citizens, Experts, and the Environment: The Politics of Local Knowledge*, Duke University Press, Durham, NC

Fischer, F. (2003) *Reframing Public Policy: Discursive Politics and Deliberative Practices*, Oxford University Press, Oxford

Fischer, F. and Forester, J. (eds) (1993) *The Argumentative Turn in Policy Analysis and Planning*, Duke University Press, Durham, NC

Fisher, W. F. (ed) (1995) *Toward Sustainable Development? Struggling over India's Narmada River*, M.E. Sharpe Publishers, Armonk, NY

Flam, E. (ed) (1994) *States and Anti-nuclear Movements*, Edinburgh University Press, Edinburgh

Flyvbjerg, B. (1998) *Rationality and Power: Democracy in Practice*, Chicago University Press, Chicago

Flyvbjerg, B. (2001) *Making Social Science Matter: Why Social Science Fails and How it Can Succeed Again*, Cambridge University Press, Cambridge

Folke, C., Carpenter, S., Elmquist, T., Gunderson, L., Holling, C. S. and Walker, B. (2002) 'Resilience and sustainable development: Building adaptive capacity in a world of transformations', *Ambio*, vol 31, pp437–440

Folke, C., Carpenter, S. R., Walker, B. H., Scheffer, M. Elmqvist, T., Gunderson, L. H. and Holling, C. S. (2004) 'Regime shifts, resilience, and biodiversity in ecosystem management', *Annual Review of Ecology, Evolution and Systematics*, vol 35, pp557–581

Folke, C., Hahn, T., Olsson, P. and Norberg, J. (2005) 'Adaptive governance of social-ecological knowledge', *Annual Review of Environment and Resources*, vol 30, pp441–473

Forester, J. (1994) 'Systems thinking, systems dynamics and soft OR', *Systems Dynamics Review*, vol 10, pp245–256

Forsyth, T. (2003) *Critical Political Ecology*, Routledge, London

Freeman, C. (1974) *The Economics of Industrial Innovation*, Routledge, London

Freire, P. (1970) *Pedagogy of the Oppressed*, Continuum, New York (2007 edn)

Fromm, J. (2004) *The Emergence of Complexity*, Kassel University Press, Kassel

Fukuyama, F. (2004) *State Building: Governance and World Order in the Twenty-First Century*, Cornell University Press, Cornell

Funtowicz, S. and Ravetz, J. (1990) *Uncertainty and Quality in Science for Policy*, Kluwer, Amsterdam

Garud, R. and Karnøe, P. (2001) *Path Creation and Path Dependence*, Lawrence Erlbaum and Associates, New Jersey

Gaventa, J. (2006) 'Triumph, deficit or contestation? Deepening the "deepening democracy debate"', *IDS Working Paper*, 264, Brighton, UK

Gaventa, J. and Valderrama, C. (1999) 'Participation, citizenship and local governance', background note prepared for workshop on 'Strengthening participation in local governance', Institute of Development Studies, 21–24 June, www.ids.ac.uk/ids/particip/research/citizen/gavval.pdf, accessed 11 August 2009

GEC (1999) *The Politics of GM Food: Risk, Science and Public Trust*, ESRC Global Environmental Change Programme, University of Sussex

Gee, D., Harremoës, P., MacGarvin, M., Stirling, A., Keys, J., Wynne, B. and Vaz, S. (eds) (2002) *The Precautionary Principle in the Twentieth Century: Late Lessons from Early Warnings*, Earthscan, London

Geels, F. (2002) 'Technological transitions as evolutionary reconfiguration processes: A multi-level perspective and a case-study', *Research Policy*, vol 31, no 8–9, pp1257–1274

Geels, F. (2004) 'From sectoral systems of innovation to socio-technical systems: Insights about dynamics and change from sociology and institutional theory', *Research Policy*, vol 33, no 6–7, pp897–920

Geels, F. (2007) 'Transformations of large technical systems: A multi-level analysis of the Dutch highway system (1950–2000)', *Science Technology & Human Values*, vol 32, no 2, pp123–149

Georgescu-Roegen, N. (1976) *Energy and Economic Myths: Institutional and Analytical Economic Essays*, Pergamon Press, New York

Gerstman, B. (2006) *Epidemiology Kept Simple: An Introduction to Classic and Modern Epidemiology*, 2nd edn, Wiley-Liss, New York

Giddens, A. (1984) *The Constitution of Society: An Outline of the Theory of Structuration*, Polity Press, Cambridge, UK

Giddens, A. (2009) *The Politics of Climate Change*, Polity Press, Cambridge, UK

Gieryn, T. F. (1983) 'Boundary-work and the demarcation of science from non-science: Strains and interests in professional ideologies of scientists', *American Sociological Review*, Vol. 48, No. 6. (1983), pp. 781–795.

Gilbert, E. H., Norman, D. W. and Winch, F. E. (1980) *Farming Systems Research: A Critical Appraisal*, MSU Rural Development Paper No. 6. Department of Agricultural Economics, Michigan State University, East Lansing, MI

Gilbert, N. and Troitzsch, K. (2005) *Simulation for the Social Scientist*, Open University Press, Buckingham, UK

Gladwell, M. (2000) *The Tipping Point: How Little Things Can Make a Big Difference*, Little, Brown and Co., New York

Gleick, J. (1988) *Chaos: Making a New Science*, Penguin, New York

Global Health Watch (2008) *Global Health Watch II*, Zed Books, London

Glover, D. (2009) *Undying Promise: Agricultural Biotechnology's Pro-poor Narrative, Ten Years On*, STEPS Working Paper 15, STEPS Centre, Brighton, UK

Goffman, E. (1975) *Frame Analysis: An Essay on the Organisation of Experience*, Harper & Row, New York

Goldsmith, E. and Hildyard, N. (1992) *The Social and Environmental Effects of Large Dams, Volume III, A Review of the Literature*, Wadebride Ecological Centre, Cornwall, UK

Goodland, R. (1975) 'History of "ecology"', *Science*, vol 188, pp313

Goodland, R. (1995) 'The concept of environmental sustainability', *Annual Review of Ecology and Systematics*, vol 26, pp1–24

Goodland, R. and Daly, H. (1996) 'Environmental sustainability: Universal and non-negotiable', *Ecological Applications*, vol 6, no 4, pp1002–1017

Goodwin, B. (2001) *How the Leopard Changed its Spots: The Evolution of Complexity*, Princeton University Press, Princeton, NJ

Gowdy, J. M. (1994) *Coevolutionary Economics: The Economy, Society and the Environment*, Kluwer Academic Publishers, Boston, MA

Greger, M. (2006) *Bird Flu: A Virus of Our Own Hatching*, Lantern Books, New York

Gribbin, J. (2004) *Deep Simplicity*, Penguin, London

Grillo, R. (1997) 'Discourses of development: The view from anthropology', in Stirrat, R. and Grillo, R. (eds) *Discourses of Development: Anthropological Perspectives*, Berg Publishers, Oxford

Grindle, M. and Thomas, J. (1991) *Public Choices and Policy Change*, Johns Hopkins University Press, Baltimore, MD

Grove-White, R., Macnaghten, P., Mayer, S. and Wynne, B. (1997) *Uncertain World. Genetically Modified Organisms, Food and Public Attitudes in Britain*, Centre for the Study of Environmental Change, Lancaster University, Lancaster

Grove-White, R., Macnaghten, P. and Wynne, B. (2000) *Wising Up: The Public and New Technologies*, Centre for the Study of Environmental Change, Lancaster University, Lancaster, UK

Gunderson, L. H. (2001) 'Managing surprising ecosystems in southern Florida', *Ecological Economics*, vol 37, pp371–378

Gunderson, L. H. and Holling, C. S. (eds) (2002) *Panarchy: Understanding Transformations in Human and Natural Systems*, Island Press, Washington, DC

Haas, P. (1992) 'Introduction: Epistemic communities and international policy coordination', *International Organisation*, vol 46, pp1–36

Habermas, J. (1987) *The Theory of Communicative Action*, Beacon Press, Boston, MA

Habermas, J. (1996) 'Three normative models of democracy', in Behnabib, S. (ed) *Democracy and Difference: Contesting the Boundaries of the Political*, Princeton University Press, Princeton, NJ

Hacking, I. (1991) 'How should we do the history of statistics?', in Burchell, G., Gordon, C. and Miller, P. (eds) *The Foucault Effect: Studies in Governmentality*, University of Chicago Press, Chicago/Harvester Wheatsheaf, Hemel Hempstead

Hajer, M. (1995) *The Politics of Environmental Discourse*, Clarendon, Oxford

Hajer, M. and Wagenaar, H. (2003) 'Introduction', in Hajer, M. and Wagenaar, H. (eds) *Deliberative Policy Analysis*, Cambridge University Press, Cambridge

Hanley, N. and Atkinson, G. (2003) 'Economics and sustainable development: What have we learnt, and what do we still need to learn?', in Berkhout, F., Leach, M. and Scoones, I. (eds) *Negotiating Environmental Change: New Perspectives from Social Science*, Edward Elgar, London

Hanley, N. and Spash, C. L. (1993) *Cost-Benefit Analysis and the Environment*, Edward Elgar, London

Hardin, R. (ed) (2008) *Socioemergence: Cultural Economy and Historical Ecology of Viral Disease in Tropical Forests*, unpublished manuscript

Harding, R. and Fisher, E. (eds) (1999) *Perspectives on the Precautionary Principle*, Federation Press, Sydney

Hargreaves, I., Lewis, J. and Spears, T. (2002) *Towards a Better Map: Science, the Public and the Media*, ESRC, Swindon

Harper, P. (1976) *Radical Technology*, Pantheon, London

Hempel, L. (1996) *Environmental Governance: The Global Challenge*, Island Press, Washington DC

Hewlett, B. and Hewlett, B. (2008) *Ebola, Culture and Politics: The Anthropology of an Emerging Disease*, Wadsworth Books, Kentucky

Heymann, D. L., Barakamfitiye, D., Szczeniowski, M., Muyembe-Tamfum, J. J., Bele, O. and Rodier, G. (1999) 'Ebola hemorrhagic fever: Lessons from Kikwit, Democratic Republic of the Congo', *Journal of Infectious Diseases*, vol 179, Suppl. 1, ppS283–S286

Hilborn, R. (2004) 'Sea gulls, butterflies, and grasshoppers: A brief history of the butterfly effect in nonlinear dynamics', *American Journal of Physics*, vol 72, pp425–427

Hilborn, R. and Gunderson, D. (1996) 'Chaos and paradigms for fisheries management', *Marine Policy*, vol 20, pp87–89

Hill, M. (1997) *The Policy Process in the Modern State*, Prentice Hall, London

Hjern, B. and Porter, D. (1981) 'Implementation structures: a new unit of administrative analysis', *Organization Studies*, vol 2, pp211–227

Hodgson, G. (2000) *Evolution and Institutions: On Evolutionary Economics and the Evolution of Economics*, Edward Elgar, Cheltenham, UK/Northhampton, MA

Hoffman, L. M. (1989) *The Politics of Knowledge: Activist Movements in Medicine and Planning*, State University of New York Press, Albany

Hogwood, B. and Gunn, L. (1984) *Policy Analysis and the Real World*, Oxford University Press, Oxford

Holliday, C., Schmidheiny, S. and Watts, P. (2002) *Walking the Talk: The Business Case for Sustainable Development*, Greenleaf, Sheffield

Holling, C. (1973) 'Resilience and stability of ecological systems', *Annual Review of Ecological Systematics*, vol 4, pp1–23

Holling, C. (1978) *Adaptive Environmental Assessment and Management*, Wiley, London

Holling, C. (1993) 'Investing in Research for Sustainability' *Ecological Applications*, vol 3, no 4, pp552–555

Holling, C. S. (1998) 'Two cultures of ecology', *Conservation Ecology*, vol 2, www.consecol.org/vol2/iss2/art4, accessed 11 August 2009

Holling, C. S. and Meffe, G. K. (1996) 'Command and control and the pathology of natural resource management', *Conservation Biology*, vol 10, pp328–337

Holmberg, J., Bass, S. and Timberlake, L. (1991) Defending the future: A guide to sustainable development, Earthscan, London

Holmes, T., Scoones, I. (2000) Participatory environmental policy processes: experiences from north and south, *IDS Working Paper*, 113, IDS, Brighton, UK

Homewood, K. (2008) *Ecology of African Pastoral Societies*, James Currey, Oxford

Hoogma, R., Kemp, R., Schot, J. and Truffer, B. (2002) *Experimenting for Sustainable Transport: The Approach of Strategic Niche Management*, Spon Press, London

Horgan, J. (1995) 'From complexity to perplexity', *Scientific American*, vol 272, no 6, pp104–109

Houghton, J. (2008) 'Foreword' in *Climate Safety: In Case of Emergency*, report by The Public Interest Research Centre, http://climatesafety.org/wp-content/uploads/climatesafety.pdf, accessed 12 August 2009

Howarth, R. and Norgaard. R. (1997) 'Intergenerational transfers and the social discount rate', in Ackerman, F., Kiron, D., Goodwin, N. R., Harris, J. M. and Gallagher, K. (eds) *Human Wellbeing and Economic Goals*, vol 3 of *Frontier Issues in Economic Thought*, Island Press, Washington, DC

Howes, M. and Chambers, R. (1979) 'Indigenous technical knowledge: Analysis, implications and issues', *IDS Bulletin*, vol 10, no 2, pp5–11

Hughes, T. P. (1983) *Networks of Power Electrification in Western Society, 1880–1930*, Johns Hopkins University Press, Baltimore, MD

Hughes, T. P., Bellwood, D. R., Folke, C., Steneck, R. S., and Wilson, J. (2005) 'New paradigms for supporting the resilience of marine ecosystems', *Trends in Ecology and Evolution*, vol 20, no 7, pp380–386

Hydén, G. (1983) *No Shortcuts to Progress: African Development Management in Perspective*, University of California Press, Berkeley

Illich, I. (1971) *Deschooling Society*, Harper and Row, New York

Illich, I. (1973) *Tools for Conviviality*, Harper and Row, New York

Institute of Development Studies (2004) 'Immersions for policy and personal change: Reflection and learning for development professionals', *IDS Policy Briefing*, Issue 22, July, IDS, Brighton, UK

International Assessment of Agricultural Knowledge, Science and Technology for Development (2008) *Agriculture at a Crossroads: The Synthesis Report*, Washington, DC, IAASTD, www.agassessment.org, accessed 12 August 2009

International Institute for Environment and Development (2006) *Citizens Space for Democratic Deliberation on GMOs and the Future of Farming in Mali*, IIED, London

Irwin, I. (1995) *Citizen Science: A Study of People, Expertise and Sustainable Development*, Routledge, London

Ison, R. (2004) 'Understanding systems approaches to managing complexity', in *T306 Managing Complexity: A Systems Approach. Block 1. Juggling with Complexity: Searching for System,* 2nd edn, The Open University, Milton Keynes

Ison, R. L., Maiteny, P. T. and Carr, S. (1997) 'Systems methodologies for sustainable natural resources research and development', *Agricultural Systems,* vol 55, pp257–272

Jackson, T. and Taylor, P. (1992) 'The precautionary principle and the prevention of marine pollution', *Chemistry and Ecology,* vol 7, pp123–134

Jamison, A. (2001) *The Making of Green Knowledge Environmental Politics and Cultural Transformation,* Cambridge University Press, Cambridge

Janssen, M. A., Anderies, J. M. and Walker, B. H. (2004) 'Robust strategies for managing rangelands with multiple stable attractors', *Environmental Economics and Management,* vol 47, pp140–162

Janssen, M. A., Bodin, Ö., Anderies, J. M., Elmqvist, T., Ernstson, H., McAllister, R. R. J., Olsson, P., and Ryan, P. (2006) 'Toward a network perspective of the study of resilience in social-ecological systems', *Ecology and Society,* vol 11, no 1, pp15, www.ecologyandsociety.org/vol11/iss1/art15/, accessed 11 August 2009

Jasanoff, S. (1990) *The Fifth Branch: Science Advisers as Policymakers,* Harvard University Press, Cambridge, MA and London

Jasanoff, S. (ed) (2004) *States of Knowledge: The Co-production of Science and Social Order,* Routledge, London

Jasanoff, S. (2005) *Designs on Nature,* Princeton University Press, Princeton, NJ

Jasanoff, S. and Martello, M. L. (2004) 'Conclusion', in Jasanoff, S. and Martello, M. L. (eds) *Earthly Politics: Local and Global in Environmental Governance,* MIT Press, Cambridge, MA and London

Jasanoff, S. and Wynne, B. (1997) *Handbook of Science and Technology Studies,* SAGE, London

Jenkins, W. (1978) *Policy Analysis: A Political and Organisational Perspective,* Martin, London

Jessop, B. (1998) 'The rise of governance and the risks of failure: The case of economic development', *International Social Science Journal,* vol 155, pp29–45

Jessop, B. (2003) 'Governance and meta-governance: On reflexivity, requisite variety and requisite irony', in Bang, H. P. (ed) *Governance as Social and Political Communication,* Manchester University Press, Manchester

Jones, K. E., Patel, N. G., Levy, M. A., Storeygard, A., Balk, D., Gittleman, J. L. and Daszak, P. (2008) 'Global trends in emerging infectious diseases', *Nature,* vol 451, no 7181, pp990

Jones, M. (1992) *Adaptive Learning Environments,* Springer, New York

Jordan, A. and Adger, N. (eds) (2009) *Governing Sustainability,* Cambridge University Press, Cambridge

Joshi, A., (1997) *Progressive Bureaucracy: An Oxymoron? The Case of Joint Forest Management in India,* Institute of Economic Growth, Delhi

Joss, S. and Durrant, J. (1995) *Public Participation in Science: The Role of Consensus Conferences in Europe,* Science Museum, London

Julian, D. (1997) 'The utilization of the logic model as a system level planning and evaluation device', *Evaluation and Program Planning,* vol 20, no 3, pp251–257

Juma, C. and Clark, N. (1995) 'Policy research in sub-Saharan Africa: An exploration', *Public Administration and Development,* vol 15, pp121–37

Kaldor, M. (1981) *The Baroque Arsenal*, London, Abacus

Kanbur, R. (ed) (2003) *Q–Squared Qualitative and Quantitative Methods of Poverty Appraisal*, Orient Longman, Hyderabad

Kates, R. W. and Kasperson, J. X. (1983) 'Comparative risk analysis of technological hazards (a review)', *Proceedings of the National Academy of Sciences*, vol 80, no 22, pp7027–7038

Kates, R. W., Clark, W. C., Corell, R., Hall, J. M., Jaeger, C., Lowe, I., McCarthy, J. J., Schellnhuber, H. J., Bolin, B., Dickson, N. M., Faucheux, S., Gallopin, G. C., Gruebler, A., Huntley, B., Jäger, J., Jodha, N. S., Kasperson, R. E., Mabogunje, A., Matson, P., Mooney, H., Moore III, B., O'Riordan, T., Svedin, U. (2001) 'Sustainability science', *Science*, vol 292, pp641–642

Kauffman, S. (1993) *The Origins of Order*, Oxford University Press, New York

Kauffman, S. (1995) *At Home in the Universe*, Oxford University Press, New York

Kaul, I., Grunberg, I. and Stern, M. (1999) *Global Public Goods*, Oxford University Press, Oxford

Keane, J. (2003) *Global Civil Society?* Cambridge University Press, Cambridge

Keeley, J. and Scoones, I. (1999) 'Understanding environmental policy processes: a review', *IDS Working Paper*, 89, Institute of Development Studies, Brighton, UK

Keeley, J. and Scoones, I. (2003) *Understanding Environmental Policy Processes. Cases from Africa*, Earthscan, London

Kelly, J. (1978) *Arrow Impossibility Theorems*, Academic Press, New York

Kemp, R., Schot, J. and Hoogma, R. (1998) 'Regime shifts to sustainability through processes of niche formation: The approach of strategic niche management', *Technology Analysis and Strategic Management*, vol 10, no 2, pp175–195

Keynes, J. (1921) *A Treatise on Probability*, Macmillan, London

Kickbusch, I. (2003) 'Global health governance: Some theoretical considerations on the new political space', in Lee, K. (ed) *Health Impacts of Globalization*, Palgrave Macmillan, Basingstoke

Kingdon, J. W. (1995) *Agendas, Alternatives and Public Policies*, 2nd edn, Longman, New York

Knight, F. (1921) *Risk, Uncertainty and Profit*, Houghton Mifflin, Boston, MA

Knowledge, Technology and Society Team (2006) *Understanding Policy Processes: A Review of IDS Research on the Environment*, KNOTS Team, Institute of Development Studies, Brighton, UK

Koestler, A. (1967) *The Ghost in the Machine*, Arkana, Penguin, London

Kolb, D. (1984) *Experiential Learning: Experience as the Source of Learning and Development*, Prentice-Hall, Englewood Cliffs, NJ

Kooiman, J. (2003) *Governing as Governance*, Sage, London

Korten, D. C. (1980) 'Community organisation and rural development – a learning process approach', *Public Administration Review*, vol 40, pp480–511

Krugman, P. (1996) *The Self-Organizing Economy*, Blackwell, Oxford

Kymlicka, W. and Norman, W. (1994) 'Return of the citizen: A survey of recent work on citizenship theory', *Ethics*, vol 104, no 2, pp352–381

Laclau, E. and Mouffe, C. (2001) *Hegemony and Socialist Strategy: Towards a Radical Democratic Politics*, 2nd edn, Verso, London

Lafferty, W. M. and Eckerberg, K. (1998) *From the Earth Summit to Local Agenda 21: Working Towards Sustainable Development*, Earthscan, London

Larkin, P. A. (1977) 'Epitaph for the concept of maximum sustained yield', *Transactions of the American Fisheries Society*, vol 106, no 1, pp1–11

Latour, B. (1987) *Science in Action*, Harvard University Press, Cambridge, MA

Latour, B. (1993) *We Have Never Been Modern*, Harvard University Press, Cambridge, MA

Latour, B. (1999) *Pandora's Hope: Essays on the Reality of Science Studies*, Harvard University Press, Cambridge, MA

Latour, B. (2004) *Politics of Nature: How to Bring the Sciences into Democracy*, Harvard University Press, Cambridge, MA

Latour, B. (2005) *Reassembling the Social: An Introduction to Actor-Network Theory*, Oxford University Press, Oxford

Lawson, T. (2005). 'The (confused) state of equilibrium analysis in modern economics: An explanation'. *Journal of Post Keynesian Economics*, vol 27, pp423–444

Leach, G. (1979) *Low Energy Strategy for the United Kingdom*, Science Reviews, London

Leach, M. (2005) 'MMR mobilisation: Citizens and science in a British vaccine controversy', *IDS Working Paper*, 254, Institute of Development Studies, Brighton, UK

Leach, M. (2008) *Haemorrhagic Fevers in Africa: Narratives, Politics and Pathways of Disease and Response*, STEPS Working Paper 14, STEPS Centre, Brighton, UK

Leach, M. and Fairhead, J. (2007) *Vaccine Anxieties: Global Science, Child Health and Society*, Earthscan, London

Leach, M. and Mearns, R. (eds) (1996) *The Lie of the Land: Challenging Received Wisdom on the African Environment*, James Currey, Oxford

Leach, M. and Scoones, I. (2007) Mobilizing Citizens: Social Movements and the Politics of Knowledge, *IDS Working Paper*, 276, IDS, Brighton, UK

Leach, M., Scoones, I. and Wynne, B. (2005) *Science and Citizens: Globalisation and the Challenge of Engagement*, Zed Press, London

Leach, M., Bloom, G., Ely, A., Nightingale, P., Scoones, I., Shah, E. and Smith, A. (2007) *Understanding Governance: Pathways to Sustainability*, STEPS Working Paper 2, STEPS Centre, Brighton, UK

Leach. M., Scoones, I. and Stirling, A. (2010) 'Governing epidemics in an age of complexity: Narratives, politics and pathways to sustainability', *Global Environmental Change*, forthcoming. Available (February 2010) at: doi:10.1016/ j.gloenvcha.2009.11.008

Lele, S. M. (1991) 'Sustainable development: A critical review', *World Development*, vol 19, no 6, pp607–621

Levett, R. (1997) 'Tools, techniques and processes for municipal environmental management', *Local Environment*, vol 2, no 2, pp189–202

Levidow, L., Carr, S., Schomberg, R. and Wield, D. (1998) 'European biotechnology regulation: Framing the risk assessment of a herbicide-tolerant crop', *Science, Technology and Human Values*, vol 22, no 4, pp472–505

Lewin, R. (2000) *Complexity – Life at the Edge of Chaos*, University of Chicago Press, Chicago

Liebowitz, S. J. and Margolis, S. E. (1995) 'Path dependence, lock-in, and history', *Journal of Law, Economics and Organization*, vol 11, no 1, pp205–226

Lindblom, C. (1959) 'The science of "muddling through"', *Public Administration Review*, vol 19 , pp79–88

Lipsky, M. (1980) *Street-Level Bureaucracy: Dilemmas of the Individual in Public Services*, Russell Sage Foundation, New York

Loasby, B. (1976) *Choice, Complexity and Ignorance: An Inquiry into Economic Theory and the Practice of Decision Making*, Cambridge University Press, Cambridge

Long, N. (2001) *Development Sociology: Actor Perspectives*, Routledge, London

Long, N. and Long, A. (eds) (1992) *Battlefields of Knowledge: The Interlocking of Theory and Practice in Social Research and Development*, Routledge, London

Longini, I. M. Jr., Nizam, A., Xu, S., Ungchusak, K., Hanshaoworakul, W., Cummings, D. A. T. and Halloran, E. (2005) 'Containing pandemic influenza at the source', *Science*, vol 309, no 5737, pp1083–1087

Lorenz, E. N. (1963) 'Deterministic non-periodic flow' *Journal of Atmospheric Sciences*, vol 20, pp130–141

Lovins, A. (1979) *Soft Energy Paths: Towards a Durable Peace*, Harper Collins, London

Lowe, P. and Morrison, D. (1984) 'Bad news or goods news: Environmental politics and the mass media', *The Sociological Review*, vol 32, no 1, pp75–90

Luce, R. and Raiffa, H. (1957) *Games and Decisions*, John Wiley, Chichester

Ludwig, D., Hilborn, R. and Walters, C. (1993) 'Uncertainty, resource exploitation and conservation: Lessons from history', *Science*, vol 260, pp17–36

Ludwig, D., Walker, B. and Holling, C. S. (1997) 'Sustainability, stability and resilience', *Conservation Ecology*, vol 1, no 1, pp7, www.consecol.org/vol1/iss1/art7/, accessed 11 August 2009

Ludwig D., Walker, B. H. and Holling, C. S. (2002) 'Models and metaphors of sustainability, stability, and resilience', in Gunderson, L. H. and Pritchard, L. (eds) *Resilience and the Behavior of Large-Scale Systems*, Island Press, Washington, DC

Luhmann, N. (1995) *Social Systems*, Stanford University Press, Stanford

MacGarvin, M. (1995) 'The implications of the precautionary principle for biological monitoring', *Helgolander Meeresuntersuchunge*, vol 49, pp647–662

MacKay, A. (1980) *Arrow's Theorem: The Paradox of Social Choice – A Case Study in the Philosophy of Economics*, Yale University Press, New Haven, CT

Mandelbrot, B. (1967) 'How long is the coast of Britain? Statistical self-similarity and fractional dimension', *Science*, vol 156, pp636–638

Mandelbrot, B. (1982) *The Fractal Geometry of Nature*, W. H. Freeman, New York

Marsh, D. and Rhodes, R. A. W. (1992) *Policy Networks in British Government*, Clarendon, Oxford

May, R. (1976) 'Simple mathematical models with very complicated dynamics', *Nature*, vol 261, pp459–476

May, R. (1977) 'Thresholds and breakpoints in ecosystems with a multiplicity of stable states', *Nature*, vol 269, pp471–477

May, R. (ed) (1981) *Theoretical Ecology: Principles and Applications*, Blackwell, Oxford

May, R. (1989) 'The chaotic rhythms of life', *New Scientist*, vol 124, pp37–41

McKeown B. and Thomas, D. (1988) *Q Methodology*, SAGE, Newbury Park

Meadowcroft, J. (1999) 'The politics of sustainable development: Emergent areas and challenges for political science', *International Political Science Review*, vol 20, pp219–237

Meadows, D. (1972) *The Limits of Growth. A Report for the Club of Rome's Project on the Predicament of Mankind*, Universe Books, New York

Mehta, L. (2005) *The Politics and Poetics of Water: Naturalising Scarcity in Western India*, Orient Longman, Delhi

Mehta, L. (2007) 'Scarcity and property rights. The case of water in western India', *Land Policy*, vol 24, no 4, pp654–663

Mehta, L., Leach, M., Newell, P., Scoones, I., Sivaramakrishnan, K. and Way, S. A. (1999) 'Exploring understanding of institutions and uncertainty: New directions in natural resource management', *IDS Discussion Paper*, 372, IDS, Brighton, UK

Mehta, L., Leach, M. and Scoones, I. (2001) 'Environmental Governance in an Uncertain World', *IDS Bulletin*, vol 32, no 4, IDS, Brighton, UK

Mehta, L., Leach, M., Marshall, F., Movik, S., Shah, E., Smith, A., Stirling, A. and Thompson J. (2007) *Liquid Dynamics: Challenges for Sustainability in Water and Sanitation*, STEPS Working Paper 6, STEPS Centre, Brighton, UK

Melucci, A. (1985) 'The symbolic challenge of contemporary movements', *Social Research*, vol 52, no 4, pp789–816

Melucci, A. (1989) *Nomads of the Present: Social Movements and Individual Needs in Contemporary Society*, Temple University Press, Philadelphia

Merry, S. E. (1992) 'Anthropology, law and transnational processes', *Annual Review of Anthropology*, vol 21, pp357–379

Merry, S. E. (1998) 'Legal pluralism', *Law and Society Review*, vol 22, pp869–896

Met Office (2009) 'Early action on climate change needed', www.metoffice.gov.uk/corporate/pressoffice/2009/pr20090215.html, accessed 12 August 2009

Miller, B. (2000) *Geography and Social Movements*, University of Minnesota Press, Minneapolis, MN

Millstone, E., Brunner, E. and Mayer, S. (1999) 'Beyond "substantial equivalence"', *Nature*, vol 401, pp525–526

Mitchell C. (2007) *The Political Economy of Sustainable Energy*, London, Palgrave

Moench M. and Doxit, A. (eds) (2004) 'Adaptive capacity and livelihood resilience: Adaptive strategies for responding to floods and droughts in South Asia', Institute for Social and Environmental Transition, International, Boulder, CO/Institute for Social and Environmental Transition, Nepal

Mokyr, J. (1992) *The Lever of Riches: Technological Creativity and Economic Progress*, Oxford University Press, Oxford

Morgan, M., Henrion, M. and Small, M. (1990) *Uncertainty: A Guide to Dealing with Uncertainty in Quantitative Risk and Policy Analysis*, Cambridge University Press, Cambridge

Mosey, D. (2006) *Reactor Accidents: Institutional Failure in the Nuclear Industry*, 2nd edn, Progressive Media Markets, Sidcup, UK

Mosse, D. (1994) 'Authority, gender and knowledge: Theoretical reflections on the practice of participatory rural appraisal', *Development and Change*, vol 25, pp 569–578

Mosse, D. (2003) *The Rule of Water: Statecraft, Ecology and Collective Action in South India*, Oxford University Press, New Delhi

Mosse, D. (2005) *Cultivating Development. An Ethnography of Aid Policy and Practice*, Pluto Press, London

Mosse, D., Farrington, J. and Rew, A. (eds) (1998) *Development as Process, Concepts and Methods for Working with Complexity*, Routledge, London

Mouffe, C. (1995) 'Democratic politics and the question of identity', in Rajchman, J. (ed) *The Identity in Question*, Routledge, New York

Mouffe, C. (2005) *On the Political*, Routledge, London, New York

Mouffe, C. (2006) *The Return of the Political*, Verso, New York

Munasinghe, M. and Swart, R. (2005) *Primer on Climate Change and Sustainable Development: Facts, Policy Analysis and Applications*, Cambridge University Press, Cambridge

Munton, R. (2003) 'Deliberative democracy and environmental decision-making', in Berkhout, F., Leach, M., and Scoones, I. (eds) *Negotiating Environmental Change: New Perspectives from Social Science*, Edward Elgar, Cheltenham

Nattrass, N. (2007) *Mortal Combat: AIDS Denialism and the Struggle for Antiretrovirals in South Africa*, University of KwaZulu-Natal Press, Scottsville, South Africa

Neill, A. S. (1960) *Summerhill: A Radical Approach to Child Rearing*, Hart Publishing Company, New York

Nelkin, D. (1987) 'Controversies and the authority of science', in Engelhardt Jr, H. T. and Caplan, A. L. (eds) *Scientific Controversies: Case Studies in the Resolution and Closure of Disputes in Science and Technology*, Cambridge University Press, Cambridge

Nelson, R. (ed) (1993) *National Innovation Systems*, Oxford University Press, Oxford

Nelson, R. (2008) 'Factors affecting the power of technological paradigms', *Industrial and Corporate Change*, vol 17, no 3, pp485–497

Nelson, R. and Winter, S. G. (1982) *An Evolutionary Theory of Economic Change*. Harvard University Press, Cambridge, MA

Newell, P. (2006) *Climate for Change: Non-State Actors and the Global Politics of the Greenhouse*, Cambridge University Press, Cambridge

Newman, M. E. J. (2005) 'Power laws, pareto distributions and Zipf's law', *Contemporary Physics* vol 46, pp323–351

Nicolis, G. and Prigogine, I. (1977) *Self Organization in Non-Equilibrium Systems*, J. Wiley and Sons, New York

North, D. C. (1990) *Institutions, Institutional Change and Economic Performance*, Cambridge University Press, Cambridge

Nowotny, H., Scott, P. and Gibbons, M. (2001) *Rethinking Science: Knowledge and the Public in an Age of Uncertainty*, Polity, Cambridge

Oberschall, A. (1973) *Social Conflict and Social Movements*, Prentice-Hall, Englewood Cliffs, NJ

O'Brien, M. (2000) *Making Better Environmental Decisions: An Alternative to Risk Assessment*, MIT Press, Cambridge, MA

O'Connor, M. and Spash, C. L. (1999) *Valuation and the Environment: Theory, Method and Practice*, Edward Elgar, London

Offe, C. (1985) 'New social movements: Challenging the boundaries of institutional politics', *Social Research*, vol 52, pp817–868

Ogilvie, J. (2002) *Creating Better Futures: Scenario Planning as a Tool for a Better Tomorrow*, EH Business, Oxford

Okwori, J. Z. (ed) (2005) *Community Theatre: An Introductory Coursebook*, Tamaza Press, Zaria, Nigeria

Olsen, M. (1965) *The Logic of Collective Action: Public Goods and the Theory of Groups*, Harvard University Press, Cambridge, MA

Olsson, P., Gunderson, L. H., Carpenter, S. R., Ryan, P., Lebel, L., Folke, C. and Holling, C. S. (2006) 'Shooting the rapids: Navigating transitions to adaptive governance of social-ecological systems', *Ecology and Society*, vol 11, no 1 p18. [online] URL: http://www.ecologyandsociety.org/vol11/iss1/art18/ accessed 12 August 2009

O'Neill, R. V., Johnson, A. R. and King, A. W. (1989) 'A hierarchical framework for the analysis of scale', *Landscape Ecology*, vol 3, no 3–4, pp193–205

O'Riordan, T. and A. Jordan (eds) (2000) *Re-Interpreting the Precautionary Principle*, Cameron May, London

Ostrom, E. (2005) *Understanding Institutional Diversity*, Princeton University Press, Princeton, NJ

Ostrom, E., Wynne, S. G. and Schroeder, L. D. (1993) *Institutional Incentives and Sustainable Development: Infrastructure Policies in Perspective*, Westview Press, Boulder, CO

Paarlberg, R. (2008) *Starved for Science: How Biotechnology is Being Kept Out of Africa*, Harvard University Press, Cambridge, MA and London

Page, S. E. (2007) *The Difference: How the Power of Diversity Creates Better Groups, Firms, Schools and Societies*, Princeton University Press, Princeton, NJ

Pannell, D. J. and Glenn, N. A. (2000) 'A framework for the economic evaluation and selection of sustainable indicators in agriculture', *Ecological Economics*, vol 33, pp135–149

Parkes, M., Bienen, L., Breilh, J., Hsu, L-N., McDonald, M., Patz, J., Rosenthal, J., Sahani, M., Sleigh, A., Waltner-Toews, D. and Yassi, A. (2004) 'All hands on deck: Transdisciplinary approaches to emerging infectious disease', *EcoHealth*, vol 2, no 4, pp258–272

Parmentier, R. (1999) 'Greenpeace and the dumping of waste at sea: A case of non-state actors' intervention in international affairs', *International Negotiation*, vol 4, no 3, pp 435–457

Parsons, A. (2008) 'World Bank poverty figures: What do they mean? Share the world's resources', September, www.stwr.org/globalization/world-bank-poverty-figures-what-do-they-mean.html, accessed 12 August 2009

Pate, A. (2002) 'Drowning in development: Repertoires of resistance and the Narmada Bachao Andolan', Paper presented at the annual meeting of the American Political Science Association, Boston Marriott Copley Place, Sheraton Boston & Hynes Convention Center, Boston, MA, August 28, www.allacademic.com/meta/p_mla_apa_research_citation/0/6/6/3/4/p66349_index.html, accessed 12 August 2009

Pateman, C. (1970) *Participation and Democratic Theory*, Cambridge University Press, New York

Patterson, W. (1976) *Nuclear Power*, Penguin, London

Patterson, W. (1999) *Transforming Electricity*, Earthscan, London

Patterson, W. (2007) *Keeping the Lights On*, Earthscan, London

Pearce, D. and Atkinson, G. D. (1993) 'Capital theory and the measurement of sustainable development: An indicator of "weak" sustainability', *Ecological Economics*, vol 8, pp103–108

Pearce, D., and Nash, C. (1981) *The Social Appraisal of Projects: A Text in Cost-Benefit Analysis*, Macmillan, London

Pearce, D. and Turner, R. K. (1990) *Economics of Natural Resources and the Environment*, Harvester Wheatsheaf, Hemel Hempstead

Pearce, D. and Warford, J. (1993) *Blueprint 3: World Without End; Economics, Environment and Sustainable Development*, Oxford University Press, Oxford

Pearce, D., Hamilton, K. and Atkinson, G. (1996) 'Measuring sustainable development: Progress on indicators', *Environment and Development Economics*, vol 1, no 1, pp85–101

Peet, R. and Watts, M. (2004) *Liberation Ecologies: Environment, Development, Social Movements*, 2nd edn, Routledge, London, New York

Pellizzoni, L. (2001) 'The myth of the best argument: Power, deliberation and reason', *British Journal of Sociology*, vol 52, no 1, pp59–86

Perez, C. (2002) *Technological Revolutions and Financial Capital: The Dynamics of Bubbles and Golden Ages*, Edward Elgar, Cheltenham

Peterson, I. (1995) *Newton's Clock: Chaos in the Solar System*, 2nd edn, W. H. Freeman, New York

Peterson, M. (2006) 'The precautionary principle is incoherent', *Risk Analysis*, vol 26, pp595–601

Pettit, J. and Musyoki, S. (2004) 'Rights, advocacy and participation: What's working?' *Participatory Learning and Action*, vol 50, pp97–106

Petts, J. (2001) 'Evaluating the effectiveness of deliberate processes: Waste management case studies', *Journal of Environmental Planning and Management*, vol 44, no 2, pp207–226

Phillips, A. (1995) *The Politics of Presence*, Oxford University Press, Oxford

Pierson, P. (2000) 'Increasing returns, path dependency, and the study of politics', *American Political Science Review*, vol 94, pp251–267

Pierson, P. and Skocpol, T. (2002) 'Historical institutionalism in contemporary political science', in Katznelson, I. and Milner, H. V. (eds) *Political Science: The State of the Discipline*, Norton, New York, pp663–721

Pieterse, J. N. (1996) 'My paradigm or yours? Alternative development, post-development, reflexive development', *ISS Working Paper*, 229, Institute of Social Studies, The Hague

Pimbert, M. (2004) *Institutionalising Participation and People-Centred Processes in Natural Resource Management*, IIED, London

Pimbert, M. and Wakeford, T. (2001) 'Overview – deliberative democracy and citizen empowerment', *PLA Notes*, 40, IIED, London

Pimbert, M. and Wakeford, T. (2002) *Prajateerpu: A Citizens Jury, Scenario Workshop on Food and Farming Futures for Andhra Pradesh, India*, IIED, London

Pimm, S. (1991) *The Balance of Nature? Ecological Issues in the Conservation of Species and Communities*, University of Chicago Press, Chicago

Pimm, S. (2002) *Food Webs*, University of Chicago Press, Chicago

Pinzon, J. E., Wilson, J. M., Tucker, C. J., Arthur, R., Jahrling, P. B. and Formenty, P. (2004) 'Trigger events: Enviroclimatic coupling of ebola hemorrhagic fever outbreaks', *American Journal of Tropical Medicine and Hygiene*, vol 71, no 5, pp664–674

Pool, R. (1999) *Beyond Engineering: How Society Shapes Technology*, Oxford University Press, Oxford

Portnes, P. and Weyant, J. (1999) *Discounting and Intergenerational Equity*, Resources for the Future, Washington DC

Prigogine, I. (1980) *From Being to Becoming*, Freeman, San Francisco

Puu, T. (1993) *Nonlinear Economic Dynamics*, Springer, New York

Raffensberger, C. and Tickner, J. (eds) (1999) *Protecting Public Health and the Environment: Implementing the Precautionary Principle*, Island Press, Washington, DC

Rawls, J. (1971) *A Theory of Justice*, The Belknap Press of Harvard University Press, Cambridge, MA

Rawls, J. (1993) *Political Liberalism*, Columbia University Press, New York

Raymond, B. and Bailey, S. (1997) *Third World Political Ecology*, Routledge, London

Reason, P. and Bradbury, H. (eds) (2007) *The SAGE Handbook of Action Research: Participative Inquiry and Practice*, Sage, London

Redclift, M. R. (1987) *Sustainable Development: Exploring the Contradiction*, Methuen, London

Redclift, M. R. (1992) 'Sustainable development and global environmental change: Implications of a changing agenda', *Global Environmental Change*, vol 2, pp32–42

Renn, O., Webler, T. and Wiedemann, P. (1995) *Fairness and Competence in Citizen Participation: Evaluating Models for Environmental Discourse*, Kluwer, Dordrecht

Rennings, K. and Wiggering, H. (1997) 'Steps toward indicators of sustainable development: Linking economic and ecological concepts', *Ecological Economics*, vol 20, pp25–36

Rhodes, R. A. W. (1997) *Understanding Governance*, Open University Press, Buckingham

Richards, D. and Smith, M. J. (2002) *Governance and Public Policy in the United Kingdom*, Oxford University Press, Oxford

Richards, P. (1985) *Indigenous Agricultural Revolution: Ecology and Food Production in West Africa*, Hutchinson, London

Richards, P. (1986) *Coping with Hunger: Hazard and Experiment in an African Rice Farming System*, Allen and Unwin, London

Richards, P. (2009) 'Knowledge networks and farmer seed systems', in Scoones, I. and Thompson, J. (eds) *Farmer First Revisited: Innovation for agricultural research and development*, Practical Action Publishing, London

Riley, J. and Fielding, W. J. (2001) 'An illustrated review of some farmer participatory research techniques', *Journal of Agricultural, Biological, and Environmental Statistics*, vol 6, no 1, pp5–18

Rip, A. and Kemp, R. (1998) 'Technological Change', in Rayner, S. and Malone, E. L. (eds) *Human Choice and Climate Change*, vol 2, Battelle Press, Columbus, OH

Roberts, J. T. and Parks, B. C. (2007) *A Climate of Injustice: Global Inequality, North–South Politics and Climate Policy*, MIT Press, Cambridge, MA

Robins, S. (2005a) 'Rights passages from "near death" to "new life": AIDS activism and treatment testimonies in South Africa', *IDS Working Paper*, 251, IDS, Brighton, UK

Robins, S. (2005b) 'From "medical miracles" to "normal(ised)" medicine: Aids treatment, activism and citizenship in the UK and South Africa', *IDS Working Paper*, 252, IDS, Brighton, UK

Robins, S. (2005c) 'AIDS, science and citizenship after apartheid', in Leach, M., Scoones, I. and Wynne, B. (eds) *Science and Citizens: Globalization and the Challenge of Engagement*, London, Zed Books

Robinson, J. (1974) *History versus Equilibrium*, Thames Polytechnic, London

Rocheleau, D., Thomas-Slayter, B. and Wangari, E. (eds) (1996) *Feminist Political Ecology: Global Issues and Local Experiences*, Routledge, London, New York

Roe, E. (1991) 'Development narratives, or making the best of blueprint development', *World Development*, vol 19, pp287–300

Roe, E. (1994) *Narrative Policy Analysis: Theory and Practice*, Duke University Press, Durham, NC

Rose, N. (2006) *The Politics of Life Itself: Biomedicine, Power and Subjectivity in the Twenty-First Century*, Princeton University Press, Princeton, NJ

Rose, S. (1982) *Against Biological Determinism*, Allison and Busby, London

Rosenberg, N. (1996) 'Uncertainty and technological change', in Landau, R., Taylor, T. and Wright, G. (eds) *The Mosaic of Economic Growth*, Stanford University Press, Stanford

Rosser, J. (2006) *From Catastrophe to Chaos: A General Theory of Economic Discontinuities: Mathematics, Microeconomics, Macroeconomics and Finance*, 2nd edn, Springer, New York

Rotmans, J., Kemp, R. and Asselt, M. van (2001) 'More evolution than revolution: Transition management in public policy', *Foresight*, vol 3, pp15–31

Rowe, G. and Frewer, L. (2000) 'Public participation methods: An evaluative review of the literature', *Science, Technology and Human Values*, vol 25, pp3–29

Rowe, W. (1994) 'Understanding uncertainty', *Risk Analysis*, vol 14, no 5, pp743–750

Roy, A. (1999) 'The greater common good', *Frontline*, vol 16, no 11

Royal Commission on Environmental Pollution (RCEP) (1998) , *Setting Environmental Standards*, HMSO, London

Rubyogo, J. C. and Sperling, L. (2009) 'Developing seed systems in Africa', in Scoones, I. and Thompson, J. (eds) *Farmer First Revisited: Innovation for Agricultural Research and Development*, Practical Action Publishing, London

Ruelle, D. (1989) *Elements of Differentiable Dynamics and Bifurcation Theory*, Academic Press, Boston, MA

Rusike, E. (2005), 'Exploring food and farming futures in Zimbabwe: A citizens' jury and scenario workshop experiment', in Leach, M., Scoones, I. and Wynne, B. (eds) *Science and Citizens: Globalization and the Challenge of Engagement*, Zed Press, London

Ruthenberg, H. (1971) *Farming Systems in the Tropics*, Clarendon Press, Oxford

Sabatier, P. (1975) 'Social movements and regulatory agencies: Toward a more adequate – and less pessimistic – theory of "clientele capture"', *Policy Sciences*, vol 6, pp301–342

Sabatier, P. and Jenkins-Smith, H. (eds) (1993) *Policy Change and Learning: An Advocacy Coalition Approach*, Westview Press, Boulder, CO

Sachs, W. (ed) (1992) *The Development Dictionary. A Guide to Knowledge as Power*, Zed Press, London

Sale, K. (1993) *The Green Revolution: The American Environmental Movement, 1962–1999*, Harper Collins, New York

Saltelli, A. (2001) 'Sensitivity analysis for importance assessment', EC Joint Research Centre, Ispra, Italy www.ce.ncsu.edu/risk/pdf/saltelli.pdf, accessed 12 August 2009

Sandford, S. (1982) 'Pastoral strategies and desertification: Opportunism and conservatism in dry lands', in Spooner, B., and Mann, H. S. (eds) *Desertification and Development: Dryland Ecology in Social Perspective*, Academic Press, London, New York

Sands, P. (1988) *Chernobyl Law and Communication: Transboundary Nuclea. Pollution – The Legal Materials*, Cambridge University Press, Cambridge

Sawyer, R. (2005) *Social Emergence: Societies as Complex Systems*, Cambridge University Press, Cambridge

Schelling, T. (1978) *Micromotives and Macrobehavior*, Norton, New York

Schlindwein, S. L. and Ison, R. (2004) 'Human knowing and perceived complexity: Implications for systems practice', *E-CO Issue* 6, pp27–32

Schmidheiny, S. (1992) *Changing Course: A Global Business Perspective on Development and the Environment*, MIT Press, Cambridge, MA

Schön, D. (1973) *Beyond the Stable State*, Norton, New York

Schön, D. (1983) *The Reflective Practioner: How Professionals Think in Action*, Basic Books, New York

Schön, D. (1995) *The Reflexive Practitioner: How Professionals Think in Action*, Ashgate-Arena Publishing, Avebury, UK

Schön, D. and Rein, M. (1994) *Frame Reflection: Towards the Resolution of Intractable Policy Controversies*, Basic Books, New York

Schot, J. (1998) 'The usefulness of evolutionary models for explaining innovation: The case of the Netherlands in the 19th Century', *History and Technology*, vol 14, pp173–200

Schulman, P. and Roe, E. (2008) *High Reliability Management: Operating on the Edge*, Stanford University Press, Stanford

Schwartz, M. and Thompson, M. (1990) *Divided We Stand: Redefining Politics, Technology and Social Choice*, Harvester Wheatsheaf, New York

Sclove, R. (1995) *Democracy and Technology*, Guilford Press, New York

Scoones, I. (ed) (1995) *Living with Uncertainty. New Directions in Pastoral Development in Africa*, Intermediate Technology Publications, London

Scoones, I. (1999) 'New ecology and the social sciences: What prospects for a fruitful engagement?' *Annual Review of Anthropology*, vol 28, pp479–507

Scoones, I. (2001) '*Dynamics and Diversity: Soil Fertility and Farming Livelihoods in Africa: Case Studies from Ethiopia*, Earthscan, London

Scoones, I. (2005) 'Contentious politics, contentious knowledge: Mobilising against genetically-modified crops in India, South Africa and Brazil', *IDS Working Paper*, 256, IDS, Brighton

Scoones, I. (2007) 'Sustainability', *Development in Practice*, vol 17, pp589–596

Scoones, I. (2010) *Avian Influenza: Science, Policy and Politics*, Earthscan, London

Scoones, I. and Forster, P. (2008) *The International Response to Highly Pathogenic Avian Influenza: Science, Policy and Politics*, STEPS Working Paper 10, STEPS Centre, Brighton, UK

Scoones, I. and Thompson, J. (eds) (1994) *Beyond Farmer First: Rural People's Knowledge, Agricultural Research and Extension Practice*, Intermediate Technology Publications, London

Scoones, I. and Thompson, J. (eds) (2009) *Farmer First Revisited*, Practical Action Publications, London

Scoones, I. and Wolmer W. (eds) (2002) *Pathways of Change. Crops, Livestock and Livelihoods in Africa. Lessons from Ethiopia, Mali and Zimbabwe*, James Currey, Oxford

Scoones, I. and Wolmer, W. (2005) *Policy Processes for Veterinary Services in Africa: A Workshop Report and Training Guide*, AU-IBAR, Nairobi

M., Smith, A., Stagl, S., Stirling, A. and Thompson, J. (2007) *and the Challenge of Sustainability*, STEPS Working Paper 1, ighton

pons of the Weak: Everyday Forms of Peasant Resistance, Yale ew Haven

‒‒‒‒, J. (1990) *Domination and the Arts of Resistance: Hidden Transcripts*, Yale University Press, New Haven

Scott, J. (1998) *Seeing Like a State. How Certain Schemes to Improve the Human Condition Have Failed*, Yale University Press, New Haven

Scrase, I. and MacKerron, G. (eds) (2009) *Energy for the Future: A New Agenda*, Palgrave, London

Scrase, I., Stirling, A., Geels, F., Smith, A. and Van Zwanenberg, P. (2009) *Transformative Innovation: A Report to the Department for Environment, Food and Rural Affairs*, SPRU – Science and Technology Policy Research, University of Sussex, Brighton

Scudder, T. (2005) *The Future of Large Dams*, Earthscan, London

Selman, P. (1998) 'Local Agenda 21: substance or spin?' *Journal of Environmental Planning and Management*, vol 41, no 5, pp533–553

Sen, A. (2001) *Development as Freedom*, Oxford University Press, Oxford

Senge, P. M. (1990) *The Fifth Discipline: The Art and Practice of the Learning Organization*, Doubleday Currency, New York

Shackley, S. and Wynne, B. (1995) 'Integrating knowledges for climate change: Pyramids, nets and uncertainties', *Global Environmental Change*, no 5, pp 113–12

Shore, C. and Wright, S. (1997) 'Policy: A new field of anthropology', in Shore, C. and Wright, S. (eds) *Anthropology of Policy: Critical Perspectives on Governance and Power*, Routledge, London

Shugart, H. H. and West, D. C. (1981) 'Long-term dynamics of forest ecosystems', *American Scientist*, vol 69, no 6, pp647–652

Simon, H. (1957) *Administrative Behaviour*, Macmillan, New York

Simpson, J. and Weiner, E. (eds) (1989) *The Oxford English Dictionary*, 2nd edn, Oxford University Press, Oxford

Slingenbergh, J., Gilbert, M., Balogh, K. de, Wint, W. (2004) 'Ecological sources of zoonotic diseases', *Revue Scientifique et Technique – Office International des Épizooties*, vol 23, no 2, pp467–484

Smith, A. (2007) 'Translating sustainabilities between green niches and socio-technical regimes', *Technology Analysis and Strategic Management*, vol 19, no 4, pp427–450

Smith, A. and Stirling, A. (2006) *Inside or Out? Open or Closed? Positioning the Governance of Sustainable Technology*, SPRU Electronic Working Paper Series, 148, SPRU, Brighton, UK, www.sussex.ac.uk/spru/1-6-1-2-1.html, accessed 12 August 2009

Smith, A. and Stirling, A. (2007) 'Moving outside or inside? Objectification and reflexivity in the governance of socio-technical systems', *Journal of Environmental Policy and Planning*, vol 8, no 3–4, pp1–23

Smith, A. and Stirling, A. (2010) 'Social-ecological resilience and socio-technical transitions: Critical issues for sustainability governance', *Ecology and Society*, forthcoming

Smith, A., Stirling, A. and Berkhout, F. (2005) 'The governance of sustainable socio-technical transitions' *Research Policy*, vol 34, pp1491–1510

Smith, G. and May, D. (1980) 'The artificial debate between rationalist and incrementalist models of decision making', *Policy and Politics*, vol 8, pp147–161

Smith, K. (2000) 'Innovation as a systemic phenomenon: Rethinking the role of policy', *Enterprise and Innovation Management Studies*, vol 1, no 1, pp73–102

Spash, C. (2001) 'Broadening democracy in environmental policy processes', *Environment and Planning C: Government and Policy*, vol 19, pp475–481

Sprugel, D. (1991) 'Disturbance, equilibrium and environmental variability: What is "natural" vegetation in a changing environment', *Biology Conservation*, vol 58, pp1–18

Stagl, S. (2007) *Rapid Research and Evidence Review on Emerging Methods for Sustainability Valuation and Appraisal*, Final Report to the Sustainable Development Research Network, January

Stagl, S. and Common, M. (2005) *Ecological Economics*, Cambridge University Press, Cambridge

Starr, R. (1997) *General Equilibrium Theory: An Introduction*, Cambridge University Press, Cambridge

Stewart, I. (1989) *Does God Play Dice? The Mathematics of Chaos*, Penguin Books, Harmondsworth, UK

Stiglitz, J. E. (2002) *Globalization and its Discontents*, Norton, New York

Stirling, A. (1997) 'Multicriteria mapping: Mitigating the problems of environmental valuation?' in Foster, J. (ed) *Valuing Nature: Economics, Ethics and Environment*, Routledge, London

Stirling, A. (1999) 'The appraisal of sustainability: Some problems and possible responses', *Local Environment*, vol 4, no 2, pp111–135

Stirling, A. (2003) 'Risk, uncertainty and precaution: Some instrumental implications from the social sciences', in Berkhout, F., Leach, M. and Scoones, I. (eds), *Negotiating Environmental Change: New Perspectives from Social Science*, Edward Elgar, Cheltenham

Stirling, A. (2005) 'Opening up or closing down? Analysis, participation and power in the social appraisal of technology', in Leach, M. and Scoones, I. and Wynne, B. (eds) *Science and Citizens: Globalisation and the Challenge of Engagement*, Zed Books, London

Stirling, A. (2006) 'Uncertainty, precaution and sustainability: Towards more reflective governance of technology', in Voss, J. and Kemp, R. (eds) *Sustainability and Reflexive Governance*, Edward Elgar, Cheltenham

Stirling, A. (2007a) 'Deliberate futures: Precaution and progress in social choice of sustainable technology', *Sustainable Development*, vol 15, pp286–295

Stirling, A. (2007b) 'Resilience, robustness, diversity: Dynamic strategies for sustainability', paper for the conference of the European Society for Ecological Economics, Leipzig, June 2007

Stirling, A. (2007c) 'Science, Precaution and Risk Assessment: towards more measured and constructive policy debate', *European Molecular Biology Organisation Reports*, vol 8, pp309–315

Stirling, A. (2007) 'A general framework for analysing diversity in science, technology and society', *Journal of the Royal Society Interface*, vol. 4, no. 15, 707–719

Stirling, A. (2008) 'Opening up and closing down: Power, participation and pluralism in the social appraisal of technology', *Science Technology and Human Values*, vol 33, no 2, pp262–294

Stirling, A. (2009a) 'The challenge of choice', in Scrase, I., MacKerron, G. (eds) *Energy for the Future: A New Agenda*, London, Palgrave, pp.251–260

Stirling, A. (2009b) 'Multicriteria diversity analysis: A novel heuristic framework for appraising energy portfolios', *Energy Policy*, 38, 1622–1634

Stirling, A. (2009c) 'Risk, uncertainty and power', *Seminar*, vol 597, pp33–39

Stirling, A. (2009d) 'What is energy security? Uncertainties, dynamics, strategies', presentation to conference Energy security: What do we know, and what should be done? Coin Street Centre, South Bank, London, 27 January

Stirling, A. (2010) 'Robustness and diversity: Reducing vulnerability by 'opening up' technological commitments', in Bijker, W., Mesman, J. and Hommels, A. (eds) *Technological Vulnerability*, Oxford University Press, Oxford

Stirling, A. and Gee, D. (2003) 'Science, precaution and practice', *Public Health Reports*, vol 117, no 6, pp521–533

Stirling, A. and Mayer, S. (1999) *Rethinking Risk: A Pilot Multi-Criteria Mapping of a Genetically Modified Crop in Agricultural Systems in the UK*, SPRU, University of Sussex, Brighton

Stirling, A. and Scoones, I. (2010) 'From risk assessment to mapping incertitude: Science, precaution and participation in disease ecology', *Ecology and Society*, 14(2): 14, http://www.ecologyandsociety.org/vol14/iss2/art14, accessed 22 February 2010

Stirling, A., Leach, M., Mehta, L., Scoones, I., Smith, A., Stagl, S. and Thompson, J. (2007) *Empowering Designs: Towards more Progressive Appraisal of Sustainability*, STEPS Working Paper 3, STEPS Centre, Brighton

Stoker, G. (1998) 'Governance as theory: Five propositions', *International Social Science Journal*, vol 50, no 155, pp17–28

Stone, D. and Maxwell, S. (2005) *Global Knowledge Networks and International Development*, Routledge, London

Stringer, R. and Johnson, P. (2001) 'Chlorine and the environment: An overview of the chlorine industry', *Environmental Science and Pollution Research*, vol 8, no 2, pp146–159

Suding, K. N., Gross, K. L. and Houseman G. R. (2004) 'Alternative states and positive feedbacks in restoration ecology', *Trends in Ecology and Evolution*, vol 19, no 1, pp46–53

Sundqvist, T., Soderholm, P. and Stirling, A. (2004) 'Electric power generation: Valuation of environmental costs', in Cleveland, C. J. (ed) *Encyclopedia of Energy*, Academic Press, San Diego

Suter, G. (1993) *Ecological Risk Assessment*, Lewis, Boca Raton

Tainter, J. (1988) *The Collapse of Complex Societies*, Cambridge University Press, Cambridge

Tarrow, S. (1998) *Power in Movement: Social Movements and Contentious Politics*, 4th edn, Cambridge Studies in Comparative Studies, Cambridge University Press, Cambridge

Thelen, K. (2003) 'How institutions evolve', in Mahoney, J. and Rueschemeyer, D. (eds) *Comparative Historical Analysis in the Social Sciences*, Cambridge University Press, Cambridge

Thom, R. (1989) *Structural Stability and Morphogenesis: An Outline of a General Theory of Models*, Addison-Wesley, Reading, MA

Thompson, J. (1995) 'Participatory approaches in government bureaucracies: Facilitating the process of institutional change', *World Development*, vol 23, pp1521–1554

Thompson, J. and Scoones, I. (2009) 'Addressing the dynamics of agri-food systems: An emerging agenda for social science research', *Environmental Science and Policy*, vol 12, pp386–397

Thompson, J., Millstone, E., Scoones, I., Ely, A., Marshall, F., Shah, E. and Stagl, S. (2007) *Agri-food System Dynamics: Pathways to Sustainability in an Era of Uncertainty*, STEPS Working Paper 4, STEPS Centre, Brighton

Thompson, M. and Warburton, M. (1985) 'Decision making under contradictory certainties: How to save the Himalayas when you can't find what's wrong with them', *Journal of Applied Systems Analysis*, vol 12, pp3–34

Thornton, J. (2000) *Pandora's Poison: On Chlorine, Health and a New Environmental Strategy*, MIT Press, Cambridge, MA

Tilly, C. (1978) *From Mobilization to Revolution*, Addison-Wesley, Reading, MA

Touraine, A. (1985) 'An introduction to the study of new social movements', *Social Research*, vol 52, no 4, pp749–787

Turner, B. L. II, Kasperson, R. E., Matsone, P. A., McCarthy, J. J., Corell, R. W., Christensene, L., Eckley, N., Kasperson, J. X., Luerse, A., Martello, M. L., Polsky, C. Pulsipher, A. and Schiller, A. (2003) 'A framework for vulnerability analysis in sustainability science', *Proceedings of the National Academy of Sciences*, vol 100, no 14, pp8074–8079

Turner, K. (1992) *Speculations on Weak and Strong Sustainability*, CSERGE Working Paper GEC 92-26, University of East Anglia, Norwich

Turner, R. K., Pearce, D. W. and Bateman, I. (1994) *Environmental Economics: An Elementary Introduction*, Harvester Wheatsheaf, London

United Nations Environment Programme (2007) *Global Environmental Outlook 4*, www.unep.org/geo/geo4/report/GEO-4_Report_Full_en.pdf, accessed 12 August 2009

United Nations International Strategy for Disaster Reduction Secretariat (2009) *Global Assessment Report on Disaster Risk Reduction*, www.preventionweb.net/english/hyogo/gar/report/index.php?id=9413&pid:36&pil:1, accessed 12 August 2009

Unruh, G. (2000) 'Understanding carbon lock in', *Energy Policy*, vol 28, pp817–830

Unruh, G. (2006) 'Globalizing carbon-lock-in', *Energy Policy*, vol 34, pp1185–1197

Uphoff, N. (1996) 'Understanding the world as a heterogeneous whole: Insights into the nature of systems gained from work on irrigation', *Systems Research*, vol 13, pp3–12

Varela, F. J., Maturana, H. R. and Uribe, R. (1974) 'Autopoiesis: The organization of living systems, its characterization and a model', *Biosystems*, vol 5, pp187–196

Vogel, S. (1995) 'New science, new nature: The Habermas-Marcuse debate revisited', in Feenberg, A. and Hannay, A. (eds) *Technology and the Politics of Knowledge*, Indiana University Press, Bloomington

Vogler, J. and Jordan, A. (2003), 'Governance and the environment', in Berkhout, F., Leach, M. and Scoones, I. (eds), *Negotiating Environmental Change: New Perspectives from Social Science*, Edward Elgar, London

Von Tunzelmann, N., Malerba, F., Nightingale, P. and Metcalfe, S. (2008) 'Technological paradigms: Past, present and future', *Industrial and Corporate Change*, vol 17, no 3, pp467–484

Voss, J-P., Bauknecht, D. and Kemp, R. (eds) (2006) *Reflexive Governance for Sustainable Development*, Edward Elgar, Cheltenham

Wakeford, T. (2001) 'A selection of methods used in deliberative and inclusionary processes', *PLA Notes*, vol 40, pp29–31

Wald, P. (2008) *Contagious: Cultures, Carriers and the Outbreak Narrative*, Duke University Press, Durham, NC

Waldman. L. and Leach, M. (2009) *Centres of Excellence? Questions of Capacity for Innovation, Sustainability, Development*, Background paper for the STEPS Centre New Manifesto Project, STEPS Centre, Brighton

Walker, B. H., Holling, C. S., Carpenter, S. R. and Kinzig, A. P. (2004) 'Resilience, adaptability, and transformability', *Ecology and Society*, vol 9, no 2, pp5, www.ecologyandsociety.org/vol9/iss2/art5/, accessed 12 August 2009

Walker, B. H., Gunderson, L. H., Kinzig, A. P., Folke, C., Carpenter, S. R. and Schultz. L. (2006) 'A handful of heuristics and some propositions for understanding resilience in social-ecological systems', *Ecology and Society*, vol 11 (1). p13, www.ecologyandsociety.org/vol11/iss1/art13/, accessed 12 August 2009

Walker, W. (1999) *Nuclear Entrapment: THORP and the Politics of Commitment*, Institute for Public Policy Research, London

Walker, W. (2000) 'Entrapment in large technical systems: Institutional commitment and power relations', *Research Policy*, vol 29, pp833–846

Walsh, P. D., Biek, R. and Real, L. A. (2005) 'Wave-like spread of Ebola Zaire', *PLoS Biol*, vol 3, no 11, pp371

Walters, C. J. and Hilborn, R. (1978) 'Ecological optimisation and adaptive management', *Annual Review of Ecology and Systematics*, vol 9, pp157–188

Walters, C. J. and Holling, C. S. (1990) 'Large scale management experiments and learning by doing', *Ecology*, vol 71, no 6, pp2060–2068

Waltner-Toews, D. and Wall, E. (1997) 'Emergent perplexity: In search of post-normal questions for community and agroecosystem health, *Social Science and Medicine*, vol 45, no 11, pp1741–1749

Warren, D. M. (1990) *Using Indigenous Knowledge in Agricultural Development*, World Bank Discussion Paper 127, World Bank, Washington DC

Watson, R. (2009) 'Global crisis, national chaos', presentation by Defra Chief Scientific Officer to the UNEP Governing Council, February 18, www.unep.org/civil_society/GCSF10/pdfs/GCpresentation-Global-Crisis-National-Chaos-Bob-Watson.pdf, accessed 12 August 2009

Watts, J., MacKay, R., Horton, D., Hall, A., Douthwaite, B., Chambers, R. and Acosta, A. (2003) 'Institutional learning and change: An introduction', *ISNAR Discussion Paper*, no 03-10

Weber, M. (1991) 'Bureaucracy', in Gerth, H. and Wright Mills, C. (eds) *From Max Weber: Essays in Sociology*, Routledge, London

Welford, R. (1995) *Environmental Strategy and Sustainable Development: The Corporate Challenge for the Twenty-first Century*, Routledge, New York

Werner, R. (2004) *Designing Strategy: Scenario Analysis and the Art of Making Business Strategy*, Praeger, Westport, CT

Wilks, S. and Wright, M. (1987) *Comparative Government–Industry Relations*, Clarendon, Oxford

Williams, R. and Edge, D. (1996) 'The social shaping of technology', *Research Policy*, vol 25, pp865–899

Wilson, R. W. (2000) 'The many voices of political culture: Assessing different approaches', *World Politics*, vol 52, pp246–273

Winner, L. (1977) *Autonomous Technology: Technics Out of Control as a Theme in Political Thought*, Cambridge, MIT Press

Winterfeldt, D. von and Edwards, W. (1986) *Decision Analysis and Behavioural Research*, Cambridge University Press, Cambridge

Wisner, B., Blaikie, P., Cannon, T. and Davis, I. (2004) *At Risk: Natural Hazards, People's Vulnerability and Disasters*, 2nd edn, Routledge, London

Wolmer, W. and Scoones, I. (2005) *Policy Processes in the Livestock Sector: Experiences from the African Union*, AU-IBAR, Nairobi

Woodcock, A. E. R. and Davis, M. (1978) *Catastrophe Theory*, E.P. Dutton, New York

Woolhouse, M. and Gaunt, E. (2007) 'Ecological origins of novel human pathogens', *Critical Reviews in Microbiology*, vol 33, no 4, pp231–242

World Commission on Dams (2000) *Dams and Development: A New Framework for Decision-making. The Report of the World Commission on Dams*, Earthscan, London

World Energy Assessment (2000) *Energy and the Challenge of Sustainability*, United Nations Development Programme, New York

World Health Organization (2005) *International Health Regulations: Guidance for National Policy-Makers and Partners*, WHO, Geneva

World Health Organization (2007) *A Safer Future: Global Public Health Security in the 21st Century*, The World Health Report 2007, WHO, Geneva

World Health Organization (2009) 'Global Outbreak Alert and Response Network', World Health Organization, www.who.int/csr/outbreaknetwork/en/, accessed 12 August 2009

Worldwatch Institute (2003) 'Rich–poor gap widening', *Vital Signs*, pp88–89, www.worldwatch.org/node/82, accessed 12 August 2009

Worster, D. (1977) *Nature's Economy. A History of Ecological Ideas*, Cambridge University Press, Cambridge

Wynne, B. (1987) 'Risk perception, decision analysis and the public acceptance problem', in Wynne, B. (ed) *Risk Management and Hazardous Waste: Implementation and the Dialectics of Credibility*, Springer, Berlin

Wynne, B. (1989) 'Establishing the rules of laws – Constructing expert authority', in Smith R. and Wynne, B. (eds) *Expert Evidence: Interpreting Science in the Law*, Routledge, London

Wynne, B. (1992) 'Uncertainty and environmental learning: Reconceiving science and policy in the preventive paradigm', *Global Environmental Change*, June, pp111–27

Wynne, B. (2001) 'Creating public alienation: Expert cultures of risk and ethics on GMOs', *Science as Culture*, vol 10, no 4, pp445–481

Wynne, B. (2002) 'Risk and environment as legitimatory discourses of technology: Reflexivity inside out?', *Current Sociology*, vol 50, no 30, pp459–477

Yahya, M. (2006) 'Polio vaccines – Difficult to swallow: The story of a controversy in Northern Nigeria', *IDS Working Paper*, 261, IDS, Brighton, UK

Young, I. M. (1990) *Justice and the Politics of Difference*, Princeton University Press, Princeton, NJ

Young, O. R. (1997) *Global Governance: Drawing Insights from Environmental Experience*, MIT Press, Cambridge, MA

Young, O. R. (ed.) (1999) *The Effectiveness of International Environmental Regimes: Causal Connections and Behavioural Mechanisms*, MIT Press, Cambridge, MA

Zeeman, E. C. (1977) *Catastrophe Theory-Selected Papers 1972–1977*, Addison-Wesley, Reading, MA

Zimmerer, K. (1994) 'Human geography and the "new ecology"' The prospect and promise of integration, *Annals of the Association of American Geographers*, vol 841, pp108–125

Zinn-Justin, J. (2002) *Quantum Field Theory and Critical Phenomena*, 4th edn, Clarendon Press, Oxford/Oxford University Press, New York

Zwanenberg, P. van and Millstone, E. (2001) 'Mad cow disease – 1980s–2000: How reassurances undermined precaution', in European Environment Agency, *Late Lessons from Early Warnings: The Precautionary Principle 1898–2000*, EEA, Copenhagen

Index

actor-network theory 72
adaptive governance 92, 96, 133, 134, 135
  of dynamic systems 89–91
adaptive management 33, 59
advocacy coalitions 75
Agenda 21 39, 41
agent-based modelling 25
Agrawal, Arun 22, 77, 113
agricultural development 6, 31–34, 161, 162
agricultural policy 134, 137
  variation in policy judgements on 52
agri-food system 40
agro-ecosystems 32
ambiguity xv, 4, 5, 12, 34, 53–58, 78–83, 92, 102, 104, 108–111, 123, 143, 156–166
anti-apartheid movement 146
anti-dam movements 139, 146
anti-globalization movement 148
anti-nuclear movement 143, 148
appraisal
  approaches 10, 100–102, 110, 111, 112, 120, 156, 158, 160, 163, 166, 169
  characteristics of 106
  effect on decision-making 106
  empowering designs for 99
  expert-analytic methods 103
  expert-based assessment techniques 103
  framing and 111–112
  methods and tools for 107, 125
  methods for addressing contrasting aspects of incomplete knowledge 109
  permutations of breadth and openness in 122
  in practice
    case 1: voice, vision and rural futures in Zimbabwe 117–119
    case 2: appraisal for design of HIV/AIDS prevention programmes 119–120
  quantitative assessment techniques 103
  reflexivity in 116–117
  for sustainability 100, 123
avian flu 8, 40, 46, 55, 57, 58, 63, 80, 81, 110, 162

Biosafety Protocol 41
  see also Kyoto Protocol
bovine spongiform encephalopathy (BSE) 55
Brundtland, Gro 37, 41, 42
BSE see bovine spongiform encephalopathy (BSE)
Burawoy, Michael 152
bureaucratic politics 71, 72, 132
business practices 29

carbon emissions 3, 165
Carlowitz, Hans Carl von 37
catastrophe theory 24
Centre for Social and Economic Research on the Global Environment (CSERGE) 39
chaos theory 24
Chapman, J. 31, 151
citizen action and mobilization 138–142
  policy processes and forms of 150–153, 172
  strategies, tactics and spaces of 145–150
citizen science 144, 175

civic epistemologies 74
civil society 39, 44, 69, 70, 77, 81, 87,
        88, 101, 129, 131, 168, 170
climate change 3, 48
    challenges associated with 16
    energy and 8–9
    Kyoto Protocol 40
communicative rationality 94
complexity science 11, 23–25, 27
complex system dynamics 17, 32, 34,
        78
Connell, J. 19
Conservation Ecology 33
contingency planning 8
Conway, G. R. 32
cost-benefit analysis 103, 104, 106, 107,
        114, 158, 175
CSERGE *see* Centre for Social and
        Economic Research on the Global
        Environment (CSERGE)
cybernetics 30
cyberspace 149, 150

Daly, Herman 38, 175
Deb, Debal 77–78
decision-making 107, 108, 115, 12
    appraisal for 100, 103, 105, 167
    effect of appraisal outputs on 106
    involvement of citizens in 140
    and policy processes 112
deliberative governance 91–95
developmentality, concept of 78
Dobson, Andrew 38
durability xv, 12, 59–63, 83, 85, 111,
        123, 156, 160, 169–170
dynamics xv
dynamic property xv–xvi
dynamic sustainabilities 58–63, 170–173

Ebola 8, 47, 60
ecological economic theory 24
'ecological' resilience 34
ecology 2, 18, 32, 38, 47, 57, 81, 86, 89
    and complexity in the natural sciences
        10
    genome 17
    new perspectives in 25–27

and politics of nature and technology
        72–73
    social 111
    and social science 19
ecosystem 25, 26, 33, 38, 47, 91, 135,
        164
    collaborative and learning-based
        approaches to management of 90
    inter-relationship with human societies
        15
electricity production, social cost of 50
electricity supply, variability in assessment
        of policy options for 50
Ellison, N. 71, 141
Elton, Charles 19
empowering designs, for sustainability 13
    appraisal
        approaches 100–102
        framing and 111–112
        in practice 117–120
    broadening out and opening up of
        102–111
    principles of 112–113, 121
        choice amongst different options
            114–115
        dynamic perspective and incomplete
            knowledge 115–116
        knowledge through participatory
            engagement 113–114
        reflexivity in appraisal 116–117
        rights, equity and power 116
energy
    and climate change 8–9, 16, 165–168
    low-carbon alternatives for 9, 16
    renewable sources of 9
    security 9, 45, 85, 167
    sustainable 16, 85
    transition to low-carbon system of 16
energy system
    technology policy for 20
    trans-continental infrastructures for 16
    transition to low-carbon 16
environmental sustainability 2, 21
Environment and Development, World
        Conference on 38
epidemics and health systems 7–8, 13,
        155, 162–164

Epstein, S. 75, 142, 143, 144, 175
evidence-based policy 83, 127

'farmer first' approach, for rural
    development 7, 32, 175
farming systems 31, 32, 40
Farming Systems Research (FSR) 31–32
food crisis 7, 66, 159
forum shopping 148
FSR *see* Farming Systems Research (FSR)

genetically modified (GM) crops 40, 41,
    51, 55, 118, 161
dimensions of incomplete knowledge in
    Africa 56
global food supplies 3
Global Fund 70, 141
Global Outbreak Alert and Response
    Network (GOARN) 47, 60
Global Polio Eradication Initiative 135
GM crops *see* genetically modified (GM)
    crops
GOARN *see* Global Outbreak Alert and
    Response Network (GOARN)
governance
    adaptive governance of dynamic
        systems 89–91
    comparison of adaptive, deliberative
        and reflexive approaches to 95
    concept of contemporary governance
        governance in practice 71–72
    government to networked, multi-
        levelled governance 67–70
    participatory governance 70–71
    political culture and context 73
    politics of knowledge 74–75
    politics of nature and technology
        72–73
    towards an integrated approach 75–
        76
    deliberative and reflexive governance
        91–95
    multi-levelled 150
    nature of 65
    pathways to sustainability 76–78
        politics of incomplete knowledge
            78–83

pressures towards planned
    equilibrium 83–86
in world of dynamism and
    incomplete knowledge 86–88
processes, styles and practices 89
grass-roots globalization 139
Grass Roots Immersion Programme
    (GRIP) 134
grassroots organization 138
greenhouse gases 9
Green Revolution 7, 32, 66, 159
GRIP *see* Grass Roots Immersion
    Programme (GRIP)

Habermas, Jurgen 71, 94
health security 47
health systems, epidemics and 162–164
hierarchical causal relationships 25
highly pathogenic avian influenza (HPAI)
    8, 46, 47, 55
Holling, C. (Buzz) 32, 38, 64
HPAI *see* highly pathogenic avian
    influenza (HPAI)
human–animal demography 16
human–animal–environment interactions
    47
human societies, inter-relationship with
    ecosystem 15
Hyden, Goran 21

IAASTD *see* International Assessment of
    Knowledge, Agriculture, Science
    and Technology for Development
    (IAASTD)
ignorance xv, 4, 5, 53–58, 78–83,
    109–111, 121, 123, 143, 156–166
incomplete knowledge
    appraisal methods for addressing
        contrasting aspects of 109
    dimensions of 57
        avian and human pandemic
            influenza 58
        GM foods and crops 56
        risk and uncertainty 53
    dynamic perspectives 115–116
    politics of 78–83
infectious diseases 7, 15, 16, 48, 58

Institutional Learning and Change
    initiative 136
integrated vector management 47
inter-coupled systems 25
International Assessment of Knowledge,
    Agriculture, Science and
    Technology for Development
    (IAASTD) 161–162
International Health Regulations 47
International Monetary Fund 68
irrigation systems 31
Ison, Ray 30

Jamison, A. 140, 145
Jasanoff, Sheila 69, 73, 74, 111, 129,
    145, 147, 153

Kates, Robert 34, 39
Keeley, J. 22, 74, 126, 128, 129, 131
knowledge
    dimensions of incomplete 57
        avian and human pandemic
        influenza 58
        GM foods and crops 56
        risk and uncertainty 53
    diversity through participatory
        engagement 113–114
    and dynamics of mobilization
        142–145
    incomplete *see* incomplete knowledge
    politics of 74–75, 78–83, 150
    uncertainties 91
knowledge making
    challenges of subjectivity and
        reflexivity in 153
    and communication 150–153
    types of 152
Korten, D. C. 31
Kutch, India 48–49
Kyoto Protocol 40, 167
    see also Biosafety Protocol

learning organization 31
livelihood strategies 49
London Dumping Convention 149
low-carbon energy system, development
    of 16

May, Robert 17, 26, 38, 128
MCM *see* multi-criteria mapping
    (MCM); multi-criteria methods
    (MCM)
Mehta, L. 15, 31, 48, 49, 72, 85, 91,
    103, 139, 157, 159, 175
mobilization
    citizen action and 138–142
    science-related 145
    strategies, tactics and spaces of
        145–150
multi-criteria mapping (MCM) 51, 107,
    109, 163
multi-criteria methods (MCM) 101

natural resource management 31–34
natural sciences 10, 64, 135
Nature 57
New Public Management 68
non-equilibrium thermodynamics 24
normative xvi, 5, 10, 11, 64, 93, 94,
    143, 168–169

Olsson, Per 89, 90, 133, 135
One World, One Health (OWOH)
    programme 164

pandemic influenza 57, 58
participatory governance 70–71, 75,
    96
participatory rural appraisal (PRA) 32,
    102, 119
Pearce, David 38, 39, 100, 103
People's Development Plans 144
policy entrepreneurs 135
policymaking 6, 16, 17, 21, 29, 50, 51,
    59, 68, 74, 85, 107, 114, 120,
    127–132, 138, 172
policy narratives 45, 59, 60, 81–83,
    129, 130, 132, 133
policy processes
    citizen action and mobilization
        138–142, 150
    conventional view on 127–128
    for creating and using policy spaces
        137–138
    dynamics of mobilization 142–145

for effecting policy change
  by building networks and
    encouraging champions of change
    133
  building new skills and professionals
    135–136
  by encouraging reflexivity 134
  opportunism, flexibility and adaptive
    governance 134–135
  by telling persuasive stories 132–133
  factors influencing 126–127
  features of 128–132
  mutually constructed 128
  for problem-solving 128
  strategies, tactics and spaces of
    mobilization 145–150
  ways of understanding 128–132
policy space 131, 136, 169
  concept of 137
  and strategies for opening them up 138
'political windows' 135
poverty reduction 2, 21, 161
power law distributions, in social
    phenomena 23, 25
PRA see participatory rural appraisal
    (PRA)
public–private partnerships 8, 66, 70

rapid rural appraisal (RRA) 32, 102
rational choice theory 54–55
reflective practitioner 30–31
reflexive governance 12, 89, 91–95, 169
renewable energy 165, 167
  sources of 9, 144
  trans-continental infrastructures for 16
Resilience Alliance 33, 89
risk and uncertainty 2, 52–58
risk assessment 47, 54, 55, 82, 87, 107,
    108, 109, 110, 113, 123
Robinson, Joan 19
robustness xvi, 12, 59–67, 83, 85, 96,
    111, 123, 156–166, 169–170
RRA see rapid rural appraisal (RRA)
rural development 31, 32, 126, 134, 161

Sardar Sarovar (Narmada) movement
    48, 139

Sardar Sarovar Project (SSP) 48
SARS see severe acute respiratory
    syndrome (SARS)
Schlindwein, S. L. 30
Schön, Donald 30, 31, 93, 128
Science 57
science of complexity see complexity
    science
Scoones, I. 21, 22, 25, 26, 32, 38, 40, 47,
    55, 56, 57, 70, 71, 74, 103, 113,
    114, 126, 128, 129, 130, 131, 132,
    134, 141, 142, 143, 147, 162, 175
Scott, James 22, 31, 68, 77, 85, 87, 146
seeds system in Africa 7, 31, 55, 159–162
self-organization, in evolutionary studies 25
severe acute respiratory syndrome
    (SARS) 40, 47
shocks xvi, 5, 12, 31, 38, 59–63, 83,
    85–86, 158–166, 169–170
social appraisal 13
  designs xv
social capital 135
social–ecological systems 34, 89
social–ecological–technological systems
    15, 66, 76, 89
social justice 2, 4, 12, 13, 21, 38, 48, 99,
    116, 142, 155, 157, 159, 161, 162,
    168, 171
social movements 138, 140
  and engagement with science 142
social science 19, 34, 44, 64, 86, 93, 135
social solidarity and identification 141
social–technological–environmental
    systems 96
socio-ecological systems 7, 89, 90
  rates of change of 17
socio-ecological-technology systems 15
socio-technical regimes 28, 29
soft-systems approach, for management
    and organizational change 30
Sousa, W. 19
SSP see Sardar Sarovar Project (SSP)
stability xvi, 1, 5, 12, 23, 59–63, 83–88,
    96, 102, 104, 108, 110–111, 123,
    125–127, 156–166, 169–171
'stable' states 31
stakeholder negotiation 102, 106

STEPS Centre 6
stress xvi, 5, 12, 31, 38, 59–63, 83, 85,
    158–166, 169–170
structural modelling 30
sustainability
  appraisal for 114, 123
  challenges of 2, 3, 10, 13, 22–34
  concepts and application of 11
  dynamic properties of 58–63, 171–173
  dynamics and complexity associated
    with 3–6, 34–35, 37
  empowering designs for *see*
    empowering designs, for
    sustainability
  environment and development
    challenges
    energy and climate 8–9
    epidemics and health systems 7–8
    seeds in Africa 7
    water in dryland India 6–7
  equilibrium thinking for 22–23
    agricultural development and
      natural resource management
      31–34
    complexity science 23–25
    dynamics of ecological systems 25–27
    dynamics of technological change
      27–29
    policies, organizations and
      management responses 30–31
  framing and narratives 45–52
  governance pathways to 76–78
    politics of incomplete knowledge
      78–83
    pressures towards planned
      equilibrium 83–86
    in world of dynamism and
      incomplete knowledge 86–88
  normative policy 41–43
  pathways to 11–13, 168–169
  policymaking and intervention
    strategies for 17
  politics of mobilization for 140
  science 34, 39, 63–64
  strategies for 169–171
  and sustainable development 10, 39
  systems perspective of 43, 48

sustainable development 30, 38
  Brundtland definition of 37, 41
  economic vision of 38
  political economy of 40
  sustainability and 10, 39
Sustainable Development, World
    Business Council for 38
sustainable energy 85
  systems 16
swine flu 40, 58
Sylvicultura Oeconomica 37
system governance 34

TAC *see* Treatment Action Campaign
    (TAC)
Thompson, J. 15, 31, 32, 33, 40, 74,
    111, 113, 175
Treatment Action Campaign (TAC)
    138, 139, 142, 146
Turner, Kerry 38, 39, 103

uncertainty xvi, 2, 4, 5, 11–13, 15–18,
    26, 31–35, 52–58, 63, 78–82, 89,
    95, 96, 108–111, 123, 136, 139,
    143, 156–166, 172
Uphoff, N. 31
urban water supply 42

value judgements 44, 45, 128
Voss, J-P. 92

Wald, P. 46
water-agro-ecological system 43
water crisis, community-based solutions
    for 6
water management 43
  doctrinal models 20
  in India 6–7, 42, 48, 61, 139
water resources in dryland India 6–7, 42,
    48, 61, 139, 157–159
water supply, urban 42
World Bank 3, 68, 139
  Grass Roots Immersion Programme
    (GRIP) 134
World Commission on Dams 157

zoonosis 16